THE TACO TRUCK

THE
TACO TRUCK

HOW MEXICAN STREET FOOD IS TRANSFORMING THE AMERICAN CITY

ROBERT LEMON

FOREWORD BY JEFFREY M. PILCHER

UNIVERSITY OF
ILLINOIS PRESS
Urbana, Chicago, and Springfield

Maps of the areas discussed in this book can be found at
https://www.press.uillinois.edu/books.lemon/taco_truck

Library of Congress Cataloging-in-Publication Data
Names: Lemon, Robert, 1979– author.
Title: The taco truck : how Mexican street food is transforming
    the American city / Robert Lemon.
Description: Urbana : University of Illinois Press, 2019. | Includes
    bibliographical references and index.
Identifiers: LCCN 2018056752| ISBN 9780252042454 (hardback) |
    ISBN 9780252084232 (paperback)
Subjects: LCSH: Hispanic Americans—Social life and customs.
    | Mexican Americans—Nutrition. | Food trucks—United
    States. | Tacos—United States. . | Food habits—Social
    aspects—United States. | United States—Social life and
    customs—21st century. | BISAC: SOCIAL SCIENCE / Ethnic
    Studies / Hispanic American Studies. | COOKING / Regional
    & Ethnic / Mexican. | SOCIAL SCIENCE / Emigration &
    Immigration.
Classification: LCC TX361.H57 L47 2019 | DDC 641.84—dc23
    LC record available at https://lccn.loc.gov/2018056752

E-book ISBN 9780252051296

To my grandmother, Rosalina B. Gonzalez (1911–2006),
for all the love she gave me through her cooking.

CONTENTS

FOREWORD

JEFFREY M. PILCHER

The local mobility of taco trucks represents a microcosm of geographical and social mobility in the twenty-first century. Food vendors spread across the United States as part of the great Mexican migration that began with the peso crises of the 1970s and 1980s, accelerated with the North American Free Trade Agreement in the 1990s, and largely ended with the United States' own financial crisis in 2008. Like previous generations of migrants who found opportunities in small food businesses—think of hamburgers, pizza, chop suey, and deli—Mexicans gained a measure of social mobility by traveling to find work, or at least to find a customer willing to pay for a cheap and tasty meal of carne asada. But for a generation of Americans facing downward mobility due to corporate offshoring and anti-union politics, and who are increasingly unwilling to risk moving in search of better employment, Mexican workers who would take the most unenviable jobs became a target of nativist outrage, as during the 2016 election when populists fulminated against "a taco truck on every corner." Nevertheless, attempts to treat taco trucks as an immigration problem fundamentally misrepresent the situation for countless U.S. citizens who make a living by vending and for whom restrictive city ordinances and ongoing police harassment are civil rights issues.

In seeking to resolve these political and social conflicts around food and mobility, we would do well to remember their historical antecedents. In the 1880s, American migrants to the cities of San Antonio, Texas, and Los Angeles,

California, found the local Mexican population and food to be simultaneously threatening and alluring. Tourists eagerly sought out street vendors known as "chili queens" to sample their tamales and chili con carne, even while fearing the unaccustomedly piquant taste and the risk of gastrointestinal disease. Health reformers soon arrived on the scene, seeking not to improve Mexican neighborhoods' access to clean water and sewage, which was the real cause for concern, but rather to restrict the vendors to "zones of tolerance" that were shared with prostitutes. By essentially criminalizing chili con carne, police were free to harass Mexican food (and sex) workers, while still leaving them accessible to adventuresome tourists, an arrangement that persisted until the civil rights movement.

Today, that movement's gains have never seemed more imperiled, as taco trucks have replaced nineteenth-century tamale carts as racialized symbols of criminality. Robert Lemon's book therefore provides a timely account of the myriad small and large ways that privatization and gentrification have restricted the rights of citizens and residents to the use of our cities. Using techniques of urban geography, he maps the evolving spatial dynamics of twenty-first-century Jim Crow, which attempts to segregate racialized sites of production from elite white spaces of consumption within the neoliberal city. In interviews with taco truck vendors, Lemon describes the strategies they use to navigate this hostile urban terrain and reach their customers. The book also provides an invaluable account of community organizers and progressive municipal officials who have pioneered ways of supporting vendors with the logistical and legal infrastructure needed to prepare healthy food, thereby positively contributing to urban landscapes. But perhaps the most important point is that taco truck workers, simply through their everyday presence, occupying city streets and selling food to hungry customers, embody the democratic ideals of liberty and equality for some of the most downtrodden within American society.

ACKNOWLEDGMENTS

I would like to begin by thanking Steven Hoelscher for helping me develop a sound geographical framework for this project. His insights and critical assessments of my work were always constructive and motivating.

Indeed, very many mentors and scholars along the way provided great input to how I could bring distinct themes of urban geography, cultural geography, architecture, landscape architecture, city planning, food studies, Latino studies, and Mexican immigration together. Bill Doolittle has always provided pragmatic evaluations of theoretical issues. Elizabeth Engelhardt helped me tie the work into food studies; Rebecca Torres offered astute insights into Mexican immigration to the United States and how best to incorporate other socioeconomic Latino issues into cultural landscape studies. I owe many thanks to Paul Adams as well: his brilliant comments and suggested readings throughout my entire research process helped me to better establish many of my theoretical points, and he kept me from following blindly into a number of prevailing dogmatic positions. Furthermore, I would like to thank John Radke, who encouraged me to pursue the cultural geography of taco trucks. And I owe a debt of gratitude to Jefferey Pilcher for his historical perspective of Mexican food as well as his time in writing the foreword to this book.

This research would not have come to fruition without all the people I interviewed over the past few years, especially the taco truck owners who so generously shared their personal stories and their cuisines with me. Without their big-heartedness and willingness to work with me on this study, I would not have had a book to write. Moreover, my interaction and experience with these individuals gave me keen insight to the hopes and aspirations of so many migrants who struggle every single day to carve out a space for themselves in the United States. I cannot mention many individuals by name because they are undocumented. But they know who they are; and I have made it clear to them, throughout my research, that this work is as much a chronicle of their stories and struggles as it is a scholarly explanation of their everyday spaces. However, I can name two individuals: George Azar and his mother, Mercedes Azar. George Azar owns a taco truck in Sacramento, California. When I first met George, he was kind enough to spend countless hours with me going through personal taco truck archives and recounting the history of taco trucks in Sacramento. His recordkeeping of the taco truck conflicts in Sacramento provided me incredible documentation to strengthen my argument in chapter 4. His and his parents' generosity to me not only made my research attainable but also pleasurable.

Additionally, I would like to acknowledge all other individuals who graciously agreed to be questioned. I interviewed numerous city planners, council members, city staff, and business owners in Austin, Texas; Oakland, California; San Francisco, California; Sacramento, California; and Columbus, Ohio. I do not have the space to name each individual, but I appreciate their time and interest in my work. However, I would especially like to thank some of the people whose business operations I critically and spatially deconstruct throughout this book: Emilia Otero, operator of La Placita; Caleb Zigas, director of La Cocina; Matt Cohen, owner of Off the Grid; Randall Selland, principal and chef at The Selland Group; and Bethia Woolf and Andy Dehus, owners and operators of Columbus Food Adventures. I really valued their time and appreciated that they opened up their business operations for me to evaluate from a very critical geographical framework. They are all good-hearted individuals trying to bring immigrant cuisine practices to the forefront of American society.

I would also like to thank Charlotte Friedley, who created and designed the beautiful online maps that complement this book. Tim Mollette-Parks helped me rework a few sections of this book where I was having some difficulties with clairvoyantly making my points. A huge thank you to my copyeditor, Catherine Vanhentenryck, for reviewing my writing for most every chapter of this book. And I must thank all the dedicated individuals I worked with at the University of Illinois Press for getting this manuscript onto bookshelves.

Last but not least, I need to thank my immediate family. First my cats, thank you Demi, Dani, and Alli. My three cats sat on my lap or by my side (often literally holding my hand) many endless nights. It is no surprise that Demi naps by my side and Alli purrs in my lap as I write this. I would have never been able to make it through so many all-nighters without the emotional support of my furry feline family. And I must thank my parents, Carl and Maria Lemon. My parents have given me nothing but love and encouragement during the eight demanding years I have been working on this book.

THE TACO TRUCK

ENGAGING TACO TRUCK SPACE

Ok. I suck in a lot of ways. I am snobby about food. I can't stand dirty dishes in the sink and I don't want anyone touching my stuff that is in "order." I also, would never THINK of going to Boyes Hot Springs [in Sonoma County, California] and eating from a TACO TRUCK. Never. EVER.—Enter Brown Eyes—With knowledge of all the ins-and-outs of Sonoma that I never even KNEW existed, here we suddenly are, in front of a TACO TRUCK. In BOYES HOT SPRINGS. Hand TO PEARLS. So, I said nothing. I waited in line . . . I expected not much - not NOTHING . . . It was a TACO TRUCK. In BOYES HOT SPRINGS . . . I unwrap my foil-lined plate. It smells nice, dare I say great?? What they produce out of that truck is pretty damn tasty. I love the *carne asada* plate with the meat, the beans, the lettuce, sour cream and guacamole and the little packet of corn tortillas that I pretend I will never need, but eat ever last bite of. Should you have a craving for Mehicano flare [*sic*], take a trip to La Bamba, and have no fear!—Katie W.

—Yelp Review of La Bamba Taco Truck
in Sonoma, California, April 26, 2013

Sonoma County, California, is best known to tourists for its lush vineyards and sophisticated wines, not its taco tastings. But in Sonoma, Napa, and other agricultural counties throughout California, taco trucks are as ubiquitous to California's landscape as grapevines and tomato groves. On the outskirts of downtown Sonoma, the owner of La Bamba taco truck makes tacos for the many Mexican migrants who have arrived in Sonoma County to harvest grapes. Taco trucks follow the workers to the "factories in the field."[1] During the day, the trucks owners serve tacos from roadsides that run through vineyards. At night, some of the taco trucks park in Boyes Hot Springs or in Aguas Calientes, the little Mexican barrios just outside of Sonoma's town center. Taco trucks are nomadic. They are as migratory as the Mexican day laborers. In fact, their movements parallel one another. By feeding Mexican migrants tacos along roads that meander between the grapevines, taco trucks socially shift spaces that are designed primarily to produce capital.

When Katie W., as she identified herself in her Yelp review, came across one such taco truck, it was a "Hand TO PEARLS" moment, as she put it. Encountering an enigmatic environment where one would least expect it is enthralling, especially if it offers something exotic to eat. But it is ignorant, and perhaps a bit arrogant, not to associate taco trucks with California vineyards. Why would someone *not* expect to find a taco truck in Sonoma County? The answer relates to the spatial cloak of the capitalist mode of production, which hides production methods by removing them from consumption spaces.

Neoliberal cities are exceptionally good at concealing the circuits of capital that sustain them.[2] Urban planners and developers highlight high-end consumption spaces over less appealing functions of an urban landscape. A mixed-use shopping strip, for example, is symbolic capital, while industrial and heavy commercial zones don't positively contribute to a city's image. But it is the low-wage labor that allows the neoliberal city to flourish. In most cities, developers only present alluring images to consumers to entice urban living. Consumers are seldom, if ever, formally presented the city as a factory, and rarely do the middle and upper middle classes have to encounter the production sites/sights of cities. They must seek out these underbelly urban spaces, if they wish, but typically the middle and upper middle class do so as urban explorers, not as factory workers. There are many sides to a city, and all sides must be investigated to uncover the role that a taco truck plays within an urban environment that both produces and consumes. This is to say that a taco truck's location elucidates the social and political ways in which cities work. But a taco truck parked near vineyards conveys a different narrative.

Perhaps if a person is standing in a supermarket, she may not know the exact production methods that went into harvesting the grapes she is about to purchase. As Harvey (1990, 423) says, "The grapes that sit upon the supermarket shelves are mute; we cannot see the fingerprints of exploitation upon them or tell immediately what part of the world they are from." But if a person is standing near numerous vineyards in the middle of Sonoma County, she should know exactly where the grapes are from and that they do not pick themselves. Thus, pinot noir and tacos make a perfect pairing. The consumption end of fine wine relies heavily on Mexican day laborers and the cheap tacos they depend on. For Katie, the taco truck is mysterious because it does not fit neatly into her privileged perspective of Sonoma's picturesque landscape. And she does not care to, nor have to, unpack the myriad meanings of the truck's presence or its relationship to ethnic exploitation. Instead, she is just another actor upon its space. And as she engages the taco truck's social sphere to savor a taco, Katie innocently crosses boundaries of class, ethnicity, and gender.

Taco trucks are by-products of the capitalist mode of production, but they are also an economic response to a cultural demand. Taco trucks are foremost emblematic of Mexican cultural identity. Mexican immigrants who may or may not have U.S. citizenship typically own taco trucks. They serve inexpensive, traditional-style tacos primarily to Spanish-speaking, low-wage, mostly male, Mexican day laborers.[3] The trucks exemplify an aspect of foodways; estranged emigrants search for fond memories of home through food and through the *taquero*—the taco cook—who knows how to make such food. At most taco trucks, a visitor finds Mexican gardeners, construction workers, or families sharing tacos, conversing in Spanish in diverse Mexican dialects, and chatting with the taquero about their lives and the news from Mexico. In this genial setting, taco trucks are significant social spaces that foster various aspects of Mexican cultural identity for immigrant communities through the practices of everyday life.

Taco trucks are dynamic spaces, because not only do they create a convivial atmosphere by linking place and time through culinary customs, they are also mobile. Through a taco truck's mobility, any given space can become a temporary place for people to eat tacos. Taco trucks are capable of persistently producing new social spaces and ascribing additional meanings to places, which can challenge the ways in which people come to understand such spaces and places. For these reasons, I define *taco truck space* as an evolving cultural and culinary environment in which influences of local life continually converge with economic, political, and social forces at myriad scales. In other words, taco truck spaces are shaped by and, in turn, express the uneven flows of capital between the United States and Mexico, immigration patterns from Mexico, and foodways from Mexico. Taco truck spaces are influenced by local politics, the social structure of the neighborhoods in which the trucks are parked, and community members' personal perspectives on the presence of Mexican culinary practices in semi-public and public spaces. Taco trucks abstract space and create cultural ambiguities, which become even more pronounced by the ways in which the trucks alter streetscapes.

Taco trucks call our attention to the street simply by parking along it. It is on the prosaic public street where they poetically express socioeconomic paradoxes of capitalism, mixing and matching cuisine, culture, and urban space. Taco trucks reconfigure private space by making it public, and make public space private. Taco trucks in cities normally park on public streets, in commercial strip parking lots, or in vacant lots. A taco truck parked in a private lot invites people onto the property for socioeconomic exchange. Likewise, as a taco truck owner parks on a public street, he or she privatizes a public space by making it a place to conduct business. In addition, by taking over a section of the street to vend tacos, the taco truck culturally appropriates the space. The American street becomes a place for Mexican culinary culture. The public and private dimensions of taco trucks mix, blur, and redefine the ways in which public and private spaces have predictably functioned in the United States. For many Americans these sorts of perverse practices are unfamiliar and can be challenging to accept.

This book is a study of taco trucks' social spaces along city streets and how these spaces culturally unfurl into diverse urban environments across the United States. More specifically, it examines the evolution of taco truck space and the ways different communities have interpreted its ambiguous practices. To take on this study of a taco truck's place within a city I must also carefully evaluate how ethnicity, class, and culture operate across an urban environment. Most often, community conflicts about food trucks not only determine where taco trucks are permitted to park but also help define a city's identity. As communities collectively decide what they wish their city to represent, conversations about cuisine and culture directs urban life and shapes urban form. Examining how culinary values are entrenched in urban politics throughout a city is a critical component to the study of taco trucks. This book is as much about the politics of American cities as it is about the social practices at taco trucks.

Throughout the nation there have been legitimate concerns about the public health and public safety of taco trucks. But now that most cities and states have laws in place to address these concerns, discourses about taco trucks are primarily about the trucks' social practices. Most often they are about the type of foods they serve and the kind of people they represent. There are both negative and positive viewpoints on the trucks. Some communities perceive the trucks as nuisances, while others see them as opportunities to create culinary cultural capital. These divergent dialogues yield different degrees of cultural disputes in dissimilar cities with diverse populations of their own, and these disputes result in distinctive mixtures of inclusive and exclusive urban public spaces at myriad scales.

This introduction presents pertinent background material to better illustrate the open-ended nature of taco truck spaces. It begins by briefly reviewing Mexican street food origins, from the Aztec capital to modern-day tacos in Los Angeles. Then it takes a close look at the advent of the taco truck in California and how taco trucks mirror Mexican immigration patterns across the nation. To avoid confusing taco trucks with the new, gourmet-style food trucks, the next section defines the terms I use throughout the book to describe different types of mobile food vending. The following two sections assess the reasons why informal socioeconomic practices become culturally contested and show that Los Angeles's "taco truck war" was primarily a cultural clash. Finally, this introduction addresses landscape as an epistemology to explain how social practices sculpt landscape patterns.

A BRIEF HISTORY OF MEXICAN STREET FOOD

Mexican street food can be traced back to the Aztec market of Tlatelolco, the main market in the Aztec capital of Tenochtitlan, now Mexico City (Pilcher 1998, 8). At Tlatelolco a person could find a plethora of produce from across the region, including an assortment of maizes and chiles, as well as various prepared foods to eat and drink while at the market, such as *pulque*.[4] A common street food in the Aztec civilization was the tamale. The tamale could be found at markets and was popular at festivals (Pilcher 1998, 20 and 54).[5] Street foods were widespread throughout Mesoamerica before colonization and are still a significant part of Mexican social life to this day (Smith 2003).

Mexican street food spread throughout Texas, California, and the Southwest in the 1700s and 1800s (Pilcher 2012), well before these territories became part of the United States. The political border did not immediately alter the people or their practices. In the mid- to late 1800s and early 1900s, Mexican foods were served on streets not only in towns throughout Mexico but also in Chicago, Los Angeles, San Antonio, and San Francisco (Arellano 2013; Peters 2013; Pilcher 1998 and 2012). Mexican street food had its challenges and challengers in each of these cities, but probably nowhere more than in San Antonio.

The most mystical Mexican street food vendors in the United States during the late 1880s and early 1900s were San Antonio's "chili queens." Along San Antonio's streets, main square, and Spanish plazas, women served Mexican-style chili (Bost 2003; Pilcher 2012, 105 and 106).[6] The women were providing a little extra income for their families but also drew middle-class Anglo tourists from around the country. In fact, the chili queens became so popular that there was even a "San Antonio Chili Stand" at the 1893 Chicago World's Fair, which intensified Americans' interest in Mexican food (Bost 2003, 507). Jeffery Pilcher argues that "the chili queens' attraction came from the thrill of danger, both culinary and sexual; they were seen as simultaneously alluring and contaminating" (Pilcher 2012, 105). Over time, the chili queens' cooking became criminalized, as eating Mexican chili in front of the Alamo was deemed an indecent practice (Bost 2003; Pilcher 2012). In 1943 the chili queens' vending came to a swift end as the San Antonio Health Department made it too complicated for the women to continue to cook on the street (Pilcher 2012, 128).

Mexican street food has never completely faded out in Texas, however. Dan Arreola (2002, 183–85) notes that in the small towns of South Texas, vibrant street festivals with music and food have played a significant part in shaping Texas-Mexican social identities since the 1920s. He observes also that drive-up taco huts are a prominent part of today's South Texas Tejano cultural landscape and that flour tortilla tacos are a regional icon (166–73).

The taco is a corn or flour tortilla wrapped around some sort of filling, such as beans or chicken. Aztecs and other peoples from the Americas have been wrapping beans, *nopales*, insects, and other things in tortillas and eating them for centuries (Pilcher 2012). But the street taco did not take its present-day form until Mexico's industrial boom at the end of the nineteenth century in Mexico City (Pilcher 2008; 2012). As street food faded from the developed world during modernization and the rise of the middle class, street foods became more important in the developing world as industrialization was driving migration and uprooting traditional livelihoods.

The taco is designed to be eaten on the go, standing up, and with one's hands. There is no need for a fork or plate. In this informal way, the taco is a spatial tactic because it makes an ideal fast food for working-class people who have little time to eat as they travel between their home and factory job. In modern Mexican culture, fast food and street food are fairly synonymous. Casually eating tacos on the street while walking from one place to another is a common spatial practice for the working class. Pilcher (1998; 2008) proves that the proletarian street taco traveled with migrant workers to other industrial regions, such as Los Angeles, in the 1920s to 1940s. He details the variety of modernized and Americanized forms that the taco began to take in Los Angeles and across the nation. One example is Glen Bell's standardization of fried corn tortillas, which are still served at Taco Bell drive-throughs.[7] But the most popular tacos for Mexican immigrants in the United States more closely resemble the street tacos from Mexico City, and they are usually served from trucks to people standing on the street.

THE TACO TRUCK'S EVOLUTION

The traditional taco truck is not the only food truck that traverses the American landscape today, nor was it the first mobile kitchen operation that peddled prepared meals. The United States has a varied history of mobile food vending, which has mostly been tied to feeding the working class. We can think of chuck wagon chefs cooking chili for cowboys on cattle drives in Texas during the mid-1800s (Sochat and Cano, 1997). In the late 1800s, horse-drawn lunch wagons provided economical eats for factory laborers on their late-night shifts in the industrial cities of the Northeast (Gutman 2000; Pillsbury 1990). The mid-1900s saw the advent of the motorized lunch truck that served construction sites (Engber 2014). But the taco truck was the first motorized food truck to incorporate the traditional street taco from Mexico City, and it was the first to orient its business operations to everyday Latino street life, challenging the ways that modern-day public streets and other semi-public spaces are used.

In the 1970s, taco trucks throughout California adopted some practices of lunch trucks. During the day, taco truck owners would find Mexican day laborers at construction sites or at the "factories in the fields." Instead of sandwiches, they would serve the traditional taco for Mexicans who were familiar with its flavors. At night, the trucks would park on city streets near nightclubs and Mexican neighborhoods. And of course, other taco trucks would simply remain in one spot and sell to everyone passing by, all day and late into the night.

There are numerous taco trucks throughout urban and rural California. In fact, the taco truck was born in California. The taco truck that has been in continual operation the longest is King Taco in Los Angeles, which opened for business in 1974 (Arellano 2013, 164). In the course of my research, I also came across various reports that agricultural regions throughout the Central Valley and within the city of Sacramento have had taco trucks since the early 1970s. Unfortunately, when I tried to find the owners of these trucks, many of my leads came to a quick end. Even so, there are some very credible eyewitness accounts of a taco truck that was operating in Sacramento in 1975.

Taco trucks made their mark on California's landscape at first in the 1970s and again in the late 1990s. Both of these periods are associated with large numbers of Mexicans crossing the border to find work (Durand, Massey, and Capoferro 2005). For many decades, people from central and northern Mexico have found seasonal employment in the United States (Durand and Massey 1992), and in the 1990s a new migration pattern emerged, due to changing North American trade policies. For this reason, most of the taco truck owners I interviewed migrated during either the 1970s or the late 1990s. Mexicans who immigrated during the 1970s did so to find seasonal work in the fields, and most took U.S. amnesty in 1986.[8] Most Mexicans who migrated in the late 1990s left due to agricultural hardships, and nearly all are still without their documents.[9]

Many Mexicans who migrated to the United States in the late 1990s came from rural areas in less-industrialized Mexican states. Although many still headed to U.S.–Mexican border states, such as Arizona, California, or Texas, most moved farther north and east to states such as New Jersey, New York, and North Carolina (Durand, Massey, and Capoferro 2005). The appearance of taco trucks throughout the United States mirrors this migration pattern. Since the early 2000s, taco trucks have begun to appear across the American landscape from coast to coast. They can be found in California, Ohio, Oklahoma, Texas, Louisiana, New York, Colorado, Utah, Idaho, Oregon, and North Carolina.[10]

The proliferation of taco trucks has transformed urban space throughout the United States and has most certainly popularized the current food truck trend that has swept the nation. Mobile food trucks' rise in popularity has also confounded notions of what constitutes a taco truck. It is important to identify the differences between taco trucks and other types of mobile food vending.

FOOD TRUCK TERMINOLOGY

When I first started researching taco trucks in 2004, the trucks were fairly obscure. But with the emergence of social media hype in 2008 (via Twitter, for example), food trucks are now commonplace in most major cities across the United States. Because various types of food trucks dot the U.S. landscape, it is important to define the distinct types by describing their general differences.

I use *taco truck* or *lonchera* to describe a food truck that is owned and operated by someone who migrated from Mexico and prepares traditional Mexican street foods (such as tacos, tortas, and huaraches) mostly for other Mexican immigrants to consume. Mexicans often call taco trucks *loncheras*.[11] In California, especially Los Angeles and Oakland, most Mexicans refer to the taco truck as a *lonchera*. However, the terms are also used interchangeably: in Sacramento taco truck owners habitually use the English term *taco truck*. Taco truck owners typically use their mobility sparingly, because of language issues, lack of citizenship, or mechanical problems with the truck. Therefore, taco trucks usually stay parked in one place along well-transited arterial roads within commercial strips and near Mexican neighborhoods. Conversely, a lunch truck remains in motion and makes frequent stops.

The traditional *lunch truck* typically frequents job sites and carries mostly premade sandwiches, chips, and candy bars for construction workers. When lunch truck operators are done making their rounds to construction sites and industrial districts, they park their trucks in a commissary for the night.

The third category of truck is what I refer to as the *gourmet, artisanal*, or *boutique food truck*. These trucks emerged in 2007 and 2008 and saturated American cities from 2009 to 2012. Today, more than four thousand artisanal food trucks are rolling across cities in the United States (Swanbrow 2014). These trucks are commonly owned and operated by people with American citizenship and serve artisanal foods to a mainly Anglo, middle-class clientele. These trucks are both mobile and stationary, and their owners rely heavily on Facebook, Twitter, and other social media outlets to announce their locations and special offers.

Additionally there are *pushcarts* and *trailers*. A pushcart is a piece of vending equipment that is typically no longer than six feet, has two wheels, and can be pushed by one person. A trailer has a small space inside from which one or two people can sell food, but it is also large and heavy enough that a motorized vehicle must move it.

Each piece of mobile food vending equipment has a distinct purpose. Some pushcarts are designed for selling tamales, fruits, or *paletas* (popsicles) on sidewalks. Trucks are ideal for making tacos, and trucks are, for myriad reasons, also optimal for moving about the city. In fact, distinct types of culinary practices are associated with each mobile vending unit, and each mobile vending unit has spatial practices that are typically associated with particular places. Usually these practices fit into the perception of these places neatly—for example, as pushcarts fit within Mexican barrios. But when social practices cross cultural boundaries, the practices can be considered disorderly.

ORDERLY DISORDER

City planners like urban space to be rationally ordered and controlled. Their planning mentality seldom allows them to foresee unexpected social and cultural phenomena such as taco trucks creeping into their cities. A taco truck disrupts the well-ordered spaces of the rational city. From a planner's perspective, taco truck space is wild and must be tamed. This means putting pernicious taco truck space in its proper place.

There is a tension that arises between top-down planning initiatives and bottom-up social practices. I define this tension as *orderly disorder*, and it describes planners' efforts to formalize social informalities. Informalities derive from socioeconomic pressures, such as the need for familiar foods at affordable prices. In many ways, the formal economy is responsible for creating informal commerce, because the laborers who support it were not originally considered to be part of it. The parochial urban vision of consumerism is what makes the taco truck ingenious as well as controversial.

Taco truck owners have produced a space to provide inexpensive comfort cuisine to an immigrant clientele. In so doing, they have found an economic avenue to tap into. A cultural demand creates an economic opportunity. The taco truck's design and function allow it to seamlessly integrate into the social fabric of Mexican immigrant communities. Unfortunately, its practice does not always fit into the ways that many Americans wish to perceive their neighborhood spaces. Some consider taco truck space and other informal socioeconomic practices disorderly.

Many Eurocentric-minded Americans perceive Mexican practices as anarchic. James Rojas (2003) notes that when he was growing up in a vibrant Mexican neighborhood in East Los Angeles, where life took place on the streets, there were social practices that created community but that outsiders would interpret as disorganized. "While life on the street may have looked *chaotic to outsiders, to us it was orderly* because we understood it" (276; emphasis added). What may look chaotic to one group is a highly organized sociospatial system of operation for another.

Jane Jacobs (1992) first made the argument that there are unspoken social codes of the street that keep society in check. Mitchell Duneier (2001) reconfirms her assertion in his study of informal sidewalk vending; *Sidewalk* demonstrates that a high level of social structure and moral order is embedded within such sidewalk-vending practices. "Not only do the vendors and scavengers, often unhoused, abide by codes and norms; but mostly their presence on the street enhances the social order. They keep their eyes upon the street, and the structure of sidewalk life encourages them to support one another" (43). There is social order within what may appear as social decay or disarray, and the ability to perceive that order depends on your perspective and knowledge of another group's cultural practices—in other words, whether you find yourself inside or outside a group's social boundaries. There is a social order within perceived disorder, but the dominant community typically strives to reorder it to suit their understanding. I argue that informal social practices in American cities are almost always manipulated or controlled by people with capitalist motives.

Modern Western cities have always been associated with economic development. Their patterns in many respects represent their power. The rapacious urban elite has a storied history of directing the flow of capital through razing slums for roads and highways. Haussman's magnificent boulevards in Paris ripped out housing for the poor to accelerate the movement and flow of capital (Harvey 1991), and the City Beautiful movement in the United States used tree-lined, baroque boulevards to drive up property values (Boyer 1986). Both are prime examples of the use of streets to direct and aesthetically accumulate capital. Because city planners and urban boosters are interested in attracting dollars to their city, they must determine what to do with the informal practices that have abruptly interrupted their vision for the city. Informal street food practices do not necessarily fit into most people's ideal of a pristine urban environment.

But the bottom line is economics. City planners and urban boosters appropriate informal street food practices for capital gains by trying to eliminate them, regulate them, or commoditize them. This decision almost always reflects city planners', city councils', and urban boosters' attitudes about the trucks. In most cases, mayors and municipalities decide to exclude informal commerce because it reduces the "quality of life" that their kind of city would like to represent.

Duneier (1999) asserts that city planners and officials often invoke the term "quality of life" as a reason to enact laws so that they can remove informal street-vending practices. City officials across the country regularly allege that to produce and sustain an elevated "quality of life," the city must foster immaculate environments with opulent, tree-lined streets void of trash and vagrants. "Quality of life," Duneier argues, is related to the "broken windows" theory. George L. Kelling and James Q. Wilson's 1982 article "Broken Windows," published in the *Atlantic Monthly*, finds that minor forms of disorder, such as graffiti and informal commerce, contribute to criminal activity and neighborhood decline. City officials eager to eradicate informal activities have blindly followed this theory in hopes of reducing crime and restoring neighborhood pride. But "quality of life," I have found in performing this research, has come to take on other social meanings over the past decade. And at times, a bit of spontaneity and disorder positively contribute to a city's "quality of life."

"Quality of life"—although not always termed as such—is heavily debated by community groups throughout the country. Everyone wants a high "quality of life," but not everyone has the same idea of what "quality of life" is supposed to encompass. But most seem to agree on one thing: "quality of life" relates to the visual quality of one's immediate urban surroundings. Taco trucks are lightning rods of controversy in this debate because the trucks induce a certain level of disarray in a city's streetscapes. The trucks are either welcome or unwelcome transgressions to residents and business owners, depending on such individuals' class, cultural background, education level, and financial interests in the area, as well as the city's location in the nation. Debates about taco trucks cover issues ranging from aspects of restaurant competition to cultural perceptions of how public and semi-public space should be used. The debates over taco trucks reveal various American ideologies about the cultural landscape, and these attitudes in turn influence spatial relationships.

Disputes over whether people are permitted to vend from taco trucks in public and semi-public spaces must take freedom of expression into consideration. According to Henri Lefebvre (1996), the right to express one's identity and being in the world is a fundamental right of inhabiting a city. For most Mexican immigrants, traditional street food practices represent who they are as migrants from the developing world trying to make ends meet in a society driven by capitalism. At the same time, the presence of someone vending tacos from a truck along the street may be seen by community members as threatening their own social identity. It is ultimately a cultural debate, and almost always an uneven one.

CULTURAL CONTESTATION

On May 4, 2008, Los Angeles County toughened its regulations for taco trucks on streets. A new ordinance would make the trucks move a half-mile every thirty minutes. Failure to do so would result in a misdemeanor, a $1,000 citation to the operator, and a possible penalty of incarceration. The stricter regulations threatened taco trucks in East Los Angeles. The following day, which happened to be Cinco de Mayo, a petition started online to "save our taco trucks" (Saveourtacotrucks.org 2008).[12] The organization asserted, "Carne asada is not a crime" and "The revolution will be served on a paper plate." The issue made national news. *Time* magazine called it "The Great Taco Truck War" (Keegan 2008), and the *New York Times* reported, "In Taco Truck Battle, Mild Angelenos Turn Hot" (Steinhauer 2008). The law, once in effect, made its way into the courtroom, where it was soon struck down (Rogers 2008).

Ernesto Hernández-López (2010) writes that "the taco truck war" was created through social disputes over culinary practices. Owners of Mexican brick-and-mortar restaurants disliked the trucks because they were competition, and other community residents perceived them as blight. Conversely, Latino immigrants argued that the altercations were about their ethnicity and economic standing.[13] Consequently, cultural conflicts become political debates.

Hernández-López argues that these disagreements were primarily "cultural concerns for neighborhood identity," which in turn influenced food truck litigation (241). He writes, "Cultural issues intrinsic to food practices serve as the driving force for these public space debates. Deciding what is permitted in public space effectively shapes food's place in local culture" (263). He claims that the fundamental issue over food-vending regulations is the taco truck owner's right to occupy public space—and that California law, not public opinion about culinary practices or "quality of life," governs the social order of the street.

California Vehicle Code Section 22455 permits municipalities to regulate the time, manner, and location of mobile food truck vending to protect public safety (California Vehicles Code Section 22455). From a narrow legal perspective, a city or county is entitled to regulate only aspects of food truck vending that relate to health and public safety. A food truck is no more hazardous than any other vehicle on the road, and laws regulating motorized vehicles are already established. Moreover, health departments inspect food trucks across the nation. If a food truck has passed its health inspection and has obtained its business permit, it should fundamentally have a right to vend anywhere in public or semi-public spaces. However, throughout the Los Angeles metropolis and the state of California, local governments continuously write laws forbidding food vending from trucks, and they are continuously challenged in court.

The first landmark case was *Barajas v. City of Anaheim* (1993). The Superior Court of Orange County, California, determined that the City of Anaheim was prohibiting food truck vending in public streets without positing a public safety concern. Since this ruling, attorney Jeffrey Dermer and his law partners have fought and won a number of court cases in Southern California based on this precedent (Dermer Behrendt Legal Advisors 2011). The attorneys adamantly assert that municipal food truck laws are blatantly based on the premise of competition and that food trucks pose no threat to public safety. Dermer argues further that food truck regulations actually threaten the freedom to use public space—a fundamental aspect of American democracy (Food Trucks vs. The Establishment, 2012). I take a similar standpoint about taco truck spaces for the purpose of my analysis throughout this book. Focusing on this basic logic better enables me to investigate how communities construct beliefs about what constitutes appropriate behavior in their culture through their efforts to regulate taco trucks. Ultimately, struggles among social groups' ideologies influence the cultural dimensions of streetscapes and urban landscapes.

SPATIAL PRACTICES AS CULTURAL LANDSCAPE PATTERNS

Geographers have long been interested in how societies structure the look of the land. When geographers *read* a landscape, they are deciphering the meanings of the assemblage of elements within it, such as roads, fences, houses, commercial strips, skyscrapers, and factories. Geographers have traditionally contended that these ordinary environments are culturally important because people unconsciously project their values onto the earth's surface. (Groth and Bressi 1997; Jackson 1986 and 2000; Lewis 1979; Meinig 1979; Zelinsky 1994). By studying cultural landscapes and interpreting the meanings that landscapes express, they claim, we can better come to terms with who we are and what we are becoming as human beings in the world.

In 1925 Carl Sauer was the first to point American geographers to the philosophy of landscape that was prevalent in Germany at the time. Sauer (1967) made a case for "landscape morphology," an approach to studying how people and places mutually evolve. Cultural landscape studies became popular, and geographers pursued them for decades. But by the 1980s the number of geographers interested in cultural landscapes had dwindled. Studying cultural landscapes became unfashionable as many turned to Marxist theory or statistics to explain spatial phenomena. A few geographers, however, began to scrutinize landscapes from more critical perspectives. In 1984 Denis Cosgrove (1998) introduced Marxist theory to landscape studies. In doing so, he argued that the elites of renaissance Italy used landscape iconography to implement their ideologies as a way to subjugate subordinate classes.[14] In a more contemporary approach to the epistemology of landscape, James and Nancy Duncan (2003) examined how the Anglo upper class's convictions about suburban countryside aesthetics in Bedford, New York, produced peculiar zoning codes and policies, which ultimately excluded the low-wage Mexican population that manicured these "landscapes of privilege." Similarly, Richard Schein (2006) has proved that racial injustices are deeply ingrained into the common features of the American landscape. Paralleling these themes of landscape and power, Sharon Zukin (1996) has maintained that developers imbue cityscapes with the "right kinds" of cultural symbols to accrue capital, which leads to the preclusion of people who cannot afford to consume them.[15] And Don Mitchell (1996) has brought the idea of landscape back to morphology by asserting that landscapes are continually shaped through social struggles. Mitchell demonstrates that Mexican migrants in California's scenic agricultural fields are regularly making landscape through their labor as well as by fighting for more humane living conditions. For Duncan, Schein, Zukin, and Mitchell, landscapes are never innocent of their production processes.

Much theoretical ground about landscape has been trodden.[16] But these frameworks mostly focus on the fixed aesthetics of landscapes, not the habitual spatial practices of people living within them. In geography, human behavior and movement have been incorporated into other realms of study, such as studies of the representation of social practices and their appropriate and inappropriate places (Cresswell 1996; Sibley 1995), how people move through and experience places (Amin and Thrift 2009; Cresswell 2006 and 2010; Pile and Thrift 1995), and how social practices ascribe meaning to spaces (Cresswell 1996; Slocum 2006).[17] A missing link in cultural-landscape studies is the analysis of social practices as spatial patterns. My aim in this text is to bring about a new way of seeing landscape: through the lens of spatial practices. To do this, I assert that the visual spatial organization of social practices is part of landscape. Put simply, people complete a landscape's composition.

This approach makes the taco truck fascinating from a philosophical perspective because the taco truck is not only a landscape feature, it is also a spatial practice. It sets the landscape in motion. If we want to understand how everyday social practices actively render landscape, the taco truck is a perfect subject. A city's cultural landscape morphology can be observed through its trucks' mobility practices. Mexican immigration has changed and will continue to change the form and function of American cities. By examining the spatial arrangements of taco trucks in urban environments, we can better decipher how Mexicans are integrating and being integrated into American society.

Taco trucks cannot be completely eradicated from any particular urban setting because their owners can use their mobility to circumnavigate stringent policies. Because of this dynamic capability, mobility empowers the taco truck owner and the Mexican immigrant community the taquero serves. Seen in this light, taco trucks come to represent resistance against a community that may try to prohibit them and simultaneously become symbols of Mexican cultural perseverance. Disadvantaged people almost always find ways to sustain themselves in inhospitable environments. People from all walks of life almost always make a space for themselves in a city, even when not provided with a proper place. As David Sibley (1995, 76) reminds us, "We cannot understand the role of space in the reproduction of social relations without recognizing that the relatively powerless still have enough power to 'carve out spaces of control' in respect of their day-to-day lives." I argue that because the taco truck is spatially versatile, it is always carving out social spaces for Mexican daily customs.

Taco truck owners motor around cities seeking spaces where they are most appreciated and least threatened. The truck owner is capable of spatially responding to the social parameters of space and place based on the ideologies and urban policies that govern the landscape. Their methodical movements produce atypical rhythms in municipalities across the nation. These fluctuating patterns denote various American ideologies toward taco trucks in particular and Mexican immigrants in general. Different U.S. cities influence taco trucks' spatial practices in various and irregular ways. And in turn, these dynamic landscape patterns express a city's evolving cultural identity.

OVERVIEW OF CHAPTERS

This book evaluates three different metropolises in the United States: the Bay Area, California; Sacramento, California; and Columbus, Ohio. I chose these urban areas because of their distinct histories and contemporary issues with mobile food vending. In addition, the ways in which current culinary trends and urban policies influence urban life and urban form in each region is remarkably unique. Each chapter of this book demonstrates how urban culinary culture and local politics influence where and how taco trucks operate.

Social discourses and urban planning initiatives throughout the country affect where taco trucks can park in any given municipality. These distinct spatial configurations represent American attitudes toward taco trucks as well as the ways that Mexican immigrants traverse American urban landscapes. To better unravel these entangled relationships, the chapters in this book examine different urban policies and share various personal taco truck vignettes that pertain to the production of taco truck space.

In addition, the contrasting urban cultures exemplify the ways in which diverse taste preferences influence urban space. One's foods preferences and class standing are integral in defining sociospatial relationships across a city. In other words, culinary culture influences how cities operate socially and politically, which ultimately determines where certain cuisines and social groups can be found. These diverse, multiscalar factors must be taken into consideration when evaluating the ways in which taco truck space operates. For this reason, chapters in this book engage different social and political aspects of taco truck space at varied scales, which expand from a truck to the city. While some chapters look closely at the social life along the streets that takes place within the microcosms of taco truck space, others tackle the city at large and the ways in which citizens, elected officials, and urban planners use cuisine to construct spaces to create a collective sense of place.

Chapters 1 and 2 examine street food practices across the Bay Area. They focus on how street food vending reemerged in the 1990s in Latino districts in Oakland and San Francisco, California. In Oakland, community activist Emilia Otero fights for street food vendors' right to occupy public space in the city's eastside barrios. She helps legitimize street food vending in Oakland and paves the way for street food vendors to develop their businesses—from pushcarts and taco trucks to restaurants. In San Francisco, young economic developers help immigrant women turn their small, informal businesses into thriving corporations, while others try to take advantage of the boom in boutique food trucks. These entrepreneurs discuss how they package and market street foods for middle-class consumption.

Chapters 3 and 4 examine the various tensions that have emerged between restaurants and food trucks over culinary practices in Sacramento, California. As the city promotes its new marketing brand, "The Farm to Fork Capital of America," restaurateurs refashion the aesthetics of downtown to reinforce their motto. In so doing, they try to regulate food truck practices out of downtown. The city's code-enforcement department becomes a mediator between food trucks and restaurateurs. Meanwhile, traditional taco trucks, which have been present in Sacramento since 1975, struggle to remain within the city limits. Their issues are increasingly conflated with the influx of gourmet trucks, and their existence is threatened. Chapter 3 evaluates Sacramento's marketing campaign to explore how class, culture, cuisine, and urban politics influence urban design and urban from. It presents, deconstructs, and defines the phenomenon of gastronomic gentrification. Then chapter 4 mirrors the issues chapter 3 presents to show how such large-scale political and gentrification processes affect the livelihoods of taco truck owners.

Chapters 5, 6, and 7 investigate how taco trucks and gourmet food trucks have transformed Columbus's urban image. Chapter 5 looks at the appearance of taco trucks in Columbus's West Side in the early 2000s and the progression of the community's initially negative perception of the trucks to a positive one as the trucks have become a more integral part of the neighborhood. Chapter 6 then expands to scale of the city to show how urban branding and the influx of gourmet food trucks has further eased the acceptance of taco trucks into the city. Since the City of Columbus rebranded itself as "a smart and open city," taco trucks have become markers of ethnic diversity that enhance the city's cultural capital. However, taco trucks somehow still seem to be missing from the city's central consumption spaces. Chapter 7 investigates what other factors contribute to this unusual spatial arrangement. It concludes the exploration of taco trucks in Columbus by taking a detailed look at how taco truck owners must continually develop new ways of adapting spatially to the political and social dimensions of Columbus's landscape. For most taco truck owners in the city, deportation is a legitimate business concern. Taco truck owners use their mobility as a spatial strategy for survival in an uncertain and unsettling urban landscape. As taco truck owners navigate the social terrains of Columbus, they must modify their menus to suit their newfound neighborhoods. Most often, a community's culinary preference depends on whether they prefer tacos with extra sour cream and yellow cheese, or simply with onion and cilantro.

CHAPTER 1

REMAKING OAKLAND'S STREETS

In east Oakland, a woman physically struggles with a police officer over a food cart operated on a sidewalk by a Latina vendor. As the police officer attempts to discard the vendor's tamales, the woman cries, "No, you can't take her livelihood away!" The woman battling on behalf of others is Emilia Otero. She is a civic activist in Oakland who has been both physically and politically fighting with city officials over the right for Latinos to vend on the streets, along the sidewalks, and within vacant lots scattered throughout Oakland's east side.

Otero is a community organizer. She operates La Placita, a communal prep kitchen designed for poor street food vendors to prepare and cook their foods. The Alameda County Health Department (ACHD) inspects La Placita regularly, and Emilia has been working diligently with the City of Oakland's city council and planners to legitimize informal street food vending. As she contends with city officials to allow Latinos to sell food in public spaces, she asserts Latinos' right to the city.

In this chapter, I argue that immigrant street food dynamics propagate empowerment, and I demonstrate how the Latino immigrant population shapes Oakland's landscape order to their collective will. More specifically, I analyze the ways in which Latino street food practices challenge city officials' conventional concepts of how public and semi-public spaces across Oakland should function and for whom. In this regard, I borrow from Lefebvre's notion of what constitutes one's right to the city. For Lefebvre (1996, 173) the right to the city is to inhabit. The city is a living representation, where individual identity and social interactions express its form organically. This is to say that the city is lived through the daily routines of its dwellers. And for many destitute street food vendors, spatial tactics define their vending practices. They must find ways to occupy space in order to produce a profit and ultimately survive the currents of a capitalist-driven city. I also borrow from Certeau's (1986) concept of spatial practices, wherein he argues that individuals must devise cultural codes and tactics to endure social constraints. These habitual practices shape everyday life and contribute to the social fabric of ordinary environments.

The chapter is divided into four parts. I begin by considering Oakland's informality and how Latinos contribute to the capitalist mode of production. In the second part, I experientially explore Fruitvale's ambiance and the ways in which Latino immigrants express their identity through the landscape. Next, I review how Emilia Otero has challenged the city's restrictive approach to informal street food vending. Thus, part three looks at Oakland's landscape through Otero's eyes. At this point, I turn to how other disenfranchised groups have socially latched onto the performances of Latino street food vendors to produce other informal sustainable habitats. While in the first three parts I address how the city is fashioned from the bottom up, in the fourth part I examine street food practices from the top down. I interview city and county officials about their approach to the Latino street food phenomenon. Overall, in this chapter I scrutinize the ways in which city officials modify Oakland's policies and zoning laws to encompass new forms of food vending, and I analyze the extent to which such modifications help or hinder such practices.

INFORMAL OAKLAND

The spontaneous food-vending practices that have sprung to life on Oakland's streets are due to a spike in immigration from Mexico in the mid-1990s. For many Latino immigrants fleeing Mexico, Oakland is their destination, a gateway city to the First World's economy. It is geographically a pivotal city in terms of human migration to job opportunities throughout Northern California. A few immigrants told me that they came from Mexico or Central America with Oakland in mind. One man from Guatemala disclosed to me that it was particularly terrifying to travel across Mexico to California. But he was confident that he would find a job once he arrived. Eventually, he obtained a job picking fruit in Lodi and Watsonville, but he makes Oakland his base when he's not working.

The foreign-born population in Oakland and Fruitvale is 24 percent. The majority of the foreign-born in the Fruitvale and San Antonio areas are Latinos

from Mexico and Central America (U.S. Census 2000 and 2010). Many immigrants, when they first reach Oakland, will have migrated via Arizona or
Southern California. Once they arrive in Oakland, they may take a job in the
service industry, somewhere within the Bay Area. Many work as housekeepers,
cooks, dishwashers, busboys, and landscapers. But not all immigrants remain
in the region; others will continue to Sonoma, Napa, Sacramento, Livingston,
and Watsonville, or they will move east to California's Central Valley to toil in
the fields. Oakland's centrality to many economic opportunities has created a
cultural migrant node within an intricate economic network. It definitely offers
a sense of permanence to its fairly nomadic Latino population.

Much of Oakland's informal commerce has developed to cater to the Latino
population's cultural preferences. Many Latino immigrants desire familiar cuisines from home. A demand develops, which in turn creates economic opportunities for those same immigrants. Cheap eats are also essential. The late 1990s
and early 2000s have been difficult times for both the U.S. and Mexican economies. Eating at restaurants is an extravagance, especially for Latino immigrants
who are trying to save every penny they earn—not to mention that for many
immigrants, the opportunity to cook for themselves is seldom a possibility, as
they have no access to a decent kitchen space. Essentially, street food vending
fills a niche, catering to cultural preferences and to one's own pocketbook.

Many in the community already have the cultural know-how, at least in
preparing cuisine to sell on the street. Certainly, the Bay Area's middle and
upper classes rely on Latinos for menial labor, but many Latinos also exploit
themselves, tapping into their own culture to generate new economic opportunities; they become entrepreneurs who must reveal their cultural identity to
turn a profit. As they take to the street, they further expose themselves to the
social dangers and legal formalities of the city. Hence, they must develop new
tactics and cultural codes to sustain their place. This is what it means to say
that Latino street food practices are not simply cultural but also symbolic of
socioeconomic struggles. And in Oakland, these struggles most often manifest
themselves on Fruitvale's streets.

FRUITVALE'S AMBIANCE

Oakland residents consider the Fruitvale district to be the city's barrio. Its Mexican murals, Spanish-speaking business district, large Catholic Church, and
informal Latino commercial practices contribute considerably to the neighborhood's cultural landscape. Additionally, taco trucks dominate the district. The
social practices of the Fruitvale district have changed radically over the past

one hundred years. Fruitvale once boasted orchards of cherries and apricots; before that, it was a cattle ranch that was gifted as a land grant from Spain to the Peralta family (Maly 2008; Bagwell 1996). The Peralta family lost the land title when California became part of the United States (Peralta Hacienda Historical Park 2012). Fruitvale's social history has certainly modified the landscape. Probably the district's most dramatic urbanization took place after the 1906 San Francisco earthquake, due to out-migration from San Francisco to the East Bay.

Fruitvale is still very much a hybrid of its rural past and historic urbanization; there are still numerous fruit trees throughout the neighborhood and within people's yards, and the prevailing street pattern follows the former suburban streetcar rail lines. The area may have once been bursting with cherry and apricot orchards, but the most popular fruits in Fruitvale are now the tropical ones. On nearly every corner one can buy coconuts, pineapples, and mangos, with a sprinkle of chile powder and a squeeze of lime.

Fruitvale's transition to a Latino-dominated neighborhood coincides with the emergence of Spanish-speaking civic-rights organizations and the marginalization of the Latino community; all the while, freeway development begins to spatially fragment and racially segregate the city (Maly 2008; Self 2003). The leadership of Jack Ortega with the Spanish Speaking Unity Council is prominent in uniting Latinos and becomes a dominant draw for Latinos to move into the Fruitvale neighborhood (Self 2003, 236). City council member Ignacio de la Fuente is also instrumental in fighting for Latino issues in Fruitvale.[1] Furthermore, Saint Elizabeth Catholic Church draws many Latino Catholics to the area. The church serves to unite diverse Spanish-speaking Catholic groups, such as Salvadorans, Cubans, Puerto Ricans, and Mexicans (Maly 2008, 175).

Because Spanish speakers and Catholicism have dominated Fruitvale over the past fifty years, the neighborhood attracted new Latino migrants in the mid- to late 1990s. Of course, some of the draw to the neighborhood during this period was also due to low rents (Maly 2008). According to the 2010 U.S. Census (the most recent complete data available), the population of the Fruitvale district numbers 50,294. Fifty-four percent of this population is Hispanic or Latino: 38.8 percent is of Mexican descent, and 10.5 percent is Central American (U.S. Census 2010). The area is a multicultural milieu, but the majority of residents are Mexican and Central American. It is this most recent wave of immigrants who bring informal practices with them, practices that prior to their immigration were, for the most part, absent.

In 1984 the first taco truck began vending tacos along International Boulevard near Fruitvale Avenue.[2] The truck, *Mi Grullense*, apparently hailed from a family that owned several taco trucks in Los Angeles (see plate 5).[3] The following year, the taco truck El Guadalajara opened (see plate 6). For several years, there were only a few taco trucks in Oakland; today, there are approximately one hundred traditional taco trucks throughout the city. The vast majority of the trucks are in Fruitvale, almost one on every corner.[4] While a few food trucks could be found throughout Fruitvale from the mid-1980s onward, all types of street food vending really began to flourish in the mid- to late 1990s due to an influx of Latino immigrants.[5] This arrival of immigrants started tamale carts, Michoacán ice cream and paleta carts, churro carts, chicharrones carts, and fruit carts, as well as superspontaneous vending from foldable tables and the back ends of vehicles (see plate 7). Clearly, the more recent Latino immigrants are using spatial tactics to connect with other Latinos who are seeking out familiar foodstuffs.

Everyday movements, which take the form of spatial practices and tactics, are ways of bending space (Certeau 1986). To be sure, Latino practices in Fruitvale erode the prescribed meaning of the street as they socially recode the built environment. As Certeau has contended, spatial practices create a "poetic geography" superimposed upon "the geography of the literal, forbidden or permitted meaning" (105). As Latino street food vendors' practices weave with other social routines, they produce new forms of social space. And these evolving practices become patterns that imbue the landscape with new aesthetic values.

While conducting interviews in the neighborhood, I noted some intriguing perceptions by recent immigrants about how they discern the Fruitvale district. Most Latino immigrants in the neighborhood identify with the streets that are associated with food practices. Often, they do not necessarily know the name of the district, nor do they orientate their mental maps as being part of the Fruitvale boundaries at large. City officials define the neighborhood as Fruitvale, and long-term residents refer to it by that name as well. However, recent immigrants would say that their neighborhood was defined through intimate interactions, ones directly associated with their daily activities, such as talking to friends while eating tacos. In other words, they do not interpret the neighborhood to be an area but, rather, a street, or two or three streets. Many immigrants would tell me that their neighborhood was called "Thirty-Fourth Street," "International Boulevard," and/or "Fruitvale Avenue."

The Latinos' perceived spatial order of their neighborhood tends to be centered on Saint Elizabeth Catholic Church on Thirty-Fourth Street. The church is surrounded by a high concentration of Mexican stores and taco trucks on International Boulevard, Fruitvale Avenue, and Foothill Boulevard—all central corridors of Mexican commerce. Moreover, their perceived spatial order coincides with Oakland's zoning ordinances that permit mobile food vending, which allow taco trucks and food pushcarts to operate solely within the industrial and commercial zones, primarily along Foothill Boulevard and International Boulevard.

It is interesting to note the differences in the perceived spatial relationships between planned urban space and Latino spatial practices. The bottom-up Latino practices do not fit into the ways in which city planners have defined their neighborhoods. Thus the two ways of seeing the landscape are at odds. Henri Lefebvre (1991, 143) in considering the ways in which space is produced through spatial practices argues, "Space [is] produced before being read, nor was it produced in order to be read and grasped, but rather in order to be lived by people with bodies and lives in their own particular urban context." The cultural practices associated with the Latino landscape are central to the social spatial structure that defines the Latino landscape. This observation may seem obvious, but it is important to emphasize that the residents of Fruitvale do not necessarily consider their neighborhood an area that city planners have demarcated with lines on maps. Rather, it is much more about lived space, about the spatial dimensions of the Latino landscape practices associated with the ebbs and flows of the street.[6]

When I spoke with the residents in the community, many would mention how the activities on the street would evoke memories of where they grew up. One man from Mexico City told me that he enjoyed sitting at the corner of International Boulevard and Thirty-Fifth Street to watch the cars. He said the traffic congestion and the exhaust reminded him of Mexico City's hustle and bustle. He relished the rhythms of the street.

For many Latinos, munching on Mexican street food while being in Oakland becomes synonymous with eating at home. It is not just eating the food that stirs their memories, but also the street food ambiance, as well as the life and social practices that stem from the food. Eating on the street becomes a symbolic experience: it provides a way for them to embody place, to link time and space, to find comfort within their unfamiliar surroundings, and to make firsthand social connections.

The foods that are primarily available in Fruitvale are associated with the State of Jalisco, Mexico. Most of the food vendors I spoke with were from Jalisco, Michoacán, or from a nearby region along Mexico's Pacific coast, such as Colima, Guerrero, or Sinaloa. Some of the foods found in Oakland are tortas ahogadas (drowned tortas, a Guadalajara specialty), which are sandwiches on thick buns that are then bathed or rather dipped in a chile de árbol salsa. There are also Jalisco-style tamales (the standard cornhusk tamales), cabeza barbacoa tacos (head meat tacos), goat meat tacos, as well as a variety of seafood specialties from Sinaloa, such as ceviche and shrimp tacos.

In Oakland, most food cart vendors are undocumented immigrants, while the owners of restaurants are generally documented. Taco truck owners are a mix of documented and undocumented immigrants. The hierarchy of business operations almost always starts from the bottom with a pushcart. Then, once that operation succeeds, the owners will move to a truck; if they have their papers, then they may even open a brick-and-mortar restaurant at a later date (see plate 8). There are exceptions—for instance, some restaurants that have established a truck—but almost always it is the other way around. Often, when a business moves its practice from a pushcart to a truck, and then later to a restaurant, it nearly always keeps the truck or even adds another.[7] Latino food vending in Oakland is a mix of documented and undocumented workers, licensed and unlicensed vendors, nearly all of whom are struggling to make ends meet.

When food-vending carts first appeared in Oakland in the late 1990s, the city, the police, and the Health Department did not know how to respond to the practice, other than to shut down the food vendors and dispose of their food immediately. Street food vending was deemed an illegal activity. Oakland is not the first or only city that had to deal with immigrant food cart vendors in the United States during the 1990s, but it was the first city to address the phenomenon through a progressive planning initiative to help protect the practice. I spoke with Emilia Otero—the community advocate who fought on behalf of the immigrant food cart vendors and taco truck owners—about how city officials came to expand their policies.

LA PLACITA

Emilia Otero worked closely with the Oakland officials from the late 1990s to 2001 to create policies and health codes that would legitimize food vendors' practices. In the process, she established a commercial and communal kitchen, La Placita (The Little Plaza). It is a place where vendors can prepare their foods in a controlled and hygienic environment, and the ACHD inspects the kitchen on a regular basis. Today, some of the vendors in Oakland are fully licensed, although a large number still are not. To meet licensing requirements, street food vendors must obtain a health permit from the ACHD and a business license from the City of Oakland. Additionally, the practice of mobile street food vending—whether from a pushcart or a motorized truck—is also restricted through zoning laws to primarily the Fruitvale and San Antonio areas.

I met with Otero at her office at La Placita commissary kitchen. She began by showing me all the accolades she has received over the years, now hanging on the wall behind her desk, and expressed how much the community meant to her (see plate 9).[8] We talked about the manifestation of the Latino street food practices in Oakland and when and why she became involved. She explained that she worked as a community organizer helping Fruitvale's schools with the Latino population. The community approached her in 1998 to address the various issues and concerns about street food vendors. She agreed, and once she started to work with the vendors she became passionate about their cause. She elaborated,

> All these people have families, families to support. Some of these people used to live in crowded small garages, five or six people in a small garage. . . . This is America. These people have a right; these people have a future here! Most of these people back then had no documents.

For Otero, informal street food vending was a way to legitimize one's place in the United States because it allowed people to gain a foothold in the new market economy. In 1998 Otero established the *Asociación de Comerciantes Ambulantes de Fruitvale* (ACAF), which fought for immigrant food vendors' rights to sell food in Oakland's public spaces. In other words, Otero was advocating for Latino immigrant food vendors' right to the city.

Otero's objective was to devise a way to legalize informal street food vending. This meant to render Mexican street food practices socially acceptable to the city officials and citizens. It was a complex process that involved working with myriad city offices—from the Police Department and City Planning Offices to the ACHD.

> The city had no idea what it was I wanted to do. We were the first in the country and there was no book, no instructions. Even the city didn't know how to legalize the practice. . . . They have no idea; even the health department had no idea. The City of Oakland was asking me how much they should charge for permits. I had to figure it out; I didn't have the city's financial skills . . . but the first step was to legalize them [the food carts] with Alameda County [Health Department].

For the City of Oakland and ACHD, the gravest problem with the street food vendors was that they were cooking their food in their homes. Often, the foods were being prepared in small garages where several immigrants were living. Needless to say, the food prep spaces were not very sanitary, and there was no way to know if the food was being prepped and cooked in a salubrious environment or not. Thus ACHD had no other choice than to throw out the vendor's foods. This, of course, led to dramatic confrontations between the food vendors, Otero, and the ACHD:

> [A food cart vendor] would call me and say: "The health department is here and wants to take my food." I [used] to run from my house because I didn't have a car.

I used to run! "Where are you?!" [She would ask the food vendors, and they would respond] "I'm here on International and Thirty-Ninth," or, "I'm here on Twenty-Seventh." I would go there and I used to argue with the health department. Back then they [the food vendors] had the supermarket pushcarts, the shopping carts. And I used to go over to the carts and throw myself on top of them! And say, no you aren't going to take their fruit! You're not going to throw away their tamales! They have a family to feed! And a couple of times the inspector called the police. I would tell the police my name, Emilia Otero. And the police would say, "Oohhh, *you're* Emilia Otero." By that time the city and the community knew what I was doing and the police knew who I was. . . . Believe me, when you see me, prepare yourself, because it's war! (Emphasis in original.)

Over time Otero's street battles with ACHD turned into practical solutions. At the time there was also no such concept as a commissary kitchen for street food vendors anywhere in the United States. Emilia developed the idea of a shared kitchen space for the food vendors, a central cooking location that could also be inspected by the Health Department. Fortunately, the City of Oakland awarded her a $75,000 loan to start the business, on which she still owes $35,000. Emilia began La Placita Commissary Kitchen in 2001, the first of its kind in the country. Founding the kitchen provided a stable and sanitary environment for the food vendors to prep their foods; nonetheless, the practice of street food vending in Oakland was still controversial.

Traditionally, Latino immigrants played the role of low-wage workers in the formal North American economy. Emilia put it this way: "You see, capitalists don't want Mexicans here, *but they want to use them [for their labor]*" (emphasis in original). Mexican social and cultural visibility in the formal economic (or corporate) landscape is not necessarily acceptable to property owners. Otero explained that half of the struggle was opening a kitchen; the other half was changing people's perceptions about the aesthetics of food vending. At first, city officials were extremely reluctant to permit the practice, even legally. Otero would attend city council meetings regularly and tried to educate the council members about the positive facets of microbusinesses.

The city had no idea of what I was trying to do. I used to go to the city council and yell at them. . . . Many would tell me that this is great, and this is wonderful [in reference to helping street vendors with their business]. But not in my backyard!

The City Council eventually did approve the practice; however, it was constrained to the Latino limits of the city.

In 2001 the city began a pilot program that allowed for thirty pushcarts. This ordinance at the time covered all of the food cart operators who were working with Otero and wanted to obtain an operating permit. Over the next several years, street food vending did fairly well, and nearly everyone obtained an operating permit. Otero told me that there was new animation of the street. She indicated that the legalization of informal street food practices had transformed the community positively:

> The practice [of street food vending] was bringing benefits to the community. They were bringing life to the community. Before the vending, the neighborhood was dark. Everyone was afraid to go down International Boulevard. People today say they are afraid of International Boulevard, and I will say, you should've seen 1998. You couldn't even walk at three o'clock in the afternoon on International Boulevard! These people were bringing a new face, a new business, and a new idea of progress to this community.

I could not find any statistics that confirmed a reduced crime rate in the area; however, almost everybody perceived the new street life as a positive attribute. The neighborhood did feel alive and animated. And certainly the permits allowed Latinos to more fully express their cultural identity.

Within the next few years, the City of Oakland continued to put into place some of the first policies and permits for mobile food vending in the United States—for food trucks and pushcarts alike. City officials permitted pushcarts to operate on public property as long as they did not block pedestrian traffic flows on the sidewalk. Taco trucks, however, were allowed to operate only on private property and not on public streets (Oakland, California, Code of Ordinances 5.49 and 8.09). The policies controlled aspects of mobility and social practices as well as where these performances could take place. For example, some of the behavioral ordinances around the food trucks mandated that customers had to pay before receiving their food and had to order and pick up from separate and designated windows. The owners also had to provide space for a line, and customers had only fifteen minutes to eat their food before they were to leave the premises. By controlling the spatial practices of impromptu informal commerce, the city was trying to establish a certain level of orderliness. Otero notes:

> After everything was said and done with organizing with the health department, we started on the zoning. This is the only zone we are allowed to work in. . . . If you have a license, you can only work here within this zone [*points to a zoning map and the food vending permitted zones*].

The regulations allowed for mobile food vending primarily within industrial and commercial zones along International Boulevard, Fruitvale Avenue, and

Foothill Boulevard, but only within east Oakland, predominately associated with the political boundaries of the Fruitvale and San Antonio districts. Additionally, other spatial constraints for the food trucks, according to "Permit conditions and issuance code 8.09.050," were as follows:

> The vehicular food vendor shall not locate within two hundred (200) feet (as measured from the parcel boundary) of any fast food restaurant or other vehicular food vendor, full-service restaurant or delicatessen, or within five hundred (500) feet of any public park or primary or secondary school.

Essentially, what the City of Oakland did was create a spatial code of conduct that would allow for Latino informal food performances to take place, but these spaces were only within what was already considered part of the Latino landscape. The food truck permits based on zoning codes along particular streets were established to protect Mexican practices but were done so in a manner that would conceal their presence from the city's more affluent areas. Emilia remarked,

> These people [food vendors] pay taxes, are working from commissaries, and have all their permits, but aren't allowed to work throughout the city. . . . The city wants to treat us like animals and put us in a cage. But we are not animals! We are human beings! We have a right to all spaces throughout the city!

The City of Oakland officials and council members perceive the aesthetics of Latino informal street food practices as entropic and wish to contain them to the Fruitvale and San Antonio areas. In other words, these are spatial ordinances written specifically for Latino practices and are consequently based on the ethnicity of a people and their place within the city. Emilia combats these exclusive policies by maintaining that public space should be inclusive and representative of all people: "We have a right to all spaces throughout the city!" Mitchell (2003, 133) notes that these sorts of proclamations to public space allow for minority groups to "make claim for a right to the city." Even though Latinos may not have the right to vend in all public spaces throughout the city today, it may be the beginning of a movement to refashion public spaces throughout Oakland so as to include all its inhabitants.

The new food permits and policies are by no means perfect, especially in the eyes of many Latinos. For some, the policies paradoxically represent aspects of both justice and injustice. They are a reminder of Latinos' marginalized place within society and within the city. Even though the mandatory licenses may protect Latino mobile food vending in select places, they may also inadvertently exacerbate the spatial segregation of Latinos from the rest of Oakland. Otero fumes: "They treat us like we aren't educated enough . . . like we were children! They give us a piece of candy and then tell us to shut our mouths!"

The ordinances and policies that the City of Oakland has put into place are contentious beyond their discriminatory implications. In the State of California, a city has no authority to regulate mobile food vending beyond aspects of health and public safety. Food trucks pose no more threat to public safety than any other moving vehicle. Essentially, if a food truck is regulated for any reason other than for health concerns, it calls into question the underlying motive of the ordinance. If policies are put into place, then they are nearly always developed because there is a controlling cultural construct that has developed toward the practice of street food vending. According to California law, any mobile food vendor who has a tax ID and a business permit and has passed a health inspection can operate anywhere within public space throughout the state (California Department of Motor Vehicles 2009). Although Oakland's policies are unjustifiable, most food vendors do obey most aspects of Oakland's codes, even if they do not have an operating permit.

Despite the convoluted food-vending policies, the legalization of a few carts has sparked additional forms of informality throughout Oakland, probably what Oakland city officials feared would happen, and why they would want to contain the carts in both space and practice. The permitted presence of food vendors working with Otero ignited a second wave of illegal vendors and new forms of informal commerce. Many of these illegal practices were directly related to the operation of taco trucks. For instance, socioeconomic opportunities tended to spring up alongside the food trucks, such as window washing, particularly by African Americans. Subsequently, a secondary informal commerce emerged where other disenfranchised individuals would try to extend their right to the city.

A SECONDARY INFORMAL COMMERCE

The permitting of some food trucks and pushcarts opened the floodgates of informal street food vending in general. The food-vending practice became perceived as permissible and no longer divisive, and the police came to leave the food vendors alone for the most part. Today, Fruitvale is inundated with taco trucks and pushcarts. Very few have operating permits, although many do have a health permit. Surely, for immigrant street food vendors, obtaining an operating license, a business license, and a health permit must be bewildering. However, regardless of whether vendors are aware of the regulations, informal commerce predominates Fruitvale. In this section I examine the new informal commerce that has arisen in Oakland, and the ways in which new life on the street has manifested itself and further altered Fruitvale's cultural landscape.

Sociologist Mitchell Duneier (2001, 85–90) has noted that informal vending generates complex webs of social codes as well as additional informalities. In Fruitvale, informal street food vending animates urban space while simultaneously creating places of possibility. Street food in Oakland not only promotes new jobs for Latino vendors, it also improves the neighborhood by offering other microeconomic opportunities. These new opportunities especially benefit the lifelong African American residents of Fruitvale, who, like the Latino community, have been plagued by extremely strenuous socioeconomic circumstances.

At Marisco Sinaloa, Anthony, a black man, works next to the taco truck, washing clientele's car windows and wheels by hand for a dollar or two. Anthony grew up near this neighborhood and has spent his entire adult life—approximately thirty-five years—working at a nearby car wash. He still lives in the same house where he grew up, and he comes to the taco truck to clean cars to make a few extra bucks so he can eat. After he earns a dollar or two, he goes up to the truck's window and orders himself a couple of tacos.

There is also Melvin, a black, elderly, houseless man who has lived on the street for the past fourteen years of his life.[9] He revealed that he is from San Francisco and has spent almost a decade in prison. When he was released, he ended up in Fruitvale. He pointed to a small grass strip next to a four-foot-tall concrete wall at the edge of Forty-Second Street near International Boulevard. "I've slept there in that grass for the last fourteen years of my life; that's my home." Needless to say, Melvin does not have much, but he does have a job at El Gordo taco truck (see plate 10). In the evening, Melvin puts on a battered El Gordo employee T-shirt and goes to work. When anyone arrives at El Gordo by car, Melvin is there to help the driver find a parking spot and keep an eye on his or her vehicle. When Melvin is not directing traffic, he is cleaning up after people. All night, he wipes down the counter at the truck, sweeps the street, picks up trash, and throws out people's paper plates. He also tries to provide the customers with a pleasant eating experience. He fends off beggars and the drug addicts who hang out across the street. He informs me that he really has to hold his turf and also protect the customers at the truck:

> Crackheads are always trying to rob me out here. One night a crackhead got mad at me for chasing him away because he was bothering a Mexican family trying to eat. I told him that he needed to show some respect and not to bother people while they are eating, especially a family with children. Later he came back and tried to rob me. He busted my lip and kicked me to the ground under

the truck. I'm an old man. I couldn't get up. . . . Finally the workers in the truck called the police.

Melvin takes pride in his job duties. He eagerly takes out the trash, is always singing, and makes a point to talk to everyone. The cooks and operators like to harass Melvin endearingly and are always whistling jovially at him. Melvin, who may otherwise have very little, does lead an eventful existence through living and socializing around a taco truck. My chat with Melvin ended with him asking me, "By the way, could I get a dollar or two from you?"

The street food vending seems to keep growing. At night and on weekends, I witnessed Latinos setting up tables and making fresh tortillas sporadically along International Boulevard. But I also observed several black people with barbecue businesses. African Americans in the area are getting in on the act. One Saturday afternoon, across the street from La Placita, I watched two black men set up a barbecue grill and a foldable table. They then played rap music from a 1980s-style jam box and sat outside grilling chickens. I asked Emilia if they had permits to sell food, and she replied, "No." Further down International Boulevard at the corner of Sixty-Ninth Street—at the heart of the "kill zone" and just catty-corner from a mobile police surveillance station—is another barbecue smoker. This one seems to be very popular, and there are always a number of people gathered around it. It is not uncommon to see black people grilling chicken in east Oakland along International Boulevard. The grilling and barbecuing seem to blend in well with the Latino street food scene.

As informal street food vending has grown over the past twenty years in Fruitvale, it has put a strain on the resources of the City of Oakland and Alameda County. Today, Oakland's informal commerce has become exceptionally difficult to regulate. The city no longer has a cap on the number of permits issued; however, only a small number of street food vendors actually obtain a permit. Remarkably, Fruitvale has become a swamp of informal commercial practices with regard to street food. Most people operate without a city permit and many even without a health permit. Anyone who knows how to cook food can set up a table on the sidewalk and sell food any given weekend. Because street food vending is ephemeral, it is extremely difficult for the city or the Health Department to control.

PLANNING INFORMALITY

Nancy Marcus, who works for Special Activity Permits, Office of the City Administrator, City of Oakland, informed me that currently there are only sixteen trucks and four pushcarts with an operating permit.[10] When I talked to her in April 2013 (April is the month permits are due), she noted that many had not had a chance to renew yet, and the number of permitted vendors may be higher. Regardless, when I am in Fruitvale, I see a number of pushcarts on each block, and most vendors do not have their proper permits.

Part of the problem is obtaining a city-operating permit. Current city licensing fees for a food truck are $2,090 per year, $455 for a pushcart. For some immigrants who are living in or near poverty and are trying to start a business, or to continue their microbusiness, these fees are exorbitant. For most immigrants, navigating the various department regulations is difficult—language barriers notwithstanding. Moreover, nondocumented immigrants do not have a driver's license, so they cannot obtain a truck permit anyway.[11]

Many of the trucks operate without city permits because the vendors know it is difficult for the city to enforce street-food-vending codes. Some intentionally use their mobility to evade city regulations. Marcus explained to me how difficult it was to enforce vending regulations in Oakland. She told me that there are some trucks that drive in from other parts of the Bay Area, such as San Jose. They will move around the city and then drive out. Additionally, there are other trucks that simply will move around all the time. But mainly, Oakland's officials are unable to enforce vending codes because they are understaffed and the police have bigger issues to contend with, such as high homicide rate and substantial gang activity. Currently, there is no Oakland city official responsible for enforcing the mobile-food-vending code. Even if there were someone, one employee would not be sufficient. Marcus concluded, "Lots are out vending without city permits—as for Alameda County Health certificates, probably some too [are vending without them]!"

Presently, the ACHD's mobile food program "consists of over six hundred Mobile Food Facilities including carts, trucks and vehicles of various types" (Alameda County Environmental Health 2014). A vendor's health permit costs $608 for a truck and more than $300 for a pushcart. Some immigrants starting a food business cannot afford a license; still, there are far more food vendors with a health permit than with a city permit.

I spoke with Don Atkinson-Adams, who is the office supervisor of mobile food facilities at the Alameda County Health Department. He sounded overworked when I spoke to him by telephone in March 2013 and then again in May 2014. He said that mobile food vending in Alameda County, especially in Oakland, had been growing considerably over the past decade and that the department was understaffed. He informed me that the department was hiring two new employees and that they would help reduce his workload. The last time I spoke with him, he told me that he now has four employees and that the department is four to five times larger than any other health department in the East Bay.[12]

In California, each county is responsible for health regulations. Permits are not transferable from county to county throughout the state. I asked Atkinson-Adams how many mobile health permits the department distributed in 2014. He responded,

> For what we call 1830s [mobile-food-vending code], these are mobile food prep units where people work from inside a truck. We have about 345 to 350. . . . Roughly this can be broken down in thirds for what are gourmet trucks, taco trucks, or construction food-vending/lunch trucks. But this is a very rough cut. We don't keep these numbers, so I could be off by fifty for any one category. . . . The number of pushcart permits issued, I don't have those numbers in front of me, but I'd say nine hundred.

I then inquired whether or not the Alameda County Health Department knew the number of nonpermitted trucks that may be operating in the area.

> I don't have those numbers. We are always trying to find people without permits, but it is very difficult. They are mobile, and mobile is hard to catch up with. After five or six [P.M.], or on the weekend, the probability of a nonpermitted vendor getting caught is significantly less. I'm sure many vendors are aware of this and that's when many of the illegal vendors operate. The plus for us is that the staff is up by four. For a long time we only had one person patrolling the streets for vendors without a health permit; now we are doing more patrolling. We now have as much staff as all of the surrounding counties combined.

Many food vendors use their mobility as a spatial tactic to evade city enforcement. Others simply wait for times of the day (evenings), or days of the week (weekends) when health code policies are not implemented. This often coincides with demand and supply of Latino foodstuffs. Many Latinos want to eat in the evening and desire more elaborate foods on the weekends, especially if there is a festivity such as a birthday party or other celebration. Accordingly, Latino food practices seem to work well because they take place during times ACHD vending-code regulations are not actively enforced. Still, many food vendors have no other professional occupation and therefore have no choice other than to work every day and throughout the day.

Atkinson-Adams told me that if officials came across a food vendor without a permit vending hazardous food, they would discard the food and, if possible, confiscate the mobile unit. "If the vendor is selling from a unit that we can pick up and put in our truck, we will take it. Such as plywood pushcarts. Safeway and Lucky shopping carts." I asked him why they would even take a shopping cart because it is something the vendor could just grab again the next day. He retorted, "We can't control that."

Atkinson-Adams informed me that food vendors must display their health inspection rating, something they are reluctant to do. He also confided that the sanitation of mobile food units is hit-or-miss across the city, regardless of the type of food-vending unit. And checking on city operating permits, he explained, is not their responsibility. He added that he tried to keep up the health inspection of the growing number of trucks, while "the city has been trying to control their location."[13] Evidently, economic circumstances have generated Latino social practices that inundate the city and overwhelm city officials.

= = =

Throughout this chapter I have examined the ways in which Latinos occupy Oakland's public spaces and defy city regulations through their street food-vending practices. Consequently, Oakland city officials are struggling to plan for Latino's informal way of remaking the city's streets. And as both planners and Latino activists carry out their initiatives, street life in Oakland evolves.

For Otero, the mission is to challenge the status quo; she explicitly argues that immigrants have an inherent right to the city and that street food vending is one such way that immigrants can economically avail themselves in the United States. Marcus and Atkinson-Adams both note the logistical issues with street food vending in Oakland, especially the fact that city officials simply do not have the financial resources or manpower to regulate the vast number of mobile units inundating the city's streets. Through both these bottom-up and top-down pressures, city officials, with the help of Otero, implemented ways to permit some street food vendors within the Latino district of the city.

Otero established La Placita as a kitchen space for food vendors to prep and cook their food, as well as a fixed place where ACHD could easily inspect mobile practices. City planners also developed zoning laws to permit street food vending in the Fruitvale and San Antonio districts. Despite these progressive zoning laws and urban policies, old issues persisted and new socioeconomic practices developed. Many in the Latino community complained that their street food practices were still being marginalized. The bottom-up and top-down forces were exerting new forms of social space. More illegal food vendors were taking to the streets. Secondary informal practices increased exponentially as more people found ways to tap into this informal economy—like Anthony, who washes car wheels, and Melvin, who cleans up around El Gordo taco truck.

Moreover, African Americans were also engaging the street food scene by erecting their portable grills and barbeque pits. In sum, informal commerce relentlessly took to the streets and mutated Oakland's socioeconomic landscape order.

Oakland is America's city where one is expected to challenge authority and the status quo. Whether street food vending in Oakland could be formally regulated or not, the informal economy would most likely socially negotiate its own means of existence—which in many ways it definitely has. Otero, who is incensed by Oakland's food-vending zoning laws, has now called for civil disobedience. She has told many food vendors to take to the streets throughout Oakland. Taco trucks are popping up in west Oakland and occasionally downtown. If one drives around Oakland today, one would think that there are no ordinances regulating street food space. Without a doubt, street food vending throughout Oakland perseveres. And its unplanned, ephemeral practices and resistance to Oakland's established order noticeably contribute to the city's grittiness.

Oakland's Latino food vending practices could now legally expand throughout the city in 2019, since Governor Brown signed the Safe Sidewalk Vending Act SB 946 in September of 2018 (SB 946 Sidewalk Vendors). SB 946 makes it legal for food to be sold from pushcarts along city sidewalks and in parks throughout California cities. It is important to note that this state law does not apply to food trucks and that city planning departments still have a responsibility to license and regulate street food vending. How Oakland city officials and city council interpret this new law with respect to public health and public safety remains to be seen.

Despite what one may consider to be problems with Latino street food vending, overall the effect has contributed positively to Oakland's image. The street food vending in east Oakland has helped create a vibrant sense of place for residents and visitors alike. In many ways, it has increased Fruitvale's quality of life. Fruitvale has become a popular destination for people across the Bay Area to go taste Latino cuisines and just absorb the colorful street atmosphere.[14]

Emilia Otero, with the help of city officials, the community, and the street food vendors, has altered Oakland's landscape. Not only has she helped change the social rhythms of the spaces in Fruitvale, she has also helped microbusinesses blossom. In 2001, Otero combined Oakland's Cinco de Mayo festival with a street food market in Fruitvale. The community event attracted people and money from all parts of the Bay Area. The tremendous success of the event certainly caught the attention of economic developers from both Oakland and San Francisco, and the perception of what street food vending represented was evolving. What started as a forbidden practice had slowly turned into a model for other cities and individuals to follow, albeit primarily for economic motives. Emilia put it this way:

> You know, when I first started this, I went to the [then] mayor of San Francisco for help, Gavin Newsom. He said, "I love what you are doing, but that could never happen in San Francisco. It'll be great for the East Bay but that's not really something we can pursue here." But now San Francisco has seen how successful we are with informal commercial [vending] and how it attracts people to spend money. And now they are trying to do the same thing.

CHAPTER 2

FORMALIZING SAN FRANCISCO'S INFORMAL STREET FOOD VENDORS

San Francisco's street food scene can be traced back to the 1880s and 1890s when men roamed the city peddling tamales from pushcarts (Peters 2013, 34). Anglo San Franciscans were suspicious of the tamale fillings. Historian Erica Peters notes, "Rumors about small-scale street vendors using seagull in their 'hot chicken tamales!' may have given people a reason to seek assurances of higher quality" (2013, 32). In 1892 Robert H. Putnam decided to formalize the tamale vending practice. He established an enterprise of street food vendors, suited them in white linen uniforms, and equipped them with steam pails. Putnam was successful—so successful that he expanded his business to New York City and Chicago (Arellano 2013, 42).

Over the years, Mexican street food vending faded out in San Francisco (Peters 2013, 34). And by the mid-1900s, most Mexicans in the city had moved to the Mission District. Many there owned *taquerías* (taco shops), where they created new cuisines, such as the burrito. Then, in the late 1990s a new wave of Mexican immigrants began to inundate the streets of the Mission District with their food-vending practices. They were selling tamales and tacos from pushcarts, baskets, and folding tables. And much as one hundred years earlier, there were various entrepreneurs finding ways to formalize the informality of food-vending practices—albeit perhaps for more progressive-minded motives.

Today in San Francisco there are two companies that work with street food vendors: La Cocina and Off the Grid. La Cocina, a nonprofit organization in the Mission District, helps underprivileged street food vendors develop their microbusinesses into corporations. Off the Grid, on the other hand, organizes and orchestrates boutique-food-truck street festivals. Oddly, the traditional taco truck is absent at Off the Grid food truck festivals. It appears that informal Mexican street food vending in San Francisco is becoming formalized for capital gain as the practice is replicated, marketed, and sold to the middle and upper-middle classes. And from this system flow inequalities in the ways in which urban space is socially organized.

To elucidate how the informal street food vending practices of pushcarts and food trucks are formalized, I employ the frameworks of cultural capital, cosmopolitanism, and symbolic capital. I also explore how one's geographic imagination factors into such concepts. For Bourdieu (1984), cultural capital is the way in which an individual demonstrates cultural knowhow and taste preferences in order to express social identity to others. Accordingly, cultural capital helps classify the cosmopolitan—an individual who appreciates societal differences and knows how to navigate multiple cultures (Binnie et al. 2006, 8). Moreover, cosmopolitans are people who can afford to do so, and consequently, regardless of the motive, the very act of consuming cultural differences is a sign of social distinction.

Another way social distinction is made evident is through one's geographic imagination. According to Gregory (1994), the geographic imagination is how one describes and defines what one believes constitutes another group's culture. In so doing, one marks one's social position in the world. For cosmopolitans, this is almost always a privileged perspective. In San Francisco, cosmopolitans are mostly middle to upper-middle class and tend to be young Anglos (ages twenty-five to forty).

San Francisco entrepreneurs realize it is profitable to engage the middle and upper-middle-classes' consumption practices. One way they do this is by using semiotic markers to play on a cosmopolitan's geographic imagination. Savvy business owners market their cuisines with pretty packaging and decoratively designed food trucks. Sometimes these packages provide the subliminal narrative of a foreign culture, but, more important, the beautiful wrappings of foods and the nicely decorated food trucks are designed to attract attention and visually entice people to buy the product. Sharon Zukin (1993) contends that such visual pleasures function as symbolic capital, which stimulate the economy aesthetically. Therefore, through marketing, traditional cuisines are taken out of their original social context and ascribed new meanings for a consumer culture.

Whereas chapter 1 of this book outlined how Latinos employ their own culture to remain financially viable in Oakland, chapter 2 addresses how, in San

Francisco, others exploit (or help Latinos exploit) Latino street-vending practices.

Specifically, I examine how traditional Latino street food practices are refashioned for cosmopolitan consumption and argue that formalizing these practices is an act of cultural imperialism that can lead to exclusion and exacerbate social inequalities throughout the Bay Area. The chapter is divided into two parts. In the first part, I explore La Cocina and the ways in which the organization markets ethnic cuisine to middle- and upper-middle-class San Franciscans. In the second part, I look at how Off the Grid relies on boutique-food-truck vending practices to transform urban space aesthetically to accrue capital. I conclude the chapter by critiquing what such commodification processes represent to Latinos and how unembellished Latino street food practices remain marginalized.

LA COCINA

La Cocina, founded in 2005, is a nonprofit 501(c)(3) business established as an incubator program for immigrants, especially women immigrants of color, to transition from informal street food commerce to the formal economy. La Cocina is located on Folsom Street near the south end of the Mission. They provide a kitchen space and educate immigrants on how to prepare their street foods, but this is just a minor aspect to the overall operation. La Cocina also offers immigrants economic tools, resources, educational opportunities, and valuable advice on how to succeed in the United States' First World economy.

Caleb Zigas, executive director of La Cocina, is a white male in his early to mid-thirties. Young, energetic, and passionate about his work, Zigas worked as a cook from age sixteen until he enrolled at the University of Michigan, where he earned a degree in globalization and culture. After completing his university studies, he traveled extensively in Bolivia and Costa Rica. Following his travels, he arrived in San Francisco and fell in love with the city. He then decided to combine his love of cooking with his interests in cultural studies and began working as a volunteer for La Cocina in 2005.[1]

La Cocina developed from two organizations in the Mission District: The Women's Initiative for Self-Employment and the Mission Economic Development Agency. Zigas explains:

> Both [organizations] were doing development with low-income entrepreneurs, mostly women. They found that many women were writing small-business plans and never launching, and when they found out why they weren't launching, the answer was lack of an affordable kitchen space. So the strategy was to come up with a place that would deliver affordable kitchen space to these talented en-

trepreneurs and in doing so transition them from passive employment to active income generation.

Zigas insists that La Cocina does not provide a kitchen space for just anyone to come off the street and start cooking. Rather, it is a selective program where individuals are chosen from a pool of applicants by the goals they have established for themselves, as well as the type and quality of foods they have to offer. "There will always be people making food in their houses and selling on the street," Zigas says. "And that is fine for those people trying to make a little extra money on the side." However, La Cocina aims to build companies from informal practices. The organization is not about helping all immigrants in need with meeting city and health codes per se; instead, Zigas emphasizes, La Cocina is dedicated to assisting people who want to grow their small business into a corporation. "It is about transitioning people [from] making a little bit of money on the side to asset generation. . . . We help people go into a full business and become profitable."

Based on the company's goals, La Cocina has been very successful. Levi Strauss & Co. financially sponsored the program's kitchen, and La Cocina also supplements its income from donors and grants. The company claims that they have created more than one hundred jobs; of those, 90 percent have gone to women, and 73 percent have gone to immigrants from fourteen different countries (*La Cocina* 2014).

Some of the "graduates" from the incubator program have gone on to have their own brick-and-mortar establishments and are doing well financially. Some of the immigrant entrepreneurs started making $1,000 to $2,000 per month in 2005, have grown their businesses to several thousand dollars per month, and operate with multiple employees. According to Zigas, one of La Cocina's greatest success stories has been working with Veronica Salazar and her business, Huarache Loco. Originally from Mexico City, Veronica brought her practice of making *huaraches* (a typical street food found throughout Mexico City) to San Francisco. In 2005 she started making $8,600 per month; currently, she makes $81,200 (gross income) per month and operates with twenty-two employees. She upgraded the humble huarache to accommodate middle- to upper-class San Franciscans. Recently she opened a brick-and-mortar restaurant in Marin County, although she still sells at Alemany Flea Market in South San Francisco.

La Cocina currently has thirty-five street food operations in the process of formalizing, and they have graduated fifteen companies. It is a four-year program wherein La Cocina's twelve board members guide incoming entrepreneurs through the American financial, legal, and cultural system. They help the cooks manage finances, understand San Francisco's food-trade networks, and navigate San Francisco's food policies. Most important, they help immigrants understand San Francisco's marketing mentality. Zigas puts it this way: "Our product at La Cocina is the success of the women in this program. They cook what they make, and we try to market that." Zigas also made clear that San Franciscans are interested in ethnic food at affordable prices.

La Cocina places a strong emphasis on the marketing and packaging of ethnic foods toward middle- to upper-middle-class San Franciscans. It is a relationship that speaks volumes about American attitudes toward food—especially middle- and upper-middle-class San Franciscans' mindsets toward immigrant ethnic food. Likewise, this process reveals how immigrants perceive American taste preferences. The marketing of ethnic food also changes the traditional significance of food by ascribing new social attributes to it. Foods actively take on fresh meanings simply by the change in their geographic location (Cook and Crang 1996, 140).

It is an interesting dynamic that takes place around food at La Cocina. Immigrant ethnic food is spun into a package that appeals primarily to middle-class San Franciscans. In March 2014 I interviewed La Cocina's business-development manager, Geetika Agrawal, an Indian American who received her undergraduate degree in computer science—with a minor in cultural anthropology—from Stanford University. She also holds an MBA from New York University. In her late twenties or early thirties, Agrawal is very pleasant to talk to and eager to discuss the marketing attributes of food. She reiterates the importance of formalizing the informal in order to be successful in the American marketplace and addresses how La Cocina helps immigrants make the economic transition:

> La Cocina's mission is to support entrepreneurs who are successful informal entrepreneurs and to remove the barriers to entry that exist for them to enter and be successful in the formal marketplace. So we are all about transitioning people from *informal to formal*. So when we work with our clients, it's more about giving [them] the access to the skills, tools, and . . . resources that will allow them to compete successfully in the formal marketplace (emphasis added).

She told me that one of her favorite aspects of her job is helping immigrants understand the cultural barriers that exist in the food industry. She emphasized that being able to transcend cultural perceptions is essential to formalize the informal:

> I feel like new food is like new technology. Everybody still faces the innovator's dilemma. There are your early adopters—[as,] for instance, [with] quinoa and kale. There are people here who have been eating quinoa and kale for ten years,

but now it's standard on every menu. . . . We spend a lot of time on menu design and cultural translation. In our marketing curriculum the most useful thing we do is not only targeting a market but also really working on figuring out how to translate the thing that we are talking about into something that will sound familiar enough for a San Franciscan to try it.

I asked Agrawal to provide an example of how her organization formalizes a traditional Mexican cuisine for the San Francisco marketplace. What might a Mexican immigrant want to make, and how does La Cocina work with him or her to sell it?

Part of how we differentiate ourselves with our clients is not serving the same Mexican food that everyone is used to, but serving regional Mexican cuisine. It came out of need, that every round of interviews, when we get immigrants, especially Mexicans, their perception of what they think they should present to the American market. And right now tamales are popular, so everyone wants to make tamales. But we ask them: Are tamales part of your regional culture? Do you ever make a tamale at home? And it won't be [that this is the case]. But they have an idea of what the American market needs. And I think it comes from this idea of what should be cooked for a foreigner or what should be cooked outside of the home. Or if you had a bunch of your friends over, you would never serve them tamales. Tamales is an especial occasion thing that they eat for Christmas. . . . An activity that we often have our clients do is: do not think about feeding me, but save leftovers from dinner. Whatever you made for dinner. *Just save leftovers* (emphasis in original).

La Cocina assists Mexican immigrants with pinpointing the distinctive aspects of their cuisine to market to cosmopolitans. Mexican immigrants are aware that middle-class Americans tend to like tamales, but they are not aware that cosmopolitans are more interested in exotic foods—foods that the average middle-class American would not find at a typical Mexican restaurant. When trying to figure out what is a unique and exotic item for cosmopolitans, Mexicans must first realize that just their daily cultural practices already look exotic to middle-class Americans. Certainly, the geographic imagination of each other's culture comes into play, and Mexican immigrants must figure out how their culture fits into a cosmopolitan's geographic perception. (Perhaps this is why tamales are so popular in the United States: because Mexicans perceive them to be specialty items in their own culture. Thus, the tamale becomes an ideal transcultural food between Mexicans and Anglo middle-class Americans.) Because it is difficult to see one's own culture, La Cocina asks Mexican immigrants simply to prepare what they would cook at home for friends.

La Cocina becomes a mediator of cultural ideologies as well as an exploiter of intimate ethnic practices. Searching for unknown cuisines not typically associated with a national identity or with Mexican restaurants means finding more individualized cuisines that emphasize place of origin and personal practices. These "at home" cuisines are uncharacteristic aspects of Mexico's working-class taquería landscape.

After choosing the uncommon food item a client will vend, La Cocina then must convince middle-class San Franciscans to eat it. The company works with the client to develop a marketing image for the food, organizing focus groups that discuss and describe textures and flavors, then designing a way for the distinctive food tastes to carry over into the packaging, presentation, and buying experience of the food. Agrawal explains:

> We have a culinary director on staff who used to be a sous-chef at Spruce. So his livelihood is based on marketing food. I mean, even at a fancy restaurant that is doing all sorts of crazy things, they basically have to solve the same problem, which is to present a dish in a way that makes you want to eat it. Led by him and our culinary staff, we have a binder that we keep of great menus, which is an ongoing thing on staff. So if we are ever traveling somewhere we can take pictures of great menus and put it in the binder. . . . We look at it as a marketing task. . . . Then we do a lot of focus group testing . . . a lot of activities for people trying new foods. Before we even say what the food is traditionally called, we will have a bunch of people who have never tasted the food before describe the dish. . . . It's like a lot of branding exercises. We are learning to move from what one would most intuitively describe it [the food] as, which a lot of cooks will just describe it as the ingredients in the dish, to what will make somebody want to try it.

It is through the marketing of cuisine that the food's inherent meaning is distanced from the social significance of its original place and injected into a new social dimension. As bell hooks (1992, 31) contends, "The commodification of difference promotes paradigms of consumption wherein whatever difference the Other inhabits is eradicated, via exchange, by a consumer cannibalism that not only displaces Other, but denies the significance of that Other's history through a process of de-contextualization." The food becomes hybridized through the process of formalization, both in its making and the ways in which it is understood. The cuisine is interpreted and reinterpreted based on the social discourses of cosmopolitans for consumption purposes. And for a cosmopolitan, place of origin is still important.

Most cosmopolitans yearn to experience exotic places through taste. Therefore the marketing of the food must incorporate a food's place of origin into the consumer experience. The image of place must be evoked, and this is achieved by infiltrating a cosmopolitan's geographic imagination. Foods are symbolic of place, and their symbolism can be manipulated. As Cook and Crang (1996, 140) maintain, foods become "symbolic constructs, being deployed in the discursive construction of various imaginative geographies." At La Cocina, using the imagery of street food menus from foreign lands helps to link detached social practices by providing a mental construct of a foreign place's food practices. Additionally, the repackaging also allows the cultural cosmopolitan to try exotic foods within a local perspective and a familiar practice of consumption.

Agrawal and I discussed various cuisines and how they might be marketed in San Francisco versus other cities in the United States. She noted that middle- and upper-middle-class San Franciscans generally possess a more in-depth culinary knowledge than most other urban Americans due to the city's proximity to fresh produce and prime vineyards. When it comes to Mexican food, San Francisco cosmopolitans tend to think they already know what constitutes Mexican food. Many are familiar with Mexico's regional cuisines, more so than with the regional specialties from other countries. Of course, much of people's cursory culinary knowledge derives from superficial sources about the regional preparations of Mexican cuisine, such as the cookbooks of Rick Bayless (2007) or Diana Kennedy (2009; 2013). Subsequently, there is a certain level of naïveté that the marketing can harness. The marketing then places food in such a way that the consumers will be able to identify it and understand it to a certain degree, but also perceive it as new—they feel as if they are still learning and experiencing something different. This holds true even when the name, packaging, and presentation of the cuisines are completely changed and transformed from their traditional characteristics. Agrawal observes:

> In San Francisco you have the fortune that people love Mexican food and people know taquería food. And also now with restaurants like Nopalito and La Cubana, you have people starting to interact with Mexican food as a fancier thing. So often in marketing Mexican food, you have to pick a region. So if they are tacos of Guanajuato, then you could add a description about what Guanajuato is. . . . So the thing that becomes important is that when you walk up to get your taco, how do you [the seller] talk about the meat and how do you translate the food idea, such as calling it "Guanajuato Carnitas"? So instead of just saying whatever the totally different traditional name is, this is giving it a regional identity with a name that Americans can relate to.

Beyond packaging food with cosmopolitan appeal, some of the packaging also has to deal with market vending and street food regulations. Navigating street food policies in San Francisco has its quirks. The San Francisco Health Department is strict about the ways in which the food is served, especially regarding food sold from pushcarts. Generally speaking, food served from a pushcart must be pre-cooked and prepackaged, and the pushcart must have the appropriate plumbing. This is another aspect of the marketing that La Cocina must take into account. If the food is going to be sold from a pushcart or a street stall without a kitchen, it must come in some sort of package. Under these guidelines, the tamale is perfect because it is nearly always served wrapped in a banana leaf or cornhusk. Agrawal calls it "the technicality around cornhusks." Appropriately, the tamale may be San Francisco's ultimate street food based on its historic street presence in the city and its natural packaging. With other foods, La Cocina has to be more creative. They either have to find different foods to put on a street cart or introduce American-style packaging. Health Department guidelines often dictate what becomes street food and what does not. Regardless of whether a vendor uses a pushcart or a street food stand, La Cocina always pays special attention to the packaging, which is professionally designed with an artisanal aesthetic. Often, the foods appear as if they belong on the shelves of a gourmet grocery rather than coming from a vendor at a flea market.

If La Cocina has been fashioning immigrant foods for cosmopolitans, the next step is to take these foods to the street and make the practice of eating on the street more acceptable. In 2009 La Cocina began a food festival in the Mission District, the San Francisco Street Food Festival. The festival was designed to create revenue for La Cocina, its vendors, and the community at large. In the process, they enhanced the image of the city through augmenting public streets with cooking and eating. They wanted to portray street food vending as a positive attribute that animates life on the streets and also showcases San Francisco's world cuisines.

Since the inception of the San Francisco Street Food Festival, the city has gone on to embrace the festival as one of the city's most enviable events: more than seventy thousand people attended the event in 2012 (San Francisco Street Food Festival 2014). These days, the celebration of street food in San Francisco is at its peak. People in the Bay Area have never been more excited about eating ethnic street foods; it is changing not only urban life but also the city's image. The City of San Francisco is benefiting greatly by capitalizing on the culture of street food vending. And, just as the practice of street food grows in San Francisco, so too is the Bay Area's boutique food truck scene. Since 2009, boutique food trucks have transformed various neighborhoods' streetscapes throughout the Bay Area—unwittingly replicating the taco trucks' social practices that have been present in California since the early 1970s and within Oakland since the mid-1980s.

OFF THE GRID

Matt Cohen, who started out working as a volunteer at the first San Francisco Street Food Festival, eventually founded his own street food business, Off the Grid, which specializes in organizing boutique food truck markets. The idea developed around Cohen's frustration in dealing with city ordinances to open up his own food truck and around his exposure to Asian night markets. Off the Grid started with a single food market at Fort Mason Park in San Francisco in 2010 and has grown to four food events per day (twenty-seven per week) throughout various municipalities and neighborhoods in the Bay Area. The events combined serve roughly thirty thousand meals per week, which trans-lates roughly to $300,000 in gross revenue, or over $1 million in street food sales per month. I interviewed Cohen in March 2014 about starting his business, his vision of street food, and how he is changing community space throughout the Bay Area. Surprisingly, the marketing of street food culture goes beyond the trucks' symbolic capital to include also the ways in which urban space is personally and socially experienced.

Cohen spent several years living in Fukuoka, Japan, a region of the country that is renowned for ramen and street food stalls (*yatai*, 屋台). While in Japan, he learned to cook ramen very well. When Cohen returned to the United States around 2007, he read an article about a Los Angeles truck called Heartschal-lenger, which was one of the first boutique food trucks in the country. The truck is well known for marketing specialty ice cream and eclectic toys toward adults. Cohen liked the idea of taking something unique and being able to vend it from a truck. He then wrote a business plan to sell ramen from a couple of trucks. He explained that he never was able to launch his business because of the broad financial difficulties in 2008 and 2009. Obtaining a permit from the City of San Francisco, Cohen commented, was virtually impossible. Because of all the city ordinances, and because he was unable to start his own ramen trucks for financial reasons, Cohen ended up as a paid consultant for food trucks:

> I quit my job; I spent a year or so writing a business plan about how I was going to open a couple of ramen trucks. Fast forward to financial crisis 2007–2008; that's not the best time to be opening my own trucks because I was doing it on a line of credit, and credit had frozen up. So I was like: what can I do? Maybe I'll just start consulting for people because the permit process was so difficult to navigate. It took me a year to figure out how to do the permits. Slowly, all of these trucks started opening, and I was the person that people started hiring to do the permitting and consulting for launching their trucks, getting their permits and finding locations where they could operate.

Cohen became, as he puts it, the "turnkey" for mobile food trucks in finding space in San Francisco. He also noticed that San Francisco's mobile-food-vending ordinances were primarily about keeping mobile food vendors apart from one another, which was contradictory to Asian night markets, whose purpose is to bring vendors together:

> The whole orientation in San Francisco was really about keeping vendors away from each other. Primarily I think it was like traditional lonchera kind of places that were really nomadic, or they would set up and be in one place for the entire day . . . or it was pretzels and hot dogs. The city didn't want pretzel and hot dog vendors lining Market Street every fifty feet the whole way down. . . . The orientation [of urban policies] was all about keeping vendors apart from each other. And it soon became apparent that after a year of doing this that grouping people together like in an Asian night market type of experience was really something that was missing from the city.

Cohen's idea of creating an American street food market composed of mobile food vendors coincided with the surge of boutique food trucks that did not necessarily want to go through the convoluted city permitting process. He then started street food events where an entire street or area of the city would be closed to vehicular traffic once a week, during the afternoon or evening. Establishing event space through event permitting allowed mobile food vendors to bypass the complicated city ordinances and individual permitting, while enabling them to work together in reconfiguring urban space.

> The [social] environment that was going on at that time was around an idea of innovation and around bootstrap artisan people that were doing something that had real energy behind it, and real passion behind it. And I think part of that was the financial crisis had driven people who had typical professional jobs into reevaluating what they wanted to do with their lives. And right at the same time was the convergence of social media. . . . There was this coming together of these two elements and it really felt like it had some energy behind it. The idea of grouping them together formally and being able to create a reoccurring kind of market experience was something that was missing.

Cohen's perspicacity regarding the various dynamics of socioeconomic issues and the culture of street food vending allowed him to help refashion San Francisco's street food scene. He organized his first food market event at Fort Mason, and it was extremely successful.[2] He was able to set up at Fort Mason because it was federal property, not city property. Fort Mason is also an area of the city that is detached from the city's iconic street grids. The food truck event was literally "Off the Grid." Eventually, Off the Grid became the name of the food truck market organization which represented a spatial practice that was figuratively "off the grid."

> Fort Mason is distinct and separate from the rest of the city. It feels distinct and separate. But also the trucks are disconnected from physical infrastructure, like a traditional brick-and-mortar restaurant. So it felt like it was off the grid. . . . I think it is more ephemeral and sort of temporary in nature. That's sort of what we were trying to get at.

Cohen is very cognizant that he is bringing foreign street food practices to the American middle class, and he finds that his success is based on creating shared community experiences around food. He describes what street food in East Asia means to him and how he thinks that he can make a business out of commoditizing the Asian street food market for the middle-class American consumer:

> I think it was the same thing that was driving the interest of street food at that time [2009–2010], which was taking an artisanal product that was relatively approachable and upscaling it and being able to market it effectively to a group of people who weren't familiar with street food at all. And I think fundamentally the reason why I invested so heavily and really committed my life for the last five years to doing this is because street food is such a powerful part of people's lives in the rest of the world and I just feel like for social-economic reasons and for cultural reasons, the United States was like, way artificially behind. . . . What we've been trying to do is just catch up as fast as we can and that's part of our success.

The people who eat the street food at Off the Grid events are primarily young professionals and families and are not by any means America's poor per se. Cohen describes the demographic: "We have young professionals [who are] twenty-five to forty years old, people who are tech savvy, and people who are defined as adventurous eaters or 'foodies.' And then we have young families, [where the parents are] twenty-five to forty-five years old." The menu items range in price from six or seven dollars, up to ten dollars. The owners of the trucks come from a variety of backgrounds as well, but they are oblivious to the idea of immigrants cooking with other immigrants in mind. Food truck entrepreneurs primarily prepare the food for middle-class Anglo customers.

> The trucks are about one-third first-time entrepreneurs, either new to the food business, or the people who used to have the best grandmother's dumplings that they used to bring to Christmas dinner. They are interested in food trucks because there is a lower capital cost to get started. [There are also] restaurants

who have an existing catering business and leverage the truck for exposure, but also to create another revenue stream. And then experienced restaurant people, such as line cooks and sous-chefs, who have an idea for a concept and are pursuing that rather than opening up their own restaurant. Those tend to be the three groups that we work with.

Besides the foods created, the spaces where the foods are consumed are of utmost importance. Cohen structures event space to feel spontaneous but also habitual. In order to be successful he has to induce social rhythms to activate the street. But the festivals also have to be predictable so that customers can become accustomed to when and where they will take place. He therefore keeps the event times and locations consistent. Any given community gathering will take place on the same day and at the same time on a weekly basis throughout the year.

> Fundamentally, when I got into doing this, there was always this sense of the traditional *lonchera* or maybe even a construction truck, they would be on a schedule but sometimes they weren't around. Maybe they broke down; maybe the weather was bad; maybe they went on vacation. There is always this uncertainty around it. . . . I'm a big believer in habit and trying to build habit. . . . In that way we are providing structure where there was less structure before.

Cohen works to establish a regular expression of extemporaneity. He also becomes more interested in developing the aspects of urban life that his food truck events are producing.

Cohen admits that at first he was mostly interested in the food aspect of the trucks, but over time it became more about the social dynamics that the practice of cooking and eating created. Cohen puts it this way:

> I had my mind on a very Asian night-market experience, creating energy around a space. I think it was about being food driven more than about the community. But what I've come to see is that it is more about the human aspect to it. And it's the community congregation point that makes our experiences powerful. The longer that we are around, the more we want to be the mechanism of those types of encounters through food.

As Off the Grid developed as a company, so too had their approach to managing and marketing the food truck events.

Off the Grid has more than sixty employees. It is a sizable business built around artisanal food trucks. The employees work various jobs, from staffing markets to web design and graphics. As in any other industry, they work on growing their business, and they do this through devising more ways in which to commoditize social practices. Off the Grid has one employee who works with vendors as a consultant in marketing their products and helping with finances. The organization also has two employees who, with an eye for new markets, scout locations within the Bay Area, and two employees who specialize in *experiential marketing*. Cohen explains:

> We look for participatory experiences in our markets. What we are trying to do is create experiences where people feel like it [the market event] is representative of the communities that we're in. . . . We have an a cappella group from Cal come to our South Side [Berkeley] market yesterday. I think it's having live painting demonstrations, or book swaps, or clothing swaps, just things that make us feel more integrated with the communities where we are. But it's participatory rather than sit back and listen. . . . It's not only necessarily about eating. The most powerful thing about our markets is that sense of shared connections that people get from it, such as running into friends and neighbors in unplanned ways. We want our markets to be as sticky as possible. And I think part of that comes from giving people activities to do that they feel are valuable.

The essence of the market is less about the food and more about the community and social practices that the street food market creates. Over time, the principle of promoting the street food market focuses on the experiential spaces designed *around* the food trucks.

Cohen also has an urban designer on staff to help with the design and function of the event spaces, to arrange the trucks, and to spatially organize all aspects of the street food market. By orchestrating the spatial arrangement and rhythms of the market, Off the Grid is able to fashion places that activate the urban environment without severely disrupting social attitudes about how the spaces are controlled. Put differently, Off the Grid successfully injects foreign street food practices into the middle- and upper-class districts of cities in a way that is socially and aesthetically acceptable to city officials and residents. Furthermore, Off the Grid's staff executes the organization's vision in a manner that emphasizes a local sense of place. Marketing experiential space, therefore, becomes crucial to a successful event:

> What we try to do is get a better sense of what the trucks are trying to do, what their general business approach is. And then [we] try to fit them into the places that might be the most appropriate for them. . . . We spend a lot of time with demographics and understanding who is coming to our market. What we are trying to do is be complementary to the places where we are and not repetitive. So what we try to do is have each place have an identity and personality of its own.

In this context, the truck's role is not only one of symbolic capital, it also creates memorable experiences by bringing people together through cooking and eating. To taste new cuisine is one aspect of experiencing place, and so is the act of sharing foods with others. A social atmosphere evolves at the market that fosters the sense of belonging to a community. The shared experience contributes to the participants' culture. Off the Grid produces community space for profit. This, I argue, is *experiential capital*—the marketing of a sense of place, through the creation of social space, for economic gain. Cooking and eating are a great way to activate social space and sell place to consumers. Ironically, Off the Grid focuses on producing a place where one is free from marketing materials. As Cohen confides, "We want to create a bubble where people feel like they are not being marketed to, even if it's in the middle of the city." For Off the Grid, its success in capital accumulation is the perceived absence of capitalism. However, with the perceived absence of the negative externalities of capitalism, such as in-your-face marketing, so too is the absence of the taco truck and the Mexican immigrant day laborer.

A distinct food-truck energy is missing from Off the Grid, and that is the traditional taco truck. I asked Cohen: How can you have food truck events without taco trucks? How can you not pay homage to the traditional taco truck, which has been ubiquitous throughout the state of California since the 1970s? Cohen is entirely aware of this conundrum. He, too, finds it perplexing that he does not have taco trucks at his events and confesses that it is not something he has been able to incorporate successfully. Cohen expounds:

> For years, we have been trying to program more traditional Mexican taco trucks into our markets. There are a variety of challenges that we have had with it. Sometimes they are coming from a background of running their own business for quite some time and they want to do their own thing . . . but our thing is really built around keeping a consistent schedule and maintaining proper documentation. And sometimes that is hard for them to do. . . . Also, the price point is really challenging. For someone who is doing $1.50 or $2 tacos, and basically our trucks need to do $1,000 in revenue in order for our fees to make sense . . . and if you're doing $1.50 or $2 tacos, [then] it's a ridiculous amount of tacos that you have to go through to have it be worthwhile in participating in our locations. . . . The traditional model of inexpensive tacos is a challenging thing to fit into our environment where there are so many choices. And the choices are clear and marketed very clearly. Generally, a Mexican taco truck or traditional lonchera has a mile-long menu list of different choices, and in some ways it has a hard time breaking through some of the noise of all the different options that are there.

What Cohen describes is an ethnic and class divide in behavior, perception, and affordability. He speaks about a conflicting divide in the world of street food and urban space. Latinos are priced out, and their cultural practices are too foreign for Off the Grid events. Mexicans are encouraged to be included, but the signifying spaces and cultural practices around the cuisine demand social and economic separation. The traditional taco truck's main demographic is the Mexican day laborer; taqueros make the cheapest thing they know how to make, using inexpensive ingredients that produce the most flavor.

Taco truck owners know their customer base and how to make the foods their clients like. They go to the spaces in the city where they know for sure that day-laboring Latinos will find them. They see and understand street food as a working-class meal associated with deprived Latino districts and do not necessarily understand how to make an artisanal taco for more affluent areas. Likewise, middle- and upper-middle-class people unfamiliar with traditional Latino street food have a difficult time deciphering the aesthetics and cuisines of a traditional taco truck. Cohen details the cultural challenges of how he once tried to incorporate the traditional taco truck El Norteño into several Off the Grid events:

> I think what is so important about the successful trucks that are coming out now is that they are not overthought. There are two or three items of what you should buy. But when you hit that truck [El Norteño] in particular, there is goat, there's tongue, there's brains. There are so many different choices and they can come in so many different formats, and it's all handwritten and somewhat unclear. And some people are turned on by that. But other people may look around and say "Well, there's Chinese bao, and there's an Indian burrito, and there's this and there's that, and then there is that other truck [El Norteño] but I really don't understand what it is." Then they are going to go to the one that is simpler.

Evidently, food consumption practices and taste preferences that stem from one's ethnicity and social class have contributed to the development of two types of food truck spaces. Although the rise of boutique food trucks has made street food vending popular in San Francisco and elsewhere, it does not include the practices of all peoples. Rather, the boutique food trucks function as a hyper-real space, where many middle- and upper-middle-class patrons celebrate new cuisines. The traditional taco truck may be welcome, but by no means is it able to compete culturally or financially. Therefore, it remains in Latino districts, where it continues to satisfy day laborers' taste preferences.

= = =

While taste contributes to the consumption spaces of the Bay Area, it can also be expressed through cultural capital. Cosmopolitans inherently demonstrate their identity through trying new cuisines. Taste can also be a food's flavor. Many Mexican immigrants, for instance, desire cuisines that remind them of home. Their identity stems from eating familiar foods, and traditional Mexican cuisines are part of their heritage. But for others, those same foods become cultural capital and are subsumed into the dominant culture.

La Cocina uses packaging of immigrant food products as symbolic capital to market immigrant foods to cosmopolitans. Through this process, they engage one's geographic imagination of what constitutes foreign cuisines and also integrate lesser-known food flavors into the dominant culture. Similarly, Off the Grid uses boutique food trucks as symbolic capital to refashion urban spaces. Realizing that one's sense of community is as significant as the foods served, Matt Cohen, the company owner, chooses to influence one's sense of place through building social cohesion. This phenomenon I defined as *experiential capital*—the way in which place is marketed through promoting social relationships and memorable interactions.

Both La Cocina and Off the Grid are quite successful at helping hundreds of entrepreneurs get started, grow their own businesses, and establish themselves in the formal economy. But they also help drive the gentrification of San Francisco. Unfortunately, these businesses can also contribute to the production of unforeseen negative externalities on the social spaces where Latino street food vending takes place. Capitalistic culinary motives, regardless of how well intentioned, often produce spatial contradictions and exacerbate socioeconomic inequalities. Non-Latinos may be inspired by the street food phenomenon, but in a capitalist system their honest sense of inspiration does not benefit everyone equally. The result is that evolving street food spaces in the Bay Area are shifted by the circuits of capital and defined predominately by ethnicity and class. As San Francisco's spaces are socially refashioned for the upper middle classes, Latinos in the Bay Area are further marginalized.

Formalizing street food practices is not the cause of gentrification, but it is most certainly an aspect of it. Cosmopolitans contribute to gentrification by completely consuming the immigrant culture that once attracted them to the neighborhood (Shaw, Bagwell, and Karmowska 2004). Paradoxically, as La Cocina helps many disenfranchised, immigrant women of color, the organization also greases the wheels of gentrification. While many immigrant street food entrepreneurs in the Mission District are able to succeed in the formal marketplace with the help of La Cocina, most Latinos in the area do not have the opportunity or resources to even remain economically viable in the neighborhood. As wealthier people move in, dispossessed Latinos must move out. And with them fades the original informal food vending of San Francisco's streets. Curiously, cosmopolitans' inclusive mentality toward ethnic differences often excludes and eradicates the culture they wish to embrace (Ley 2004; Rofe 2003).

The production of uneven spaces is even more evident in Oakland. Boutique food trucks are making their way into the East Bay. Many are challenging and changing Oakland's established food truck policies. Even though Oakland was the first city in the United States to create food vending ordinances for Latinos in southeast Oakland, city officials are now writing separate regulations for the city's more affluent spaces—such as Oakland's city center—to accommodate Off the Grid and other boutique food trucks. City planner Nancy Marcus conveyed to me that the number of artisanal food trucks coming into Oakland is "massive" and that the city doesn't "have any staff" to sufficiently regulate the trucks. From 2012 to 2014 she worked on a pilot program that allowed food trucks throughout Oakland's city center in the form of pods.

Oakland city officials realized they needed to address the new demand for mobile food truck vending. They also considered the boutique trucks as an aspect of economic growth and determined that the food trucks could be beneficial to neighborhood residents who have minimal food access. Marcus explained that it was important for Oakland to create a separate ordinance for the city center because of the demand for the food trucks, but also because it was becoming a point of controversy among downtown businesses. The solution was to designate four food truck pods downtown—locations where any food truck could get a permit to vend. Regrettably, traditional taco trucks were priced out. As a result, two ordinances for food trucks in Oakland developed: one for boutique food trucks in the city center, and one for the traditional taco trucks in East Oakland.

Class and ethnicity produce space through social practices and are often reinforced by government entities trying to control those practices. The City of Oakland's two ordinances to regulate street food vending reflect and reinforce this dichotomy. City officials predetermine place appropriateness for the types of street food vending. The City of Oakland permits food vending from taco trucks in the Latino enclave of Oakland but also reserves spaces for boutique food trucks in the city center.

I spoke again with Emilia Otero, a community advocate who works closely with Latino street food vendors in East Oakland. I asked her what she thought of the separate ordinance that allowed boutique food trucks to vend downtown. She quipped,

They want to just keep us in this section, just like animals. We are people! And here in Oakland the city is not willing to give us the credit, but every single commissary and legalizing this business all over the country, it started here! And it is good revenue for every city in this country. But here, where we started everything, city officials block us. . . . They don't want to see us here.

The blossoming of the boutique food trucks has created new challenges for traditional taco truck owners. In sum, the manifestation and popularity of boutique food trucks have added another layer of complexity to taco truck space. This is most apparent in California's capital, Sacramento, a city that takes pride in its farm-to-table initiative.

Plate 1: Taco trucks can be found throughout the country. This taco truck is parked in Tulsa, Oklahoma.

Plate 2: Mi Ranchito Mexican Market on Foothill Boulevard near Thirty-Fourth Avenue in Columbus, Ohio.

Plate 3: Murals on a Mexican restaurant along Foothill Boulevard in Oakland, California.

Plate 4: A fruit cart on Foothill Boulevard and Coolidge Avenue near a Walgreens grocery store in Oakland, California.

Plate 5: Mi Grullense taco truck on International Boulevard and Thirty-First Avenue. There are two Mi Grullense trucks on this corner in Oakland's Fruitvale district.

Plate 6: Tacos Guadalajara on International Boulevard and Forty-Fourth Avenue in East Oakland, California.

Plate 7: Vending churros in front of Saint Elizabeth Catholic Church on a Sunday morning in the heart of Oakland's Fruitvale district.

Plate 8: Tacos Sinaloa in East Oakland. The truck's owner now has a brick-and-mortar establishment where people can sit indoors and eat.

Plate 9: Emilia Otero at her desk at La Placita Commissary Kitchen in Oakland, California.

Plate 10: Taco Truck, "El Gordo," on International Boulevard in East Oakland, California.

Plate 11: Tacos Sinaloense parks in front of an auto parts store on Sacramento's east side in a pocket of county that is tucked within the city limits.

Plate 12: George Azar, owner of La Mex Taqueria. The truck is located on private property at the corner of Northgate Boulevard and Peralta Avenue in Sacramento, California.

Plate 13: Tacos Sinaloense parks in front of an auto parts store on Sacramento's east side in a pocket of the county that is tucked within the city limits.

Plate 14: Several taco trucks park in a commissary in an industrial zone in southeast Sacramento.

Plate 15: Luis Bueno, owner of the Sinaloense taco truck parked at Fruitridge Road and Forty-Fourth Street, in a pocket of county between the city limits.

Plate 16: Taqueria Los 3 Reyes was one of the first taco trucks to open in Columbus, Ohio.

Plate 17: Los Guachos taco truck serves pastor tacos on Columbus's West Side.

Plate 18: Las Delicias taco trailer is parked in front of a strip club, The Candy Stores, on Columbus's West Side.

Plate 19: Various patrons stop at El Rey's taco trailer on Columbus's West Side.

Plate 20: El Tizoncito taco truck in northeast Columbus. The owners of the truck are serving pastor tacos at midnight.

Plate 21: Inside the Dinin' Hall dining space.

Plate 22: A collage of some of the types and styles of menus found at the taco trucks in Columbus.

Plate 23: Los Chilangos' torta menu.

Plate 24: El Tizoncito taco truck in Northeast Columbus. The owner of the truck is preparing her kitchen for evening sales.

Plate 25: El Buen Sazón taco truck parks along a major intersection in northeast Columbus. There, the husband and wife owners serve traditional street and market foods from Mexico City.

Plate 26: Lisa and Dulce operating the truck at Columbus Dinin' Hall. Lisa takes orders and Dulce cooks in the kitchen.

Plate 27: Lisa shows me a calendar of where she will be moving around Columbus for lunch during the day.

Plate 28: Neighbors converse alongside a taco truck in the King Lincoln District, Columbus, Ohio.

Plate 29: José Luis Pérez, owner of El Primo and the taquero on Saturdays.

Plate 30: Los Potosinos taco truck parked in front of murals depicting famous African American musicians. The King Lincoln District, Columbus, Ohio.

CHAPTER 3

MAKING SACRAMENTO INTO AN EDIBLE CITY

Sacramento's downtown street grid occupies an area of four-and-one-half square miles, and is composed of city blocks that measure 340 feet by 320 feet. A basic grid—modified for the State of California's Capitol grounds—defines Sacramento's urban center. Recently, some streets near the capitol building have been closed to automobile traffic to function primarily as pedestrian corridors. City planners have incorporated many urban design philosophies to make the city center more pedestrian friendly, encouraging mixed-use development with small storefronts and cafés with patio seating. Developers have tried to capitalize on walkability and living downtown by employing marketing strategies for this lifestyle. The grid is not just a spatial order but also a colloquialism. Residents refer to "the grid" as a place where one goes "out on the town." Local businesses have promoted the grid's walkable infrastructure through clever marketing campaigns, such as "walk the grid" and "shop the grid" (Downtown Grid 2013).

Another chief component of Sacramento's downtown development is its innovative restaurant scene. Food has become the foremost way to attract people to downtown. Because Sacramento sits in the nation's breadbasket, Mayor Johnson recently branded the city "Farm-to-Fork Capital of America" (Lillis 2012; "Farm to Fork Capital of America" 2014). In order for city businesses to capitalize on Sacramento's agricultural hearth, city boosters have to showcase the region's agricultural aesthetics. As second-tier cities struggle to reinvent themselves, "eating local" has become Sacramento's new urban mantra. The city's economic strategists are now strongly encouraging restaurateurs to buy from local boutique farms, and the grid has become synonymous with its restaurant scene. City boosters employ semiotic markers associated with opulent food spaces to script the farm-to-fork narrative. The city's aesthetic and physical design—from the interior of restaurants to its streetscape—is being upgraded by developers who perceive culinary practices as a means for urban renewal. Not only can you walk and shop the grid, you can eat it too. "Eat the Grid" has become the business district's foremost marketing campaign. In Sacramento, the city grid is both walkable *and* edible.

Curiously, food trucks were absent from Sacramento's city center until 2015. The city council and many restaurateurs believed that food trucks blemish streetscapes and ordered city code enforcers to write stringent policies to keep food trucks on the move and away from downtown. For a city that prides itself on cuisine, it was strange that only certain culinary practices were allowed to contribute to the city's "eat local" image. When it came to the topic of taco trucks, a figurative food fight over food practices, food spaces, and food truck policies made Sacramento one of the most controversial cities in the United States.

This chapter focuses on Sacramento from 2006 to 2014, the height of when city boosters were devoted to revitalizing the city through cuisine. This was also a pivotal period when cultural and economic issues pertaining to traditional taco trucks, gourmet food trucks and restaurants clashed. Ironically, the absence of taco trucks downtown brought to light how a neoliberal city was increasingly being shaped by its evolving culinary culture as part of its marketing identity. For this reason, before I can address the taco trucks' battle to remain within Sacramento, I must first present and deconstruct the city council's and restaurateurs' urban vision. This chapter takes a step back from the Latino culinary practices at taco trucks to carefully consider the power dimensions of exclusive food spaces and the ways in which they socially structure Sacramento's landscape.

Rachel Slocum (2010) makes a strong case for studying food space through race. She claims, "Race is produced and racism reinforced through foodspace" (313). To better evaluate how Latino taco truck spaces are affected, it is critical to assess Anglo middle- and upper-class food spaces in Sacramento. In this way, social and cultural divergent food spaces are assessed in relation to each other. This chapter explores the facets of experiential capital at restaurants, while chapter 4 addresses how these social processes affect taco truck spaces.

"SAC-A-TOMATOES"

Because of peculiar soil and climatic conditions—the great variety
of soils and the division of the seasons into two periods . . . it has
been possible in California to evolve an agricultural economy without
parallel in the United States.
—Carey McWilliams, *Factories in the Field*, 1939.

Sacramento is often dubbed "Sac-a-Tomatoes" because of its central location within America's breadbasket; truly, the region's physical geography infiltrates our sense of place within the city. Located at the confluence of the Sacramento River and the American River, the city sits precariously at the base of the Sacramento–San Joaquin delta and historically has been known to flood. Joan Didion (2004) writes about seasonal flooding in Sacramento as a way of life: "Many Sacramento houses during my childhood had on their walls one or another lithograph showing the familiar downtown grid with streets of water, through which citizens could be seen going about their business by raft or rowboat" (20).

Today, modern engineering—such as the construction of levees—restrains seasonal floodwaters and separates humans from environmental processes.[1] But, because of seasonal river flooding over hundreds of years prior to the rise of monolithic hydro-engineering, some of the most fertile soils in the world, comparable to those of the Nile River delta, are found throughout Sacramento valley and San Joaquin valley (McWilliams and Sackman 2000; Parsons 1986). Sacramento is located between these two agriculturally dominant drainage basins. Geographer James Parsons (1986) once described the cultural landscape of San Joaquin valley as "the magnificent diversity of crops yielding the bumper harvests of food and fiber that make California agriculture one of the wonders of the world" (375). California continues to be the nation's largest agricultural producer and exporter. According to the California Department of Food and Agriculture,

> The State's 80,500 farms and ranches received a record $44.7 billion for their output . . . in 2011. . . . California's agricultural abundance includes more than 400 commodities. The state produces nearly half of U.S.-grown fruits, nuts, and vegetables. Across the nation, U.S. consumers regularly purchase several crops produced solely in California. (California Dept. of Food and Ag. 2012, 2)

California produces the highest diversity of produce of any state or agrarian region in the United States. And Sacramento is trying to use these regional agricultural attributes to brand its urban identity.

Contado is city-state governance. The word and concept emerged in twelfth-century Italy to describe the city's economic relationship with its hinterland (Brechin 2006, xxiii). Essentially, it is a word to express the idea of the city's reliance on its region. Geographer Gray Brechin revisits the term *contado* and presents it as a spatial concept to evaluate how cities dominate and exploit their natural environment. According to Brechin (1999), the contado is "the territory that the city [can] militarily dominate and thus draw upon. The *contado* provide[s] the city with its food, resources, labor, conscripts, and much of its taxes, while its people (the *contadini*) [receive] a marketplace and a degree of protection in return." Seen in this way, Sacramento functions much like a contado. Sacramento's city boosters and marketers use the city's propinquity to California's breadbasket to generate a sense of ownership over its agricultural hinterland and, in turn, a sense of place through food.

The notion of the contado also influenced urban design. For instance, Piazza del Campo—the central piazza in Siena, Italy—is the city's most sacred social space, a place created by the nobles of the commune (city-state) to demonstrate Siena's dominance and dependence on both the urban and rural landscapes. The name translates as "plaza of the fields" (or "plaza of the country"), and the space itself was used as a place for commerce of goods produced throughout the region since the thirteenth century. The picturesque beauty of the market space, along with the curvilinear streets that radiate out from the piazza, became "a local ideal in art as well as town planning" (Rogers 2001, 120). Lefebvre (1991) notes the significance of the formally designed Italian Renaissance piazza during the advent of perspective drawing in architecture: "[A] space was produced that was neither rural nor urban, but the result of a newly engendered spatial relationship between the two. . . . [G]rowth could only occur via the town-country relationship via those groups which were the motor of development: the urban oligarchy and a portion of the peasantry" (78). Much as in other cities in Italy, and much like the rest of the world prior to the industrialization of agriculture, the seasonal processions and social practices found throughout the region were always reflected within the city's central commercial spaces (Mumford 1989). Put simply, urban life and local agricultural practices were entwined.

The French word *terroir* best expresses the notion that foodstuff's quality and taste are primary produced by place. Terroir describes the influences that soils, slope aspects, terrain, and climate have on viticulture (Gibson 2010; Trubek 2009; Wilson 2012). The flavors of wine are produced by all the physical and cultural dimensions of place and not merely by the characteristics of the grape itself. The notion that cuisine cannot be subtracted from place—but exemplifies the characteristics of place—has been used throughout Europe to control various types of food production laws, such as the names of wines, cheeses, and hams (Bauch 2005; Trubek 2009). Although the United States does not recognize these European food laws—and Americans have a history of disregarding associations between food and place—it is becoming a more prominent global trend to search out locally produced foods (Johnston and Baumann 2009; Sims 2011). Americans are not immune to this idea, however: Idaho potatoes, Sonoma wines, Wisconsin cheese, and Texas barbecue are all examples of how Americans think about the relationship of cuisines to geographic regions. And this phenomenon is perhaps due to the perceived embodiment of place through food.

Terroir also arouses a sense of place through food. You can taste place, especially if you know where and how something was produced. Trubek (2009, 6) notes that the importance of taste is the human embodiment of nature: "In the act of tasting, when a bite of food or a sip of wine moves through the mouth and into the body, culture and nature become one. Universally, eating and drinking are processes of bringing the natural world into the human domain." In this respect, knowing a food's origins affects one's sense of place. If you are not physically in the place where a food was produced, you may feel withdrawn from place, and the food may not taste as good. However, if you are eating food in the region where it was produced, the embodiment of place is complete.

Regions around the world try to capitalize on the phenomenon of savoring the individual qualities of place through food tourism (Adema 2009; Sims 2011). "Eating local," or trying locally sourced foods and celebrity chefs' flavors, has become a rising trend in the United States. Much of it has to do with "foodies" seeking "authentic" culinary experiences, especially those that have "geographic specificity" (Johnston and Baumann 2009, 74). Americans may not know what to call it exactly, but they are yearning to experience place through taste. As Johnston and Baumann find in their research on the eating practices of "foodies," "the connection between a food and a specific place is central to determining a food's authenticity" (79).

The farm-to-table movement—as restaurateurs, gourmet chefs, and high-end grocery stores have dubbed it—best exemplifies the past decade's "eat local" phenomenon (Schoenfeld 2011). Farm-to-table is defined by the act of purchasing one's produce directly from the farmer. In the United States, the term and concept have grown in popularity along with the "slow food" movement. And because Sacramento is located at the heart of the United States' breadbasket, surrounded by hundreds of local farms and ranches, city boosters capitalize on its abundance of locally sourced foods to forge a new urban identity. The embodiment of Sacramento's agricultural region takes place and shapes space throughout Sacramento's city center. It is where contado meets terroir to produce culinary cultural capital.

California's natural resources, from gold mines and from fertile basins, have influenced the form and function of California cities (Barth 1988; Brechin 2006). Certainly, urban formation and agrarian processes have always had a symbiotic relationship in terms of capital production (Cronon 1992); however, beyond aspects of academic geographic discourse, cities and agriculture are seldom considered inseparable. Curiously, Sacramento is making an attempt to change that perception, albeit for the sake of profit. To create a marketable local sense of place, city boosters showcase regional agricultural output. These regional agricultural practices are reflected in the city's central urban spaces, much as one would have found in Piazza del Campo seven hundred years ago. Thus, farmers' markets throughout the city center, as well as restaurant spaces, are essential in experientially connecting Sacramento's urban environment with its agricultural hinterland.

In September 2013, to showcase the region's livestock and local ranchers, Sacramento commenced its "Farm-to-Fork Week" by running cattle across its iconic Tower Bridge and down its prominent city streets (Anderson 2013). It was a spectacle that demonstrated to residents and tourists alike that the city's image was interwoven into its surrounding agrarian landscape.

MARKETING A REGIONAL "SENSE OF PLACE"

The interpretation of a sense of place is subjective, but just because we cannot always define our personal "sense of place" in absolute terms does not mean our human connections and shared experiences to place(s) are irrelevant. Since the 1970s, geographers have written philosophically about the phenomenology of place (Tuan 1990, 2001, 2013; Relph 2008). Our bodies, they argue, experience space and place through our senses, and these spatial perceptions are significant in defining who we are as human beings in the world. But it was not until the late 1980s and the 1990s that city planners began to harness the experiential characteristics of place and package it for others to consume.

It is important to have a positive sense of place toward a city if we want to live and work within that city. Recognizing this phenomenon, Sacramento officials and marketers are working to redefine the city experientially for the sake of economic development. In the past, city planners devised economic development plans that focused on tax cuts for large corporate facilities (Harvey 1989b; Logan and Molotch 2007), but this model for urban economic growth is progressing. In today's financial market, Sacramento city planners, council members, and boosters realize that creating a local "sense of place" is essential to attracting and obtaining a young, well-educated demographic. This echoes Richard Florida's (2012) argument: if cities want to remain viable, they must attract the "creative class"—the top third of the money earners of society. Once the money earners have moved into the city, city officials can use their tax dollars to improve the city's infrastructure. David Harvey (1989b) has noted this trend in urban policy:

> Gentrification, cultural innovation, and physical up-grading of urban environment (including the turn to post-modernist styles of architecture and urban design), consumer attractions . . . and entertainment (*the organization of urban spectacles on a temporary or permanent basis*), have all become much more prominent facets of strategies for urban regeneration. Above all, the city has to appear as an innovative, exciting, creative, and safe place to play and consume in. (9; emphasis added)

Harvey critiques urban regeneration as a competitive strategy between cities that will ultimately produce winners and losers. Sacramento city officials believe that they have no option other than to attract young talented individuals in order to remain viable in today's service-dominant economy. And for Sacramento's city planners, creating a strong sense of place through cuisine is the chief strategy to economic success.

In March 2014 I met with Mike Testa, senior vice president of the Sacramento Convention and Visitors Bureau. The bureau is a business-league nonprofit (501(c)(6)) organization that works with the City of Sacramento as well as with local businesses to help promote Sacramento's identity. It is a public–private partnership. Testa is a specialist in marketing, media communications, and public affairs. I spoke with him about the farm-to-fork branding of the city, asked him what inspired the marketing and why city officials feel that they can make such a bold claim.

Testa explained that Josh Selland, the son of locally renowned chef Randall Selland, first introduced the idea of the "Farm-to-Fork Capital of America" to a city council member as a unique and positive way to market Sacramento's identity. Testa believed it was a great idea, because, as he put it, "there is not a demographic that is not impacted, because everybody eats." Testa went on to note that when his marketing team measured the agricultural output of the region, no other agricultural area in the country compared in abundance or variety of foods produced.

> We looked at acreage of farmland. . . . And the biggest part for us was growing, period. Most cities across the country have some element of farm-to-fork

or "farm-to-table" to them. . . . In Sacramento, we have a year-round growing climate. The reality is: it is California. There is not a time of the year where we don't have something coming out of the ground.

The Sacramento Convention and Visitors Bureau must take its agricultural hinterland and turn it into something that the general public can identify with and want to experience. The next step for Testa is to translate regional food production into an urban eating experience. This entails the restaurateurs' participation.

Of any American city that serves locally grown cuisine, Sacramento has the most restaurants, simply because the restaurants are tied to the region by default. But promoting what the restaurants have always been doing has become increasingly crucial. Testa puts it this way:

> We are farm-to-fork by the pure nature of geography (emphasis added). You are buying directly from the farmers, versus folks in New York who get a lot of their produce exported from this region. Because of convenience, restaurants here buy directly from the farmer, and they have been doing that for decades. For us, it was a matter of putting a name on it and giving it an identity. And the restaurants have said, "Yeah, of course that is what we will do, that is what we have always done." But maybe we should tell the customer that on the menu, that this product was sourced ten miles away, from this farm, and that we bought it this morning. So a lot of them started taking an active role in explaining that definition to the consumer.

It is not sufficient to tell customers only that the food is locally sourced. The built environment needs to reinforce the city's image as a "foodie" haven. Food spaces such as restaurants and farmers' markets become vital in retrofitting the city. Upgrading the urban environment through dining venues is one way to control a city's urban development while simultaneously supporting its urban brand.

City council member Jay Schenirer explained that as Sacramento grows, the City of Sacramento must be able to steer its growth by building distinct neighborhoods downtown that reflect the farm-to-fork identity. Schenirer emphasized the importance of the farm-to-fork initiative in convincing people to move to downtown Sacramento: "Our vision is to get people into the city and live in the city. . . . We want to restore our communities through arts, sports, and dining. We want people to move to and eat downtown. . . . [W]e believe that restaurants downtown will generate investment." The city of Sacramento now needs to augment its civic spaces and neighborhoods to emphasize its newly adopted identity.[2] Experiencing the qualities of that place becomes essential.

The city council and its downtown businesses must invest in transforming the urban landscape into desirable destinations where one would like to reside or visit. Ultimately, the built environment must reflect the city's marketing image as well as support the city boosters' vision for "quality of life."

Sacramento's 2007 Economic Development Strategy Report details how the city should plan and design its spaces to grow its economy by attracting the creative class through promoting a high "quality of life."

> Quality of life . . . is increasingly becoming one of the key inputs that helps determine a city or region's economic prosperity. Quality of life, although rightfully an end in itself, is also a foundational input into what a city or region must ultimately strive for—economic prosperity. Without economic prosperity, a city or region may have little room to negotiate resources to put towards improving quality of life. Economic prosperity brings wealth to a region, part of which can be invested in quality of life, which in turn helps feed economic prosperity; there is a cycle. (Sacramento Economic Development Strategy 2007, 70)

To execute this strategy, the plan focuses primarily on neighborhoods within the city and in what ways those districts could be transformed to create a strong sense of place to residents and visitors.

> *Concern for Place* has always been central to economic and community development. There is increasing awareness that the overall economic health of a city is built on a foundation of strong neighborhoods and districts. It is becoming increasingly clear that highly skilled, mobile, and innovative workers seek *environments that provide them with a unique sense of place. A set of strategies focused on Place are about building these environments and strengthening the City's sense of place.* (Ibid., 77; emphasis added)

The plan then addresses its "three core strategies related to Places" to be "Opportunity Zones; Commercial Corridors and Neighborhoods; Specialized Infrastructure" (77). Some of the proposed improvements related to the strategies are to create pedestrian-friendly streets, reduce blight, upgrade public transit, identify tourism destinations, and transform strip commercial areas to mixed-use, high-density boulevards. The plan emphasizes that every urban district needs to create a sense of place for visitors and residents. "In particular, each corridor is seeking a unique identity for itself that honors the surrounding neighborhood and population, and contributes to the overall vision for Sacramento as well" (83). Certainly, restaurants are a central piece to drive development in the farm-to-fork capital, and this means that city council must heavily invest in the city's restaurant scene.

RESTAURANT URBAN RENEWAL

City boosters are developing and promoting Sacramento's urban brand through reshaping the city's central urban spaces as places for luxury living. They are in the process of creating swank urban places to see and to be seen within. And, perhaps, there are no better ways to activate urban space socially than with bars, restaurants, and arena complexes. Urban developers constructed a new basketball arena for the Sacramento Kings. In May 2014 the city council approved $258 million in city funds to build a new arena in the heart of the city, within the blocks of J and L Streets, as well as Third and Seventh Streets (Heitner 2014). The new arena was erected in what the city's economic development plan considers to be an "opportunity zone." Additionally, it borders parts of downtown that have been relatively dilapidated since the 1950s. As far as the city council and its investment partners were concerned, northwest downtown Sacramento needed to be revitalized.

The city council allotted $8.6 million in city funds to redevelop K Street at Tenth Street with two new bars and a restaurant (Sacramento Economic Development Annual Report 2010). The concept stems from the success of other entertainment districts in cities throughout the country, such as the French Quarter in New Orleans. City boosters in most second-tier cities believe that they should have an entertainment district if they want to attract the creative class. From 2000 to 2010, Sacramento economic developers invested more than $300 million into the downtown district around K Street (Sacramento Economic Development Annual Report 2007, 2010). Much of the money has gone into lofts, hotels, and restaurants, such as the Sheraton Grande Hotel, the Citizen Hotel, the Cathedral Lofts, Esquire Grill, and Ella Restaurant.

The Paragary Group is the largest restaurant benefactor of Sacramento's economic investments. The city council fully funded the Paragary Group and the Taylor Group $6 million in developing an IMAX Theater and the Esquire Grill. The Paragary Group has also partnered with Taylor Group and the City of Sacramento to build two bars and a concert venue at the corner of Tenth and K streets for $15.45 million.

The large allotments of gifted money from the city to shape downtown spaces did not go unnoticed or uncontested by some Sacramentans. According to the *Sacramento Press*, more than three hundred concerned citizens protested the funding of KBAR and Dive Bar (Mendick 2009). The worry was that the city council played favorites in the free market and was becoming a competitor to other local businesses in the process. *Sacramento Press* quotes Matt Haines, owner of two Bistro 33 restaurants downtown: "They've spent $25 million on one corner, 10th and K. . . . The city is becoming one of our competitors" (Belcher 2009). Regardless of complaints and opposition to the city council's spending on strategically planned developments, the city council continued to favor its business partners in the belief that creating the right kind of social spaces would stimulate movement and dollars downtown and would have a ripple effect throughout the city.

As the Sacramento City Council generously gifted funds to private partners to transform districts throughout the city, they were also empowering privileged individuals and further abetting them in implementing their personal business strategies. During this contentious time between restaurants and trucks, many perceived Randy Paragary to have had the utmost influence on city council's decisions. In 2008, *Sacramento Magazine* listed Paragary as one of the one hundred most powerful and influential people in the region (Dunteman 2008). His concept of the city through restaurant space and the city council's vision of farm-to-fork marketing were closely aligned. Since working with the city council and city staff in developing Esquire Grill, Paragary continued to cooperate closely with the city council in establishing, throughout the city's grid, local-color restaurants that ostensibly enhance a neighborhood's sense of place. For example, when the City Mayor branded Sacramento the "Farm-to-Fork Capital of America," Paragary immediately embraced the propaganda. He remodeled and changed the name of his Italian bistro, Spartaro, to Hock Farm (Anderson 2013).[3] The Paragary Restaurant Group describes Hock Farm as follows:

> A celebration of the Sacramento region's rich history and bountiful terrain, the restaurant is named after John Sutter's Hock Farm. Established in 1841, the settlement was the first large-scale agricultural settlement in Northern California. From the beginning, Sutter recognized the farming potential of the Sacramento Valley and pursued many agricultural ventures including grain, cattle, orchards and vineyards, foreshadowing Sacramento's modern day designation as the "Farm-to-Fork Capital" (Paragary Restaurant Group 2014b)

A shrewd businessman, Paragary recognizes that to be financially successful he must dominate space, which he does through restaurant location and territoriality. He owns thirteen establishments throughout downtown Sacramento, nine of which are restaurants. Each restaurant is strategically tailored to its urban surroundings; each location offers a distinctive menu and a distinguishing décor to complement as well as shape the neighborhood's demographics. This strategy echoes Sacramento's economic development plan, which emphasizes that enhancing commercial corridors is vital to Sacramento's urban identity. The Paragary Restaurant Group's Web page states:

Randy has a reputation of going into neighborhoods and improving their collective dining as well as retail business. We are very proud of the diversity of our locations. We have invested abundant thought, time, energy, vigilance and resources to *create unique locations that enhance the urban landscape* and represent high quality. And we sincerely thank the people of our community who have reciprocated by embracing us as a *vital element of the local dining and entertainment scene.* (Paragary Restaurant Group 2014d; emphasis added)

Paragary and other prominent restaurateurs have invested much time and energy in shaping Sacramento's urban landscape through restaurants. Not only do the presence of restaurants reinforce the farm-to-fork agenda, they also foster a sense of place through creating a convivial atmosphere.

SACRAMENTO'S RESTAURANT SPACE

To best understand aesthetic attitudes toward Sacramento's urban landscape, it is important to ascertain how downtown Sacramento is gentrifying through a fashionable restaurant scene to create a "foodie" sense of place. Restaurants are more than iconic destinations; they are designed to create a social ambiance, which can help define one's sense of community. Simply put, restaurant space is the assemblage of cooking and eating practices, architectural design, interior decorating, and social relationships. In this section, I investigate Sacramento's restaurant spaces and demonstrate how their designs influence urban life and mirror the region's sociospatial structure.

Restaurant designs in Sacramento encourage individual interactions and promote a heightened sense of community. These spaces are intended to echo the farm-to-fork philosophy, blurring the boundaries between country and city, between producer and consumer. This relationship is conveyed either via the spatial layout or by putting the foods' origins on display. For example, The Roxy decorates its walls with the names and images of the ranches where it sources its meat and also has a large, open kitchen that showcases the chefs as they cook. The visuals heighten the restaurant experience to be more than just dining out—it also becomes a spectacle. Although the restaurants are designed to be all-inclusive, semi-public social spaces, they almost exclusively serve the middle- and upper-class customers who can afford to consume their vivid atmosphere on a regular basis. As Sharon Zukin (1996) reminds us, cities are built to "manipulate symbolic languages of exclusion and entitlement." In the socioeconomic context of Sacramento, restaurant spaces are a form of "aesthetic power" (7).

Today, restaurants are ubiquitous features of the American cultural land-scape. They may be ordinary places, but they are socially charged spaces that reinforce one's social standing and reflect cultural trends (Pillsbury 1990). In the United States during the mid-1800s, restaurants were primarily formal dining establishments associated with hotels for the socially mobile elite.[4] Paul Groth (1994, 30) details how hotel-dining spaces have affected American cuisine culture:

> In most cities by 1900, three of the top five restaurants were sure to be in palace hotels, and the creative cookery and inventive bar drinks of the era often ema-nated from hotel chefs or hotel barkeepers. Parker House rolls, Waldorf salad, Maxwell House coffee, and the Manhattan cocktail all gained their names from hotels. . . . The importance of dining in the company of an elegant crowd con-tinued into the twentieth century.

It was not until the late 1800s and early 1900s that restaurants in the United States began catering to middle-class preferences, which were often influenced by the middle class's "slumming" experiences in New York City's ethnic neigh-borhoods (Barbas 2003; Haley 2011), such as eating in Chinatown.

The functions and social meanings of restaurants, much like cuisine, are ever evolving. Perhaps there is no better place to study social change and urban cul-ture than through examining restaurant spaces (Barbas 2003; Bell and Valentine 1997; Beriss and Sutton 2007). A restaurant's ambiance is expressed through its interior design (Beriss and Sutton 2007; Ferrero 2001; Pardue 2007) and the social importance of restaurants helps construct a city's reputation (Beriss 2007), such as New Orleans's Creole cuisine. Therefore, restaurants have a deep sociospatial significance. Likewise, they showcase the people who can afford to consume such spaces and how table manners in such spaces signify belonging to a particular social class (Finkelstein 1991). Additionally, I argue that a restaurant's architecture is significant in shaping social interactions and American cuisine culture.

Goffman (1959), in his analysis of restaurants of the 1950s, divides dining places into two fundamental spaces: the "front" and "backstage." It is a metaphor for a theatrical performance setting. Historically, restaurants have always had a separation between the kitchen and dining rooms. Even today, restaurant work-ers refer to "working the front of the house" or "the back of the house," much like in a theater. In the past, the labor in the kitchen was concealed from the diner's sight, and most patrons had little interest in watching their meal being cooked (Groth 2008). Nobody of social importance wanted to sit anywhere near the kitchen because it was considered a snub by the headwaiter (Haley 2011, 34).

Furthermore, the human stress and commotion of the kitchen were not al-lowed to permeate the comforting spaces of the dining room. Although chefs were highly esteemed and their meals were to be enjoyed, their act of creat-ing the meal was not. But cooking as a "labor of love" has transcended class boundaries. Over the past few decades, middle-class Americans have come to view cooking as an act of artistic ingenuity and, perhaps, something they think they might like to try in their own kitchens. American attitudes toward culinary preparation have become domesticated primarily through cooking shows on television (Ray 2007), and food has become fetishized in magazines and movies (McBride 2010; Zimmerman 2009). These new culturally constructed mentali-ties toward cooking and eating are influencing the ways in which restaurants are now designed. Cooking is becoming center stage.

Take the kitchen. Many restaurants across the country are opening their floor plans to allow the kitchen to be in full view of the diners, and in some cases, the cocina is even placed in the center of the dining area. Food critic Richard Magee (2007) claims that when food is "removed from the kitchen, [it] becomes divorced from its nutritive or taste qualities." This suggests that elevating the kitchen space to become the focal point of the dining room exposes aspects of the food system, thus allowing the food to maintain its basic nutritive qualities. The kitchen, much like a farmers' market, becomes a spatial nexus between the country and the city. It is where food transitions from soiled and raw to cleaned and cooked. Making the cooking area transparent allows the consumers to observe the way their meal is prepared and how it arrives from the farm to the table. But the kitchen is just one aspect of the dining theme. To complete the narrative, the chef or the waiter will inform the diner about the elements of the food that are not readily observable. The entire experience of watching the performances in the cocina becomes a dining education about farm-to-table, and presumably, the food also tastes better.

Randall Selland's restaurant The Kitchen, established in 1991, is a paragon of new restaurant design. The name "The Kitchen" itself is self-explanatory in terms of design concept. The restaurant is foremost designed around a large kitchen counter to encourage communal activity, much like one might find in a family home. I interviewed Selland in June 2013; he explained that he aimed to replicate his family's cooking space to simulate and stimulate similar social in-teractions in his restaurant: "The whole concept is about getting people together around food and having a good time. . . . You will see people in here talking like they have known each other all their lives, but they've just met." For Selland, the key concept for his restaurant is conviviality. I was fortunate enough to be invited to dine at The Kitchen to partake in the social atmosphere and observe firsthand how Selland creates social synergy among strangers through cooking and eating together.

The Kitchen has two kitchen spaces: a back kitchen and a demonstration kitchen. The back cocina is where food is prepped or additional ovens are available. Although the back kitchen is partitioned from the front kitchen, there are no doors to separate the activities or disrupt one's line of sight between the two spaces. Moreover, people are allowed to walk to the back cuisine and talk with the chefs or observe, but it is really the front cuisine that is designed as the center stage.

There is a large bar seating about thirty people that wraps around the front cooking area. In other words, the back of the house is now the front of the house. What used to be behind the scenes is now the main act—a cooking extravaganza. There are no longer any boundaries that separate the patrons from the chefs. One could, perhaps, argue that the bar is a boundary. However, Selland is explicit that one is free to roam anywhere around the restaurant at any time: "Truly anything goes here at The Kitchen." (Selland's 2014).

On the night I dined there, Selland put on a performance. He came out welcoming his guests to The Kitchen and informed them about the dinner they were about to experience. He told the diners to get comfortable by taking a "stroll in the kitchen" and encouraged them to "chat" with the chefs, "relax" in the garden patio, or visit the wine cellar. Much like a theatrical performance, the dinner was designed around seven acts and one intermission: "We've learned how to build menus to create excitement. So there [are] no filler courses, every course has purpose, every course has meaning," explained Selland.

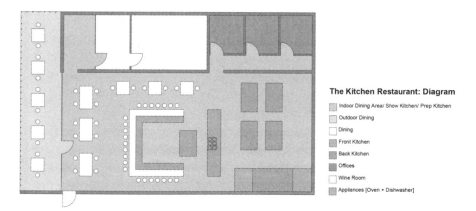

Figure 1: Diagram of The Kitchen's spatial arrangement. Source: Diagram based on drawings from author's sketchbook.

In the first act, Selland presented the ingredients he would use for the evening. He paraded around the room holding a large sockeye salmon over his shoulder. He educated his diners about the fish. He said that it was not a locally caught fish—it was from Oregon, and he had the fish flown in just for this particular feast. He spoke briefly about the environmental problems that have affected the salmon population in California, the various flavors and textures that different types of salmon have, and where they tend to spawn on the Northern Pacific Coast.

As Selland walked about the room, he showed different vegetables he would be using that night. He informed the customers where the produce was from, and even who had sold it to him. He explained what made each ingredient special in terms of the way in which it had been cultivated, why he chose that particular ingredient, and how he planned on combining it with the other ingredients.

The crowd of about sixty-five people in the room oohed and aahed at all the spectacular foods Selland showcased, and many of them asked questions. Randall invoked humor and kept the diners constantly laughing and interacting with him and with each other. He fed off the energy in the room and loved for people to participate. If someone asked a question, Randall would immediately dive deeper into the topic or tell a humorous personal story—often, it was a combination of both. If someone was interested in a cooking technique, he invited the person to get up from his or her seat and go around the counter to get a better look or maybe help out. It was a very engaging, educational, and entertaining environment. In fact, to experience it significantly contributed to the way in which I came to know Sacramento.

Selland, through the assistance of the restaurant's spatial layout and through his actions, emphasized the relationship between country and city, agriculture and urban dining. As the waiters brought out each course, they informed the patrons about how each food item had been prepared. For example, the waiter presented the first dish: "This is a duck egg from Contreras Ranch, near Half Moon Bay. This egg has been slowly poached for six hours at a constant temperature of 63 degrees." The sommelier described the terrain of each wine that he paired for the dish:

> This is a 2010 Chardonnay from Fisher Vineyards Mountain Estate in Sonoma. Fisher Vineyards grows their chardonnay vines on a steep, rocky, northeast-facing slope at an average elevation of thirteen hundred feet, receiving early morning sun and minimal exposure to hot afternoon temperatures. This allows the grape to develop bold, ripe flavors.

The servers were adept in connecting the physical geography of the place where something is produced with the consumer's experience of taste. The information the server chose to communicate about the growing environments of food, as well as the manner of his conveyance, transcended the urban dining experience. However, this description of the wine's production did not convey to me the blood and sweat that helped pick the grapes and produce the wine.

Lefebvre (1991, 81) contends, "Things lie, and when, having become commodities, they lie in order to conceal their origin, namely social labour, they tend to set themselves up as absolutes. Products and the circuits they establish (in space) are fetishized." As produce makes its ways from farm to table, the spaces around the products are transformed to convey altered imaginary geographical experiences about their production. Restaurant spaces not only reinforce social standing, they also reduce the image of how food is produced to the physical characteristics of the land.

California is a land of industrialized agriculture and always has been (Guthman 2004; McWilliams and Sackman 2000; Walker 2004). Most of the produce in California is picked by Mexican day laborers (Mitchell 1996; Walker 2004). Selland acknowledges that Mexicans represent the backbone of California's dining and agricultural economy. California is home to 11.5 million Mexican citizens (U.S. Census 2010) and an estimated 2.5 million Mexican nondocumented immigrants (Department of Homeland Security's Office of Immigration Statistics 2014). They make up approximately 30 percent of the state's population. California's economy would not survive without them working low-wage, labor-intensive tasks, from picking fruits to washing dishes. Mexican immigrants are the low-cost, intensive labor side of farm to table. I even spoke with many small farmers in the region who conceded that they rely on low-wage Mexican labor. Distance obscures the fields from urban dining, but only a wall separates the formal diners from the Mexican day laborers who are just a few feet away, performing the most menial tasks.

Other than the kitchen, bar, and the dining room, there are other important elements of restaurant space, such as the wine cellar, outdoor patio, and dishwashing room. In almost all restaurants, the dishwashing room is completely concealed from sight. When I began my research, I started to scrutinize the spatial configurations of every restaurant I stepped into. The Kitchen is the only restaurant I have ever seen in which the person washing dishes was not completely out of sight; however, the dishwashing area was farthest removed from the dining area.

The performance of labor and the ways in which those performances are interpreted by culture are reflected in restaurant spaces. The kitchen can be placed in the middle of a dining room, whereas a dishwashing room cannot. The Latino day laborers, who are indispensable in helping to produce the aesthetics and ambiance of the dining experience, must be kept out of sight.

Whether they are picking apples ten miles away in a field or washing dishes a few feet away, their services are seldom celebrated, let alone acknowledged. The consumption end of the food system becomes a spectacle for urban life that reinforces romanticized views of Jeffersonian agrarianism; it cannot and must not reveal social struggles. Sacramento's downtown restaurants, its revitalized entertainment districts and pristine streets, are all reliant on the peripheral Mexican communities that contribute to the production of these labor-abstracted utopias.

The Kitchen may be an extreme example of dining out, but it has significantly influenced contemporary trends in restaurant design. The success of The Kitchen's social atmosphere carries over to Selland's other restaurant concepts. He continues to put people-to-people interactions at the center of his business plan and restaurant floor plans. Because Selland focuses on the communal aspects of cuisine, he told me that he works closely with the architects in translating his message experientially, and that bar spaces along with patio dining are essential in creating the right ambiance.

Restaurateur Paragary is also attentive to the architectural details that form his restaurant spaces. He uses open floor plans to encourage social interaction and create a lively atmosphere. In Paragary's most opulent restaurant, Esquire Grill, the streetscape blends into the dining scene. There is a large, open-air patio that integrates with the tree-canopied, pedestrian Thirteenth Street. Eating "al fresco" along the sidewalk is part of Paragary's strategy for making the K-Street district feel more "vibrant" (Darnell 2012).

I would not entirely accredit the change in restaurant designs in Sacramento to the farm-to-fork movement. Restaurant designs throughout the United States have been shifting toward more open floor plans and also often offer outdoor seating. The change in restaurant design may be due to the adoption of European café spaces to showcase cities as cosmopolitan playgrounds (Latham 2008). Regardless of the design impetus, the number of restaurants throughout downtown Sacramento that have these spatial qualities is substantial. The Sacramento City Council and its business partners are using restaurant spaces to rejuvenate the city's downtown atmosphere with an air of urbanity.

As Sacramento gentrifies gastronomically with the farm-to-fork marketing brand, restaurateurs design restaurant space to change the feel and look of the city. The transformation of urban space, from the inside out, is significant in forging Sacramento's newfound identity. Restaurant spaces, no doubt, become places of symbolic power that experientially evoke an exclusive urban identity.

= = =

Sacramento's City Council's initiative is to increase downtown property values through cooking and eating locally sourced foods. They use regional cuisine to elevate the city economically, and, in so doing, rely on the country to define the city. Sacramento's regional agriculture augments the city's architecture. Its urban renewal through cuisine is twofold: consume locally produced foods on the one hand, foster social interaction on the other. It is a form of experiential capital that prioritizes socialization to endorse its marketing image. Accordingly, restaurants and farmers' markets become significant social spaces that reinforce Sacramento's image as the "Farm-to-Fork Capital of America."

Restaurateurs use the farm-to-fork philosophy to design restaurants that create conviviality. In this way, the taste of place is also a shared experience. Open kitchens, long bars, outdoor patios, and sidewalk cafés are all designed to accommodate the changing culture of cosmopolitan culinary practices. These design strategies not only heighten the visibility of eating together, they also encourage the social interactions of strangers. The result is a vibrant and exclusive urban dining scene.

The upgrading of the urban environment around culinary customs is associated with a process I refer to as *gastro-gentrification*—the changing character and shifting demographic of the city and/or a neighborhood through food practices. It is the creation of innovative and/or ethnic restaurants, urban agriculture, farmers' markets, food trucks, eating local, "slow food," or any other food movement that transforms the atmosphere of an urban environment and consequently the residential demographic. For sure, coffee shops, boutique bakeries, specialty grocery stores, and ethnic food stands are often catalysts for gentrification. In the past, one could perceive these spatial reconfigurations and demographic shifts as they took place organically. Now, city planners, city councils, and urban developers are conceiving these processes. Planned gentrification through cuisine has become a new agent of urban renewal.

In most scenarios, the upgrading of the urban landscape is not without aspects of exclusion and exploitation. The individuals who have the power to remake the urban landscape do so by making invisible the very people they need to shape it. Mexican day laborers pick nearly all of the produce in California, not to mention that they perform much of the work in the back kitchens. These aspects of labor in California's food system are not selling points to entice the creative class to move to Sacramento. Connecting chefs to boutique farms better fits the farm-to-fork framework because it maintains many of the customers' imaginary and idealized images of the nineteenth-century farmstead. This vision focuses on the constructed beauty of the lush green gardens but not on the laborers bent over picking grapes between the groves.

Furthermore, Mexican day laborers often depend on cheap tacos sold from roving trucks. Not only does the urban renewal of Sacramento rely on inexpensive Mexican labor to create an image of exclusiveness, it also aims to eliminate their way of eating. The city council and many restaurateurs maintain that the reprogramming of streets with farmers' markets and the redesign of restaurants enhance the city's quality of life, whereas taco trucks blight the urban landscape and thus tarnish the city's image.

Much like Siena and its Piazza del Campo seven centuries ago, Sacramento's urban boosters have developed a relationship between the city's urban center and its hinterland. Restaurant districts have become symbolic social spaces in the city center, controlled by the city elite, where people can consume the cultural and conceptual construction that connects the country to the city. But, in exuding this exclusive landscape, the city's visionaries must eliminate social practices and aesthetics that subtract "visual interest" from the streetscape, such as the taco truck and the day laborer. In chapter 4, I demonstrate how the social processes that construct Sacramento's city center marginalize the traditional taco truck and affect the city's unsung laborers.

CHAPTER 4

LANDSCAPE, LABOR, AND THE LONCHERA

From 2002 to 2014 taco trucks were fiercely contested features of Sacramento's landscape. To the Sacramento City Council, taco trucks disrupted the city's spatial order, and many restaurateurs believed food trucks were unfair competition to their brick-and-mortar establishments. Moreover, the trucks impeded the city boosters' vision to sell Sacramento as "America's Farm-to-Fork Capital." As restaurateur Randy Paragary proclaimed, "I'm literally talking about a roach coach parking in front of the Capitol building. . . . How do you legislate who can be out on the streets and who can't? Who's the gourmet police? Who's going to discriminate?" (Miller 2011). Because many influential individuals, such as Paragary, felt that taco trucks cluttered the city's posh landscape, city code regulated the visibility of taco trucks by controlling their mobility.

Prior to 2015, city code dictated that the food trucks must move at least four hundred feet every thirty minutes (Sacramento City Code 5.68). For many taco truck operators, this made mobile food vending exceptionally difficult. Traditional taco trucks in Sacramento do not typically motor about the city throughout the day because it is too problematic to their cooking operation; rather, they tend to park in one place for months or even years at a time. Consequently, these ordinances forced a few taco truck owners to develop tactics to traverse the built environment, although most circumvented the policies by merely moving a block or two outside the city limits. The City Revenue Division, however, grandfathered twelve trucks into the city code. Regardless, the strict time and place regulations created a relative absence of food trucks within Sacramento's city limits, especially downtown.

Geographers have developed philosophies about the social and political forces that determine a landscape's outward appearance. Cosgrove (1998, 8) claims that landscapes are a "way of seeing" because they lay bare the ideologies of the elite, who uninhibitedly shape the look of the land for power and profit. Through this framework, zoning taco trucks out of Sacramento demonstrates the command that the city council and city boosters have to control the city's aesthetic. But as Mitchell (1996, 6) emphasizes, "To ignore the work that makes landscape . . . is thus to ignore a lot of what landscape *is*" (emphasis in original). Landscapes are also constructed through labor, Mitchell argues, and laborers both challenge and change the representation of landscape as it is being shaped. Landscapes, therefore, are also produced through political conflicts as well as through the everyday life and social struggles of the working classes.

The taco truck is a significant feature of California's cultural landscape because it symbolizes the livelihoods of the state's Mexican workforce. Not only are taco trucks owned and operated by Mexicans, they serve inexpensive tacos to the many low-wage Mexican laborers who construct and maintain California's cities and pick the fruits and vegetables in the fields. What makes the taco truck unique from a geographic theoretical standpoint is that the truck is a mobile feature of the landscape. Even though many taco truck owners prefer to remain parked in one place, they will strategically employ their mobility when needed. Paradoxically, the taco truck is both fixed and dynamic. Cresswell (2006, 25), who researches how the representations of mobility practices are socially constructed and contested, posits "fixity and flow" as opposing principles to understand the ways in which society is spatially structured; movement and mobility function as an active form of resistance when a dominant social group tries to exclude undesirable practices from a particular place.

While chapter 3 evaluates the ways in which the city council and restaurateurs work to fashion the urban landscape with exclusive dining spaces, this chapter examines the taco truck owners' struggle from 2002 to 2014 to remain part of Sacramento's urban life and cultural identity. Sacramento City Council's and the restaurateurs' landscape ideology threatened not only taco trucks, I argue, but also the Mexican laborers' social practices—the communal life that is associated with eating at taco trucks.

"MOVE IT OR LOSE IT"

From 2002 to 2006, the City of Sacramento decided to enforce its "outdated" mobile food-vending laws on Northgate Boulevard in North Sacramento as well as on Franklin Boulevard in South Sacramento, where approximately twenty traditional taco trucks parked daily on private parking lots. City officials had received complaints about blight, crime, and unfair business competition. Based on the number of complaints about taco trucks, the city thought it was time to revamp its ordinances to erase the trucks from the city's landscape.

The April 27, 2006, front page of the *Sacramento News and Review* featured the taco truck owners' dilemma: "Move it or lose it: City cracks down on food trucks, vendors cry 'ethnic cleansing'" (Dyer 2006). That same month, the headline for the *Sacramento Bee* read: "Mobile food vendors feel threatened: Restaurant owners, city officials seek to keep catering operations moving" (Montaño 2006). The articles report that some residents were "shouting racial slurs" at the truck workers and that there were countless complaints about drug sales and blight associated with taco trucks (Dyer 2006). There were also many grievances that food trucks were unfair competition to brick-and-mortar restaurants.

Regardless of what motivated the complaints, the city council and city staff were eager to eradicate the trucks. In February 2006 a "Report to Law and Legislation Committee" by the Finance Department indicated that the mobile food-vending code should be revised because of the number and types of perceived disorders about the trucks:

> The Revenue Division, as well as other City departments, receives complaints concerning the operation of food-vending vehicles with the City. Specific concerns reported to, or observed by, City staff include, but are not limited to:

> Operation of non-permitted mobile food vehicles;
> Non-permitted operators;
> Mobile food vehicles operating during prohibited hours;
> Vending at unoccupied sites;
> Mobile food operators negatively impacting local "brick and mortar" businesses and food establishments;
> Sale of items inconsistent with health permits; and
> Violence and misconduct regarding vending routes.

> (Report to Law and Legislation Committee, City of Sacramento, Staff Report, February 7, 2006)

The report concluded with recommendations for changes to the mobile food-vending code in order to regulate the trucks. The complaints that the Revenue Office cited might have been verifiable, but they would not warrant a reworking of city code to regulate mobility and the right to vend in public or semi-public spaces. Many of the complaints turned out to be unwarranted or became excuses for city officials to harass the vendors with citations. City officials were search-ing for any reason to eliminate the trucks from the city.[1]

According to the City of Sacramento Revenue Division, taco trucks induce crime and violence, create a nuisance because they generate complaints, and/or compete with brick-and-mortar establishments. Instead of addressing each complaint through the appropriate authorities—such as the Police Depart-ment for crime or the Health Department for health regulations—the City of Sacramento Revenue Division concluded that mobile food vending should be regulated in a manner that keeps the practice mobile.

City officials and the city council operate under the assumption that they can control all land uses throughout the city in a way that best benefits the com-munity, and this extends to policing human mobility—in this case, vending in public and semi-public spaces. Zones are designated for particular practices, and food truck practices need to correspond to these places. The original regu-lations for mobile food vending were written in the 1960s and 1970s to protect the practice of lunch trucks that traveled between construction sites. The code notes that the trucks must move every fifteen minutes and may only operate between the hours of 6:00 A.M. and 8:00 P.M. during the summer, and 6:00 A.M. and 6:00 P.M. during the winter (Sacramento City Code 7.06.060). There is one exception to the mobility aspect of this code, and that applies if the trucks are parked on private property:

> [A] food-vending vehicle may be operated during the hours prescribed by said paragraphs (1) and (2) if the vehicle stops only on private property which is used for non-residential purposes, with the permission of the occupant of the property, for the primary purpose of selling food to employees of the business located on the private property and to the employees of other nearby businesses.

In 2006, the city staff and city council believed that this code was outdated and should be updated. Brad Wasson, revenue manager for the City of Sacramento, argued that food trucks were designed to be mobile and that city code should enforce their mobility. *Sacramento News and Review* quoted him as stating, "[These vendors] are getting around putting up a restaurant, [and] that wasn't the intent of the code" (Dryer 2006). Wasson eventually rewrote the code so that food trucks on both public and private property had to remain mobile, but he did make a few exceptions. He allowed twelve immobile taco trucks to be grand-fathered in. However, by 2014, only four traditional taco trucks remained of those twelve. The traditional taco trucks were slowly fading away or moving out.

George Azar is one of the traditional taco truck owners who fought the city council and city staff on the issue of mobile food vending (see plate 12). George led the battle against the City of Sacramento on behalf of taco truck owners because he has a basic understanding of his right to vend food on Sacramento's streets and parking lots. George's advantage is that he is a U.S.-born citizen with fluency in English.

Born in San Diego, California, George has lived all his life in Sacramento and, since 1998, has been operating his taco truck at the corner of Northgate Boulevard and Peralta Avenue. In April 2006 he released a media advisory titled "City to Take on Taco Trucks: City Staff Propose Changes that Will End a Centuries-Old Cultural Way of Eating."[2] The second paragraph emphasizes, "Taco Trucks have been a part of the City's *landscape* for nearly a century, if not longer" (emphasis added). Here, *landscape* is the proscenium where social life unfolds. And for George, taco trucks significantly contribute to the cultural making of California's landscape. Central to his argument is that city officials are threatening a deep-rooted way of life by belittling the cultural importance of culinary customs within Mexican working-class communities:

> No one really knows why the sudden interest in controlling the way and times that taco trucks sell in Sacramento, but city staff are recommending changes that will greatly hamper sales and basically eliminate a convenient, economic and traditional way of eating for Mexicans. . . . Taco vendors have been a part of Mexican culture for centuries in Mexico and in every other major city of California. It clearly has been a part of Sacramento Latino culture for as long as my parents, grandparents and I can remember.

From 2002 to 2015, George had to fight city ordinances to keep Mexican street-food vending active—not in terms of protecting his cultural practices but in terms of opposing what he believes are irrational and invalid city regulations enforced in a discriminatory manner.

I met with George to discuss the controversy over the mobile food regulations. He and I had several in-depth discussions about the historic practice of Mexican mobile food vending in California and the recurring battles he has had with the City of Sacramento since 2002. I also spoke with his mother, Mercedes Azar, who used to work for Governor Jerry Brown and currently works for the Sacramento City Council. Because of her job position in City Hall, she was able to keep George abreast about city/state policies and could notify him when mobile food issues were suddenly brought forward to city council meetings.

George and I began our conversations by assessing the historic significance of taco trucks in Sacramento. Sacramento without Mexican street food is unimaginable, George professed, because mobile food vending is entrenched in the social lives of the labor force that lives here. "All of my life I've gone to eat at taco

MEDIA ADVISORY

FOR IMMEDIATE RELEASE
April 11, 2006

Contact: George Azar
La Mex Taqueria
(916) 416-2918

CITY TO TAKE ON TACO TRUCKS

*City Staff Propose Changes that will End a Centuries-old
Cultural Way of Eating
Public Informational Meeting to be held Wed. April 12 at 6 pm at the
Library Galleria, 9th and I Streets*

Sacramento-A little known, antiquated and never before enforced city code is being used as the impetus for cracking down on Taco Trucks in Sacramento.

Taco Trucks have been a part of the City's landscape for nearly a century, if not longer. Customers have enjoyed the convenience of eating at these trucks for years and years. Traditionally, Taco Trucks begin selling at the lunch hour and continue sales into the late evening and on weekends until 2 a.m. These have been the eating establishments

Figure 2: Media advisory written by George Azar: "City to Take on Taco Trucks."

trucks and taco trailers. We've got deep ethnic roots here in Sacramento. It's just been part of the city. Sacramento used to be all farmlands. And who does all the farming? [*He laughs loudly*] Who picks it all? [*Laughing some more*] Those baskets of strawberries would be $15 [if Mexicans were not picking them]!"[3] Inexpensive tacos and low-wage Mexican labor have an interwoven relationship. It is impossible to write or talk about taco trucks without acknowledging that their existence is fundamentally tied to Mexican labor and migration routes from Mexico. As I spoke with George and his parents in May 2013, they told me that taco trucks have been roaming the Central Valley since the early 1970s. George's mother explained:

> The trucks have been here forever. I can't tell you how long specifically, but I know in 1975 there was a taco truck that had been parked outside the Reno Club on 12th Street. . . . We had Mexican taco trucks outside of Mexican bars until 2 A.M. These were not taco stands, they were real trucks. And we would eat tacos there all the time, and this was in 1975.

Street tacos in Sacramento have been around since at least the 1950s. George's father, Guillermo, was a taquero in Jalostotitlán, Jalisco. When he moved to

Sacramento, he sold street tacos—from a pushcart—outside a club on Franklin Boulevard during the week and in public parks on the weekends. George elaborates: "My dad has been selling tacos in the park since the 1960s, and before that there were other taco vendors. . . . My [maternal] grandfather sold the best chorizo tacos outside of church every Sunday."

Mercedes Azar adds:

> My father used to sell tacos at a stand in Mexico City [in the 1920s]. Selling tacos out of trucks and carts has been a part of Mexican culture forever. It's nothing new. And that's the part that amazed me in Sacramento. That when George opened up his truck—and it didn't happen right away—he was there for a few years . . . then, all of a sudden, he started getting harassed. . . . So suddenly it becomes an issue. And for different reasons, for different council members . . . I believe there were some council members who felt that [the trucks] were prime for criminal activities. There were other council members who don't like the sight. It's "blight" in their opinion.

The objections to the trucks throughout the city seemed to originate from biased interpretations about the aesthetics of Mexican street-food vending by ultraconservative Anglo neighbors. Many believed that taco trucks made Sacramento "look like Mexico" or "third world." Others assumed that the taco truck owners and their clientele were all "illegals." Because of the complaints, the city code enforcement officers began performing regular sweeps throughout the city in 2002. They wrote tickets for various violations and immediately shut down carts and trucks that had no health and license permits. George commented in disbelief: "It's been battles since day 1. . . . They cleaned off Franklin Boulevard and got rid of all the trailers [taco trucks]. The city seemed to think it was a blight on the community because of a few people who think, 'Those places are just hangouts. They sell drugs and this and that.'" George argued that non-Latinos tend to have negative perceptions about Mexican culinary practices. They are prejudiced against Mexicans hanging out on the street and associate their standing around at a taco truck with criminal behavior. To the contrary, George cleaned up the trash around his truck and even made the environment safer:

> If you ask the owner where I park my truck at his business . . . [he will say that] up until a month ago he had not been robbed. Nothing since I parked there. A month ago he got robbed and we sat and talked about, wow, this is the first time since 1998 that it's happened to his business. Call me crazy, but I think it helped [having my truck parked outside] we had people outside eating. . . . Eyes on the street, activity, and that's what you want in the city. You want people walking

the sidewalks and shopping and eating—things like that. So it makes no sense for the city to push the way they are pushing.

George's point of view is that Mexican food vending contributes to the city's "quality of life" because taco trucks create social activity on the street and provide a sense of security. George uses the words, "eyes on the street" to describe how people get to know a place in terms of who belongs and who doesn't. Jane Jacobs (1992, 36) actually put forth the expression "eyes on the street" as a community strategy to watch out for one another by having personal exchanges, such as shop owners surveying the sidewalk and residents watching—from their windows—children play on the street. These visual engagements, she contends, come from mixed-use spaces in mid-density neighborhoods, such as Greenwich Village, New York City, where she had resided.

While automobile commercial strips in California are the antithesis to 1950s mixed-use neighborhoods of lower Manhattan, taco trucks inject intimate individual interactions onto the street corner. It is an informal and idiosyncratic way to socially reconfigure the cold geometries of the urban landscape, which arguably ameliorates community life and could deter criminal behavior. Regardless of the positive social life taco trucks introduce, the tattered image of the trucks reinforces the notion that they generate crime.

George concedes that some of the trucks do not look that nice. If city officials have issues with the trucks' aesthetics, he insists, they should help the vendors improve their operation rather than regulate them out:

> It was a battle for a long time to get the city to realize, you know what, it's just honest people out there trying to make an honest living, you know? It's only food, you know? You got a problem with one truck doing something bad, then take care of the problem. . . . If you don't like the way it looks, create ways to regulate the trucks to look better. . . . The city never gave ethnic food owners the chance to invest in their business and their vehicles. . . . The city doesn't want to improve the trucks' image; they just want to wipe them out.

City officials were not interested in helping mobile food vendors meet code regulations or enhance their business practices. Instead, city authorities tried to displace the food vendors through intimidation. George explained that, starting in the early 2000s, code enforcement executed frequent patrols to clear out food vendors. According to George, it was fairly easy for the city health and code enforcement departments to run around the city and scare away taco truck owners, because Mexican vendors already felt like they were living at the margins of society.

In 2002 a code enforcement officer wrote George's father a ticket for vending after hours. Mrs. Azar found the citation on his record in the spring of 2013. "Can you believe my husband has a misdemeanor on his record? The city gave him a misdemeanor for operating a food truck after 8:00 P.M.! He didn't even know that it was a misdemeanor." George added, "My father speaks very broken English. He probably didn't know what really was going on, so he just signed the ticket." The officer's report reads:

> I, Belinda Losoya, responded to 2630 Northgate Blvd. to investigate a complaint from the Sacramento Police Department regarding several trucks operating and selling their wares after 8:00 P.M.. . . . I sat near by [sic] in my city vehicle observing the La Mex Taqueria. Numerous patrons came to purchase food. . . . Mr. Azar stated: ". . . We were told if we were on private property we could operate late. We have permission to park on this lot. We also, pay the property owner's [sic] here a little money. We are just trying to make a living." I advised Mr. Azar that

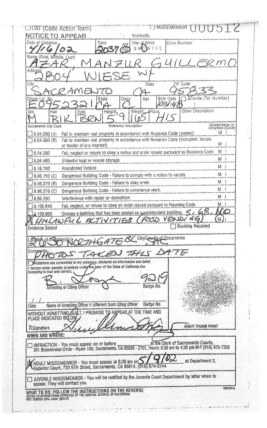

Figure 3: Citation issued to Guillermo Azar: "Unlawful Activities (Food Vending)."

he was in violation of his business tax certificate operating hours. (Sacramento Police Department Report Z-020011358).

The ticket cites "unlawful activities (food vending)" as the infraction. When we consider the reasons for a citation from code enforcement, we may think of a building not in compliance with fire regulations or an abandoned vehicle—violations that threaten public safety or health. "Food vending" by someone who holds a health permit, I argue, does not qualify as a major violation of city code. A misdemeanor in California is often associated with trespassing, public intoxication, or theft. The misdemeanor "unlawful activities (food vending)" seems strict. In what way does food vending become criminal? In this case, it is the time the food was served from the taco truck—after eight in the evening. It is not the food vending itself that is criminal; rather, it is the time and manner of the food vending that makes the practice illegal. For the City of Sacramento, selling tacos from a truck after 8 P.M. is a misdemeanor punishable by California law. Put differently, Mexican culinary culture is criminalized because it does not fit into the City of Sacramento's code, which is defined by what city officials deem socially appropriate for food vending along streets at night.

Code enforcers also evaluated other violations that fell beyond their authority. They checked employees' identifications to see if they were U.S. citizens. When the code enforcer in this instance found out that one of Azar's employees did not have his green card, she threatened to contact Immigration and Customs Enforcement. "He [Mr. Azar] was further advised that anyone working for him needed a green card or migration [sic] would be contacted regarding the violation" (Sacramento Police Department Report Z-020011358). George had been out of town and unaware of the citation until he returned. His father, perhaps not fully aware of the circumstances, was unable to contest the issue in court and willingly paid a fee of $108. The court reported:

> On or about April 16, 2002, in the City of Sacramento, defendant, Guillermo Azar, did commit a misdemeanor, namely: a violation of Section 5.68.110 (B)(1) of City Code of the City of Sacramento in that said defendant, a food-vending vehicle driver or person in the business of operating a food-vending vehicle, did unlawfully operate a food-vending vehicle for food-vending purposes between the hours of 8 P.M. . . . and 5 A.M. of the following day. (*The People of the State of California v. Guillermo Azar*, Case No. 02M05033)

George explained that this is one of the tactics that the city's Revenue Department staff used to force taco truck owners to close. He said he was going broke closing at 8:00 P.M. every night. He insisted that it is imperative to stay open until 2:00 A.M. in order to feed Mexican laborers who work late shifts. These are often people who do not have an opportunity to eat during conventional dining hours. George followed the law as he continued to struggle with city officials. He also made the issue public by giving an interview to the *Sacramento Bee* about the early closing hours.

George argued that many of the food vendors, whether they had proper business documents or not, may have been undocumented and afraid of confronting the accusation, and/or did not speak English well enough to fully comprehend the nature of the violation:

> The department [of code enforcement], all they would have to do is show a badge and they [the food vendors] were gone. There used to be one [taco truck] on every corner on Franklin Boulevard. When I first opened, and within the first six or seven years [of being open], just in this section of Northern Sacramento, there would have probably been a good twelve or thirteen trucks that popped up. And when this all started really going [the city code enforcement harassing the trucks], they totally folded. Gone!

City officials would find unclear wording in the food-vending code and interpret the code to mean what they wanted it to mean, then enforce the code in English to Spanish-speaking immigrants. It empowered them to issue expensive tickets to disadvantaged taco truck owners. In June 2006 George received a citation because an employee did not have an operating license, nor was the driver of the truck on scene with the vehicle. The code states that the employer must have a license but does not specify that the employees must have one (City Code Section 5.68.080). Moreover, the vehicle was not in motion, so the driver did not have to be present. This time George responded to the violation with a formal statement to city officials. This is an excerpt from his rebuttal:

> My reading of the section, based on the excellent English grammar teaching I received by the outstanding teachers of Christian Brothers High School, is that this section applies only to owners. It appears to me that Section 5.68.080 has a properly conjugated sentence, which clearly states, when broken down into its separate parts, that it applies only to owners.

George was born and raised in California, is a second-generation Californian, is well educated, and speaks fluent English. He explained that most of the other taco truck owners do not speak English. Almost all of them, however, are documented U.S. citizens, and most of them have the proper paperwork to own and operate a taco truck. But if the city code enforcers were to write similar tickets to other taco truck owners, the owners would not understand why they were

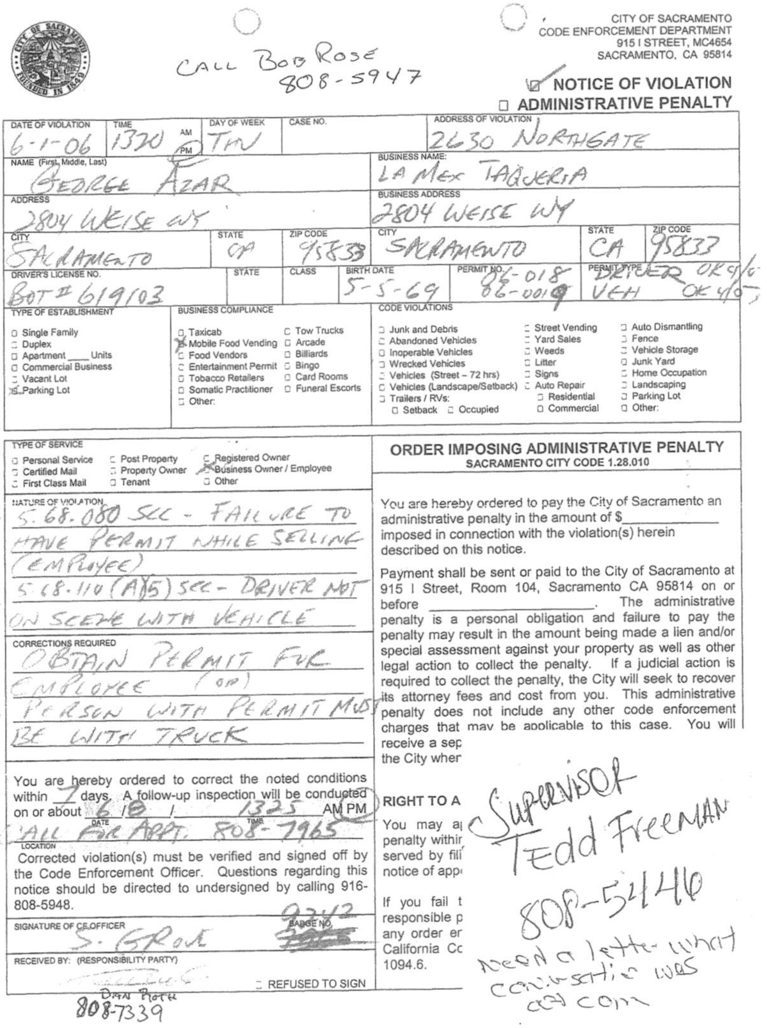
CITY OF SACRAMENTO
CODE ENFORCEMENT DEPARTMENT
915 I STREET, MC4654
SACRAMENTO, CA 95814

CALL BOB ROSE 808-5947

☑ NOTICE OF VIOLATION
☐ ADMINISTRATIVE PENALTY

DATE OF VIOLATION: 6-1-06 TIME: 1320 PM DAY OF WEEK: THU CASE NO.:
ADDRESS OF VIOLATION: 2630 NORTHGATE
NAME (First, Middle, Last): GEORGE AZAR
BUSINESS NAME: LA MEX TAQUERIA
ADDRESS: 2804 WEISE WY
BUSINESS ADDRESS: 2804 WEISE WY
CITY: SACRAMENTO STATE: CA ZIP CODE: 95833
CITY: SACRAMENTO STATE: CA ZIP CODE: 95833
DRIVER'S LICENSE NO.: BOT # 619103 STATE CLASS BIRTH DATE: 5-5-69
PERMIT NO.: 06-018 06-0019 PERMIT TYPE: DRIVER VEH

TYPE OF ESTABLISHMENT: ☐ Single Family ☐ Duplex ☐ Apartment ___ Units ☐ Commercial Business ☐ Vacant Lot ☒ Parking Lot

BUSINESS COMPLIANCE: ☐ Taxicab ☒ Mobile Food Vending ☐ Food Vendors ☐ Entertainment Permit ☐ Tobacco Retailers ☐ Somatic Practitioner ☐ Other: ☐ Tow Trucks ☐ Arcade ☐ Billiards ☐ Bingo ☐ Card Rooms ☐ Funeral Escorts

CODE VIOLATIONS: ☐ Junk and Debris ☐ Abandoned Vehicles ☐ Inoperable Vehicles ☐ Wrecked Vehicles ☐ Vehicles (Street – 72 hrs) ☐ Vehicles (Landscape/Setback) ☐ Trailers / RVs: ☐ Setback ☐ Occupied ☐ Street Vending ☐ Yard Sales ☐ Weeds ☐ Litter ☐ Signs ☐ Auto Repair ☐ Residential ☐ Commercial ☐ Auto Dismantling ☐ Fence ☐ Vehicle Storage ☐ Junk Yard ☐ Home Occupation ☐ Landscaping ☐ Parking Lot ☐ Other:

TYPE OF SERVICE: ☐ Personal Service ☐ Certified Mail ☐ First Class Mail ☐ Post Property ☐ Property Owner ☐ Tenant ☐ Registered Owner ☒ Business Owner / Employee ☐ Other

NATURE OF VIOLATION:
1. 5.68.080 SEC - FAILURE TO HAVE PERMIT WHILE SELLING (EMPLOYEE)
2. 5.68.110 (A)(5) SEC - DRIVER NOT ON SCENE WITH VEHICLE

CORRECTIONS REQUIRED:
1. OBTAIN PERMIT FOR EMPLOYEE (OR)
2. PERSON WITH PERMIT MUST BE WITH TRUCK

You are hereby ordered to correct the noted conditions within 7 days. A follow-up inspection will be conducted on or about 6/8 / 1325 AM PM
DATE TIME
CALL FOR APPT. 808-7965
LOCATION
Corrected violation(s) must be verified and signed off by the Code Enforcement Officer. Questions regarding this notice should be directed to undersigned by calling 916-808-5948.

SIGNATURE OF CE OFFICER: S. GROVE BADGE NO.
RECEIVED BY: (RESPONSIBILITY PARTY) ☐ REFUSED TO SIGN
DAN ROTH 808-7339

ORDER IMPOSING ADMINISTRATIVE PENALTY
SACRAMENTO CITY CODE 1.28.010

You are hereby ordered to pay the City of Sacramento an administrative penalty in the amount of $__________ imposed in connection with the violation(s) herein described on this notice.

Payment shall be sent or paid to the City of Sacramento at 915 I Street, Room 104, Sacramento CA 95814 on or before __________. The administrative penalty is a personal obligation and failure to pay the penalty may result in the amount being made a lien and/or special assessment against your property as well as other legal action to collect the penalty. If a judicial action is required to collect the penalty, the City will seek to recover its attorney fees and cost from you. This administrative penalty does not include any other code enforcement charges that may be applicable to this case. You will receive a sep... the City wher...

RIGHT TO A...
You may a... penalty withir... served by fil... notice of app...

If you fail t... responsible p... any order er... California Cc... 1094.6.

Supervisor Tedd Freeman 808-5446
need a letter what conversation was ...

Figure 4: Citation issued to George Azar for "failure to have permit while selling (employee)" and for "driver not on scene with vehicle."

being cited or be able to read it carefully or to comprehend the city code completely. George was sure that other truck owners were getting the same types of tickets and that the city code enforcers were slowly forcing the trucks, one by one, to fold financially. Perhaps, if it were not for George stepping up to protest the city officials' discriminatory practices, all traditional taco trucks would have been expunged from the city's landscape. In George's words: "All these other taco truck owners are a lot like my father. They don't speak much English. They really don't understand what is going on. They all look to me to do something. . . . Can you imagine the average person? They didn't stand a chance. Forget about it! Taco trucks would have been done!" George battled on the streets and in City Hall for his business; in the process, he defended a cultural way of life for many Mexicans. He emphasized that the way Mexicans eat street tacos is integral to Sacramento's cultural landscape. It is not just the aesthetics of the taco truck but also the social practices that take place around the truck. The taco truck is a space that stitches together urban life and urban form for Mexicans, highlighting their identity and social place within Sacramento. George, his mother, and many other Latinos, revere the taco truck as a symbolic and sacred space that is intrinsic to their cultural practice. Therefore, it is offensive to them that city code enforcers regulate taco trucks in a way that negates the trucks' cultural purpose to Mexican society. Ultimately, the city is discriminating against Mexican culinary customs. Mercedes Azar reasoned:

> At that time [our] point was, this is discriminatory against Mexicans because this is part of our culture. You may not like standing outside of a window asking for three tacos, eating them, and then deciding you want another one of that kind, eating it and then deciding you want a *torta*. But that's just the way we do it. And we like it quick and affordable. . . . George has customers that will come in and buy fifty tacos and take them home to feed to all the kids. You know, we do that. If I'm tired and have a million things to do, we go, "Let's go down to the taco truck."

George expounded: "I've even brought it up in City Hall before, how Mexicans eat in Mexico. And I've had people tell me, "Well, this ain't Mexico." Okay, well . . . I understand it's not Mexico, but it doesn't take away the fact that, well, first of all it used to be part of Mexico . . . [Mexican] people live here, [Mexican] people still work here." Although George and his mother surmised that the city council and city staff were discriminating against Mexican cultural practices, they did not believe that city officials were being explicitly racist. George and Mercedes Azar just presumed that the city genuinely perceived taco trucks as blight and their social atmosphere as chaos. Rather than claiming that city officials were racist or culturally insensitive, it was more imperative to prove that city officials were proceeding unjustly and enforcing regulations unlawfully. Mercedes Azar elaborated:

> When you pull the race card, you can look just as bad as they look: They being racist and you claiming racism. To me, you both are equally a problem. So we can assume that it's being driven by racism, but it doesn't do you any good because it doesn't deal with the issues. If you deal with the issues and show the illogicalness of their argument, I think you have a better chance of dealing with the city and proving your case.

George pointed out the city code enforcers' multiple flaws in logic, as well as the selective enforcement and loose interpretations of code regulations. He noted that the mobile food-vending ordinance applied only to public streets, not to private property, and that no specified times regulated mobile food-vending on private property: "It never stated anything about parking on private property. Which is why I wasn't breaking any rules." Finally, George put together a petition in 2008 to keep taco trucks open in Sacramento and presented it to the city council with more than two thousand signatures.

George temporarily won his skirmish with the city council and city officials and was allowed to stay open as late as 2:00 A.M. on weekends. In the process,

---

WHEREAS, we the undersigned:

- Are regular customers of La Mex Taqueria, a food truck from which Tacos, Tortas, Burritos and other Mexican food is sold.
- Are aware that La Mex Taqueria has been doing business parked on the lot in front of SP Liquor, at 2630 Northgate Boulevard for the past 4 years.
- Are customers of La Mex Taqueria because it is convenient, reasonably priced, clean, has the best tacos of any food establishment in Sacramento, and its employees and owners are friendly and customer-service oriented.
- Are customers of La Mex Taqueria because its operating hours had always met our needs -- whether it was for lunch, dinner on the way home even if we worked late, were out shopping, socializing, coming back from the movies or from a Kings game, or just at home and not feeling up to cooking; La Mex was always open.
- Are aware that regardless of the hours, during the past four years there have never been any safety issues, crimes or loitering at the La Mex Taqueria.
- Assert that the activity at La Mex has actually served as a deterrent to crime for the surrounding brick and mortar businesses. (After not having had a single burglary for the past four years, after La Mex was cited by the City and forced to begin closing at 8 p.m., SP Liquor was held up for the first time since La Mex began operating on its lot.)
- Want more choices for eating in the Northgate area during the late evening hours since there are no other food establishments open late (except for your usual unhealthy fast food drive-ins) leaving the area residents no other option than to cook, go hungry or travel to other parts of the city to find healthy, tasty, inexpensive fast food.
- Were informed by the City, in response to questions seeking an understanding of the foundation for the hours established by the current ordinance, that the hours were established for mobile trucks that went to "construction sites where no other food establishments were available" and the focus was placed on the ensuring the start hour was early enough for those workers (5 a.m.), without much thought going to the closing hours.

WE, THEREFORE, urge the Mayor and City Council of Sacramento to:

- Review the existing city ordinance that limits food trucks from operating beyond 8 p.m. during the summer months and 6 p.m. during the winter months, AND
- Change the ordinance to allow La Mex Taqueria to operate as it had in the past, until 10 p.m. from Sunday through Thursday and until 2 a.m. on Friday and Saturday, year round.

NAME	ADDRESS

Figure 5: George Azar's petition to the Sacramento City Council received more than two thousand signatures.

he saved a few taco trucks within the city limits. The City Revenue Office decided to grandfather the existing taco trucks into a five-year sunset clause. In 2008 the Sacramento City Council and the City Revenue Office also decided to update the mobile food-vending ordinance. Any new trucks operating in the city would have to move four hundred feet every thirty minutes, and this would be enforced on both public and private property. In addition, all mobile food-vending regulations would be reviewed in January 2013, including whether or not the grandfathered taco trucks would have to abide by the updated mobile vending ordinances.

However, it did not take until 2013 for the issue of mobile food vending to be brought back to city council's attention. In the summer of 2010, Randy Paragary wanted to ensure that all food trucks' wheels stayed spinning. Taco trucks were not the only food trucks the city council and city officials were concerned about. The boutique food trucks became the focus of the city's mobile food-vending discussions. George and his mother clarified:

> MERCEDES: When the first taco truck issues started, the [downtown] restaurants were not involved or even interested. They got interested when the gourmets got in. [At first,] they [the gourmet trucks] came in from San Francisco and Oakland. They weren't Sacramento gourmets.
> GEORGE: When Crush Burger first opened his truck it was SacTown Mini Burger. Then, when Drusky opened his truck they were doing all of downtown. And right away Randy Paragary . . .
> MERCEDES [*FINISHING SENTENCE*]: . . . and all of those restaurants that did not want that competition, gourmet [trucks] [were] getting into their market. Taco trucks weren't.

"FOOD TRUCKS [STILL] NOT WELCOME HERE"

On August 23, 2010, the *Sacramento Bee* featured on their cover: "Food Trucks Not Welcome Here: In Capital City, Rules Cool Hot New Trend." Staff writer Chris Macias (2010) reported, "The hottest new food trend literally rolls through the country, using Twitter and other social media to alert hungry customers. . . . But that food trucks wouldn't be able to stop for long in Sacramento." The 2008 revised rules requiring food trucks to remain mobile resurfaced in 2010 as boutique food trucks traversed downtown Sacramento. The emergence of gourmet food trucks changed the nature of the food truck debate. The mobile food-vending issues, driven by the apprehension over the taco trucks' appearance, became centered on the downtown restaurateurs' concern that the gourmet food trucks cut into their business. The taco trucks' practices and the gourmet food trucks' practices were conflated into a single mobile food-vending issue for the City of Sacramento. And as Sacramento's culinary scene evolved, restaurateurs and the city council decided to focus on the aesthetics of mobility.

Leading the charge against the food truck owners' investment into the city's image was Randy Paragary. Paragary is the main restaurateur to bring the issue before the city council on a regular basis. Mercedes Azar noted that when Paragary and other restaurateurs started to complain about food trucks, city officials followed suit:

> You've got a restaurant that is paying all these taxes to the city, and they say, "Hey, what's up with this truck? You guys close them down." They [the City code enforcers] would shoo them away right away, and not worry about those persons' bills, their family, or what they were out there doing. They [the restaurateurs] thought it was a problem, their problem, and that was it.

Prominent restaurateurs were now concerned about the gourmet food trucks that have reignited the food-vending issues, which appeared to have settled down in 2008. The mobile food practices again became a major point of controversy. A roundtable discussion, held on Monday, June 6, 2011, at The Kitchen restaurant, addressed the matters associated with mobile food-vending ordinances. The restaurateurs, food truck owners, city council members, city staff, and Midtown Business Association representatives all attended the discussion (First Mobile Food-Vending Ordinance Roundtable Discussion 2006). From what I surmised from George Azar and Randall Selland, who were both in attendance, Paragary was adamant that food trucks stay out of downtown and away from his restaurants, or at the very least, keep moving.

The mobility facet of the city's mobile food-vending ordinances became the point of controversy. The *Sacramento News and Review* article "What the Truck?!!" (Miller 2011), quotes Paragary: "It's supposed to be temporary. A mobile food truck. You honk your horn. Construction workers come running out on their break and you move on. If you don't limit it, they won't move on." Paragary does not like the representation of food truck practices. Food trucks are for the working class, and their presence stains the image of his white-tablecloth restaurants. Furthermore, Paragary presupposes that food trucks should stay mobile because they have wheels and, as such, are designed *to be mobile*. But, how long can they stay in one place? How far do they have to move? And must they always be moving just because they have wheels?

The spontaneous social practices of food trucks define their spatial rhythms and daily routines. However, the city council, city staff, and restaurateurs are working to redefine the food truck's business operations as they see fit—in this case, the practice of mobility, simply based on the notion that a food truck has wheels. Yes, taco trucks and gourmet food trucks do have wheels, but their mobility practices are driven by the need to traverse space and park at places that allow them to feed diverse types of people.

According to Cresswell (2006, 47), "The study of the modern world is a study of velocity and vectors. Rather than comparing mobility to place, mobilities are placed in relation to each other." Certainly, there are differences in the degrees of mobility between a taco truck and a gourmet food truck as well as myriad mobility practices among distinct types of patrons (Lemon 2017).[4]

Before California taco trucks started parking in cities, they roamed the fields following day laborers. The trucks' spatial dynamics reflected the mobility patterns of laboring Mexican migrants. Eventually, taco truck owners began to settle near urban barrios. Typically, these trucks would park along the street or in private parking lots within commercial strips. Taco trucks suddenly shifted from being highly mobile to being mostly immobile. There are various pragmatic reasons for such a modification in mobility practices.

First, we must remember that taco trucks are makeshift. They are usually worn-down buses or utility trucks that have been converted into a food service vehicle at a minimal cost. Most taco trucks cost about $20,000 to configure with a refrigerator, grill, running water, and a grease dispenser.[5] These items are not easy to lock down when the trucks try to stay in one place. Furthermore, the truck's tires and engine are not always in the best condition. The risk of taking a worn-out truck on the road everyday could mean multiple costly breakdowns. Not to mention the cost of fuel: many taco truck owners told me that the gas expense alone is enough to want to park in one place. Jaime Quintero, owner of Tacos La Piedad, explained that it was too risky and costly to be mobile. He said that you could get in an accident, have a mechanical problem with the truck, have to pay for fuel, and you were constantly looking for workers in the field. "We decided to go to the city because we could stay put and people in the neighborhood could get to know us better."[6] Staying in one place has the added benefit of allowing the truck owners to establish a regular clientele.

Taco truck owners target day laborers; if they are going to remain parked in one place, they need to find avenues to collect the most revenue. Therefore, taco truck owners will typically park along arterial roads within commercial and industrial zones, or in commercial strips near Latino neighborhoods. They strategically place their trucks where they can catch the ebbs and flows of their working-class patrons as they drive between worksites. Taco truck owners use their mobility to find the best spot to catch the most customers.

Gourmet food trucks, conversely, are not makeshift. Gourmet food trucks are most often elaborately designed. They almost always have a reliable engine and quality tires. Moreover, many have kitchens that are easy to lock into place. The drawers and refrigerator doors all have latches that can be fastened in a matter of minutes. And, because gourmet food trucks typically cater to the middle class, operating expenses, such as gas, can simply be factored into the cost of the cuisine. As a result, boutique food trucks in Sacramento are highly mobile.

Gourmet food trucks move about Sacramento effortlessly. Many will frequent food truck festivals, go to white-collar office parks, as well as to specialty breweries. For example, Roel Olivares owns a boutique food truck that serves upscale tacos to an Anglo, middle-class clientele. He remarks that breweries are really growing in number in Sacramento and that he loves to work with them: "I pair with the brewery, they do beer flights and I do a taco flight to go with it. . . . It's all about marketing." Olivares emphasizes the importance of marketing the truck through creating culinary specialties, selling merchandise such as T-shirts, and using social media throughout the day to announce the truck's next location. Traditional taco truck owners do not typically understand these marketing techniques, nor do they rely on them or need them to create a customer base. But, for most boutique trucks, marketing is essential to attract customers to the truck. The hype of eating at a particular truck has to be sold. Social media, such as Facebook and Twitter, promote the gourmet food truck to the middle class.

The notion that the boutique food truck is mobile and that you must find it becomes an attractive draw for some urban adventurers and "foodies" (Caldwell 2011). The experience of urban exploration becomes a fun factor that can be marketed as well. Not only are boutique food trucks highly mobile, they also influence their patrons' mobility practices. Unlike day laborers who typically eat at taco trucks because the food is cheap and convenient, gourmet food trucks' clientele has more leisure time and money to find a food truck parked in an obscure part of town. In this way, gourmet food trucks manipulate their patrons' movements as they themselves move.

Food trucks, much like personal automobiles, are primarily designed to move people and goods between places. For example, driving your car to work renders mobility incidental because all you really need to do is go from one place to another. Food truck owners are primarily concerned with moving between places to capture particular flows of people. A taco truck owner may experience mobility as a forced necessity for economic survival, whereas a boutique food truck vendor may enjoy the novelty of navigating the city, tweeting their next location, and having people follow them around via social media.

Regardless of the type of truck, a food truck's mobility is one of empowerment, and its owner must use the truck's mobility as a spatial tactic to navigate politics and urban policies. Truck owners must respond to flowing populations of hungry people throughout the day, week, and year. Food trucks rely not only on their own mobility but also on the social mobility, eating habits, and dining patterns of others. Restaurants, to the contrary, are completely sedentary. You move to the restaurant; the restaurant does not move to you.

When it comes to food spaces in Sacramento, the mobility practices of people who are going to restaurants are the fifth type of mobility—the four others being those of taco trucks and their customers as well as the boutique food trucks and their clientele. Someone going to eat at a restaurant doesn't have the same motives as someone headed to eat at a food truck. As George pointed out, people choose what they want to eat based on their personal taste preferences, available time, and how much they plan on spending:

> Someone who is going to [Paragary's restaurant] El Centro [Cocina Mexicana], I don't think they would go, "Hey, well this truck is parked out here, let's stand here and eat instead of going into Centro." Centro is a very nice restaurant. If I took my wife out I know I would walk right into Centro and eat. . . . The average person is not going to stop at a truck if he's headed to a restaurant just because he sees a truck there.

George also argued that the same customers could make divergent decisions based on their personal taste preferences. Acclaimed restaurateur and proponent of food trucks Randall Selland echoed George's sentiments when I asked him if he thought that food trucks cut into his restaurant business. Selland said,

> I don't think the guy in the three-piece suit, on his way down to Ella's to have lunch, who has been sitting in a business meeting and walks by a food truck and says, "Oh, damn, I could eat there for free. I am going to stand here and eat out of a napkin and drip it all down the front of me." It's just not going to happen. You make choices on what you want to do. Me, I like hamburgers, so once a month I'll go somewhere and get a hamburger, it's the same way with a food truck. . . . But to make a conscious choice, there's a brick-and-mortar and there's a food truck, [does someone say], "I'm going to the food truck because it's cheaper?" I think that's just a nonsensical argument.

Even so, most restaurateurs think food trucks are just another eating option that decreases restaurant revenue. Also, food trucks are associated with a clientele who often eats standing up. In other words, eating practices at food trucks are ascribed to the trucks' aesthetic.

Paragary quarrels, "A mobile-food truck. You honk your horn. Construction workers come running out on their break and you move on." Essentially a comment about leisure time associated with class standing, Paragary's remark ascribes working-class meaning to the social practice of eating at a food truck. A wealthy person has enough time (and money) to travel to and from a restaurant and have a sit-down lavish dining experience. Whereas a laboring person, on his or her work break, has only enough time to make a quick dash to the food truck—while still wearing work clothes—and eat standing up. And this happens at the whim of the truck's arrival, not on one's own terms—namely, when a truck happens to pull up and "honk its horn." Therefore, Paragary, from his privileged point of view, perceives the "roach coach" as an uncouth mobility practice for the lower class and ascribes that meaning to all food trucks. In reality, food trucks of all sorts are blurring the boundaries between classes. Regardless, eating outside at a truck is still deemed an informal way of eating for most societies.

Some of the city's elite restaurateurs define a food truck's mobile performance and its accompanying social practices as uncivilized. Cresswell (2006) contends that low-class mobility practices are not only perceived as chaotic, they also produce discourses of displacement:

> The consequences of a sedentarist metaphysics for mobile people are severe. Thinking of the world as rooted and bounded is reflected in language and social practice. Such thoughts actively territorialize identities in property, in region, in nation—in place. They simultaneously produce discourse and practice that treats mobility and displacement as pathological. (27)

When a truck does not continuously move, its visibility and its association with a particular place is heightened. Moreover, taco trucks have wheels, but they don't move. This paradoxical image induces the notion of "immobile mobility." As I define it, immobile mobility is the perception of something that appears to be more mobile than its most basic mobile necessity. This inverted relationship threatens the established order as well as one's own culture, traditions, community, and familiarization with place. Thus, restaurateurs pressure the city council and city staff to regulate a truck's type of movement, to keep it in its perpetual passing "place" so that they can feel as though their territory reflects a respectable spatial order. Presumably, there is an appropriate type of mobility that the city must regulate—a rhythm that renders the food trucks imperceptible. And only when this happens will the food truck conform to the city's conventional culture.

CALIFORNIA VEHICLE CODE 22455

Due to the invasion of the new gourmet food trucks, the City of Sacramento's food truck regulations have changed rapidly over the past twelve years—especially from 2010 to 2015. Brad Wasson is the city official who has had to handle both ends of the food truck controversy as the manager of the Revenue Division—a position he has held since 1999. I spoke with him at his downtown office in June 2013. Wasson began by telling me about the inundation of boutique food trucks and some of the complaints that followed in their wake:

> There was a movement of gourmet mobile food vending. They paint their trucks with fancy colors and gimmicks. Those trucks wanted to challenge the way the city was operating. They wanted to vend longer than half an hour. . . . Some people seemed to be in favor of it. Some of the restaurants were not in favor of it. They complained that the trucks often take up two parking spots making it where you can't get into the store.

Wasson expressed that the city council and city staff have a responsibility to represent the needs and desires of all residents. He conveyed that there are people who love the food trucks, and there are people who do not want the trucks downtown: "The city doesn't want to be in the middle of restaurants and food trucks. . . . There are people who like the food trucks and we want to figure out a way it [the presence of food trucks] works best for Sacramento." I asked Wasson if he made a distinction between the mobility practices of taco trucks and boutique food trucks. He replied: "The city does not differentiate between food trucks. They are all the same mobile food-vending vehicle, like an ice cream truck."

Wasson believes that the City of Sacramento has the right to regulate the location and operating practices of mobile food vending. He asserts that taco truck owners have found a loophole in the city ordinances by parking on a private parking lot and never moving. A restaurant, he explains, is associated with a land use. There are different types of land uses throughout the city, and land use types should regulate a food truck. As a governing entity, the city should be able to regulate the placement of different types of businesses throughout the city limits, Wasson argues, whether these are mobile or not.

Wasson makes a valid point. City planning departments have the right to regulate land use by what happens on a particular piece of property. They can zone areas residential, commercial, or industrial for their appropriate activities. In this way, city planners can put human practices into their "appropriate" places. The problem arises with the food truck because it is not ascribed to a particular land use. In fact, a truck can move through different zones as well as across public and private spaces. A food truck falls into a fuzzy area of the law because it has *wheels*. Therefore, the Revenue Department adopts various approaches when trying to regulate mobile food vending, either by focusing on where the truck is allowed to park or on its mobility.

Wasson notes, however, that regulating mobility is problematic, not to mention that state vehicle law strictly forbids it:

> We had a big group together of restaurant owners and trucks. The meeting concluded food trucks could vend for ninety minutes and be at least a block away from a restaurant. However, competition is competition. California vehicle code says there must be a public safety nexus. So it would be against state law to make a public safety nexus. In good faith, it doesn't support it.

California state law explicitly states that cities cannot regulate mobile food vending other than for health or public safety (California Vehicles Code Section 22455). If a food truck owner holds a county health certificate and the truck meets all vehicle regulations, there are few logical reasons for a city entity to prohibit a food truck from vending on private commercial lots or along public streets. Sacramento had a law on the books regulating the mobility and location of food trucks that the city staff acknowledged was not legitimate because they could not prove a public safety nexus.

A dispute between food truck owners and restaurateurs had impacted city policy in a way that conflicted with state law. This was not the first occurrence in California. From 2010 to 2014, Dermer Behrendt Legal Advisors, on behalf of the Southern California Mobile Food-vending Association, sued several suburban municipalities throughout the Los Angeles metropolis because they had time–place regulations similar to the ones Sacramento was trying to impose. They won each case (Dermer Behrendt Legal Advisors 2014) because they made a clear and convincing argument that municipalities cannot implement codes controlling food truck vending, especially in public space, without a significant public safety nexus. They also maintained that municipalities could not regulate public space based on competition (Linnekin, Dermer, and Geller 2011). Certainly the City of Sacramento realized this was not a court case they could win. However, no food truck owner wanted to be the one to file a lawsuit against the City of Sacramento. Sacramento gourmet food truck owners refrained from violating the city's code because they didn't want to put city officials in a position where they would have to enforce it.

Wasson admitted that since there was an agreement between the gourmet food truck owners and restaurateurs about moving every ninety minutes, he would have liked to see state law changed so that the city could have legally enforce its ordinances. In fact, city council had been putting pressure on the California Senate to adopt a bill to amend California Vehicle Code 22455 so that municipalities could fully regulate the allocation of food trucks.[7] In the interim, the Revenue Division decided to keep its old laws in place, where food trucks had to move every thirty minutes but only enforced the verbal ninety-minute agreement. While it is fairly easy for gourmet food trucks to move about in order to comply with city code, most taco truck owners found it easier to just move outside the city limits. The city's regulations not only affected the mobility dynamics of food trucks but also reconfigured Sacramento's landscape both socially and symbolically.

DYNAMIC TACO TRUCK LANDSCAPE PATTERNS

In the spring of 2009 the magazine *Edible Sacramento* published a story about the city's "vanishing taco trucks" (Kraft 2009). The article argued that the city's stringent food truck vending policies were reducing the number of taco trucks in Sacramento and, with their disappearance, diminishing the diverse cuisines that could be found throughout the city. As of 2014 there were approximately eighteen traditional taco trucks in the Sacramento metropolitan area, but only seven that operated within the city limits.[8] Indeed, the adopted policies in 2008 and the spoken agreements in 2011 affected taco trucks' spatial arrangement and therefore their presence within the city. Of the twelve taco trucks that were grandfathered into the city's food-vending ordinances in 2008, only four remained by 2014: La Mex Taqueria, La Piedad, Tacos de Oro, and El Grullense. Some of the other trucks that had been grandfathered in went out of business or moved on for other reasons. The traditional taco truck owners who did not understand how to get grandfathered into the City's mobile food regulations simply shifted their location to just outside the city limits (see plate 14).

Areolo Torres Hurelio, who opened his taco truck in 2003, disclosed to me that he had several issues with the city code enforcers throughout the years: "When things started [with the city], they [code enforcers] began giving me multiple tickets. And they kept giving me tickets without explanation of what I could do to be in compliance."[9] Language issues added to the confusion. Areolo speaks broken English and didn't fully understand the reason for the citations. He said that he received so many citations that he just wanted out of the code enforcers' jurisdiction. He eventually found a large parking lot that he thought was outside of the city limits, but he received a citation anyway. Apparently, he was just fifty feet within the city limits. It is difficult to discern the difference between what is city and what is county because Sacramento's metropolis extends into the county and is aesthetically undifferentiated. Areolo described this aesthetic confusion: "I started getting tickets for being in the city when I thought I was in the county. And I said, then, please explain to me whether I'm in the county or if I'm in the city. Eventually I figured out that the road signs in green are city, and the street signs in white are in the county." In the end, Areolo made his way outside the city limits by less than one hundred yards. Because his business is Mexican and mobile, he told me that he felt discriminated against by the city code enforcers. But, since his business is on wheels, he believed that his mobility also enabled him to find other economic opportunities. In Areolo's case, he probably could have been grandfathered into the city's mobile food-vending regulations had he more fully comprehended the food truck debates that took place between 2006 and 2008.

During this same period, a similar scenario happened to Luis Bueno (see plate 15).[10] Luis said that he had to move his taco truck east along Fruitridge Road out of the city and into the county. Luis strategically parked within a pocket of county that tucks into the city. There is no aesthetic difference in the built environment between the county and the city in this area—other than the presence of his truck and the color of the street signs. If one drives from the city eastbound along Fruitridge Road, one will pass through the county for approximately ten blocks before reentering the city. Luis found a literal spatial loophole.

Perhaps the other spatial loophole to vend within the city limits without moving periodically is to park in an industrial zone. City code allows taco trucks to vend in industrial zones until 8:00 P.M. For city officials and restaurateurs, industrial landscapes are appropriate places for taco trucks because the trucks blend in well with the tarnished industrialized infrastructure and with the ways in which factory workers eat. Three taco trucks take advantage of parking in industrial zones—they serve both workers and people passing by.

The only other option to vend food from a truck while remaining inside the city limits is to stay mobile. Only one taco truck was able to conform to the city's strict mobile regulations: El Taco Sabrozon ("The Freaking Delicious Taco"). The owner of the truck moved every thirty to ninety minutes and follows a regular route between 7:00 A.M. and 6:00 P.M. In Sacramento, traditional taco trucks either must keep moving or must move out. The taco trucks' marginal landscape order exposed the social dynamics generated by the city's prejudiced mobile food-vending policy at the time—a policy not even legal in California.

= = =

By 2014, for the most part, gourmet food trucks kept moving or attended food truck festivals or downtown special events. Most citizens in Sacramento embraced this mobile dynamic of the boutique food truck because it culturally bolstered middle-class culinary trends. Moreover, gourmet food truck owners provided more affordable cuisine options for a middle class who may not have a lot of time to seek out a sit-down restaurant or a lot of money to dine out each meal. Accordingly, gourmet food trucks have remained popular and their demand has continued to grow.

After another year of disputes and discussions among food truck owners, restaurateurs, and city officials, city code enforcers decided to amend the existing mobile food-vending ordinance. In May 26, 2015, the city council unanimously approved a new code permitting food truck owners to park their trucks along streets within the city limits as long as they obeyed parking signage (Ordinance No. 2015-0016). Food truck owners could also park their trucks on private property for more than thirty minutes, provided the vendor had obtained an additional property permit and his or her truck was not parked in a residential zone.

It is worth noting that the amendments to the existing code begin by acknowledging that food trucks play an important role in providing food to underserved communities and that food trucks offer different cuisines than what most brick-and-mortar restaurants have. The new ordinance also makes clear that it is in full compliance with California Vehicle Code 22455. Although it specifically states this, it does not mean that parts of this code could not end up being disputed in a California courthouse because many aspects of this code are questionable.[11] The city council and code enforcers have come a long way in seeing all sides of food truck vending issues. Indeed, they enacted many of the new regulations because gourmet food trucks were growing in number as they became increasingly celebrated among Sacramento's citizens.

Since 2014 Sacramento city officials have been entertaining the idea of implementing food truck pods on downtown private property. Pods would be well-landscaped lots where food trucks would park between having to move. The pods would be located in zones appropriate for a restaurant, and the trucks would be shielded with a hedge or a fence. Through this arrangement, the City of Sacramento is taking a mobile practice and regulating it like a restaurant when it is immobile. In other words, mobile food truck vending would be assigned a land use. Food trucks would finally be put into their proper place.

Lefebvre (1991) contends that when city planners designate spaces for certain activities, then those activities lose their inherent meanings because they are denied the social and spatial freedom for which they operate best. He claims, "The more space is functionalized, the more completely it falls under the sway of those "agents" that have manipulated it so as to render it unfunctional" (356). Food trucks in Sacramento are no longer operating through their own agency but under the city's supervision.

City officials are slowly eroding the very nature of what makes food trucks a dynamic and ingenious operation by implementing food truck pods. Furthermore, they are threatening the taco truck owners' traditional way of working by determining the places in the city where they can park on private property and for how long, which for the most part is away from Sacramento's city center.

As city officials implement additional regulations on food trucks, they also raise mobile food-vending fees to enforce the new regulations that they are imposing. The growing number of gourmet food trucks increases the cost of food-vending permits and puts a heavy price burden on taco truck owners. This makes it much more difficult for traditional taco trucks to survive. But city council and city officials do not seem to care too much about the financial struggles of their day-laboring residents—they are more concerned with promoting the city's farm-to-fork image.

I asked George Azar if taco trucks could play a role in the city's marketing campaign. Can the traditional taco truck take part in the farm-to-fork movement, or become "farm-to-truck?" George nodded: "Definitely! A lot of what we use in our trucks is grown here locally. It's not called 'Sac-a-tomatoes' for nothing. We use tomatoes for our salsas, come on! That's what we eat! That's all grown here! I grow my own chili peppers in the backyard!"

Food in itself does not shape space and landscape. Cooking and eating do, as well as the representational practices associated with these activities. George noted: "Well, now it's okay if you're a white guy wearing a suit eating from a truck, but if it's a landscaping crew or a Mexican family, well, that's not acceptable. Then [the taco truck] is a roach coach." The City of Sacramento did not promote taco trucks as part of its identity. Rather, it did everything to make food truck vending impossible for taco truck owners. The trucks were gradually vanishing from sight.

Sacramento's politics and policies toward taco trucks make a significant impression on California's cultural landscape.[12] The absence of taco trucks in Sacramento's city center makes Mexican labor invisible. Moreover, the discriminatory policies against the trucks had suppressed a cultural way of eating for the Mexican laborers. Although Mexican labor is welcome, their cultural imprint on Sacramento's landscape is not as prominent as it could be. But taco trucks can never completely vanish from any landscape. Even when we expand out to see Sacramento as a whole, taco trucks are still parked at Northgate Boulevard and at the outskirts of the city. Their spatial configurations and mobility patterns speak volumes about their struggle to remain part of Sacramento's social fabric.

Paragary condemned the "roach coach" because it threatens his business and Sacramento's proposed pompous appeal. But should not the state capital of Sacramento represent all people in California, including its Mexican day laborers? If social justice means acknowledging the myriad ethnic communities and social classes that contribute to a city's image and its prosperity, then perhaps there is no site/sight more suitable than a taco truck parked in front of the California state capitol building.

CHAPTER 5

COMMUNITY CONFLICT AND CUISINE IN COLUMBUS

Columbus, Ohio, may be the last place a person would expect to come across a taco truck. Named after Christopher Columbus for his "discovery of the new world," the city proudly showcases a statue of Columbus in front of Ohio's capitol building. The city even has a full replica of the *Santa Maria* at the nearby Battelle Riverfront Park. The replica ship exhibits the Columbian exchange frozen in time: "Fascinating displays show the far-ranging impact of the encounter of two worlds that existed in 1492" (Columbus Santa Maria 2013). The founding of Columbus, Ohio, may have been thousands of miles and three hundred years removed from where Columbus, the man, set foot in the Caribbean, but the midwestern city maintains strong Eurocentric ideals.

Columbus's landscape exudes an aura of white middle-class consumption patterns, from its countless commercial strip franchise advertisements, restaurant chains, and shopping strips to its conventionally dressed denizens. The city's commonplace character has become so engrained into the residents' self-consciousness that many citizens and city officials concede, "Columbus suffers from an identity crisis."[1]

Unforeseeably, the everlasting effects of European colonization in the Americas—which began with the Spanish Crown's voyages in 1492—have begun to encroach upon a predominately Anglo, conventional, suburban middle-class society. In 2001, a traditional taco truck, Little Mexico, opened on Sullivant Avenue near Georgesville Road within the Greater Hilltop Area, catering to the Mexican immigrants who had recently settled into the neighborhood (see plate 16). Shortly after, tens of other taco trucks began to emerge on Columbus's West Side. The trucks bewildered the community. Although some assessed the trucks with an ambivalent attitude, others—long-term residents and business owners—perceived cooking tacos and eating them from a truck as a primitive, pernicious practice. To them, taco trucks were an unwelcomed manifestation— magnets that attracted dirt, trash, loitering, and crime. For the West Side community, taco trucks' bizarre presence created social anarchy and disrupted the neighborhood's established spatial order.

David Sibley (1995) argues that negative judgments about unfamiliar minority practices emerging into a neighborhood derive "from feelings of anxiety, nervousness or fear" (3). He maintains that psychological perceptions toward human differences determine social boundaries. When unusual cultural practices infiltrate a familiar social setting, they generate unnerving feelings of instability, which, in turn, lead to exclusion.

Tim Cresswell (1996) takes a similar approach to Sibley's but stresses the social significance of *place* when examining cultural transgressions. Cresswell contends that *place* is defined through social practices. In other words, when people act upon an environment, they ascribe meaning to place. Vending tacos from a truck in a neighborhood that historically has not had street food ascribes a new practice—and a new meaning—to place. This cultural reappropriation of space challenges the existing community's mentality about neighborhood streets: For whom are these streets designed to look and function? Through this framework, place plays a role in how cultural transgressions are understood and regulated by dominant community groups.

In this chapter, I take a close look at how taco trucks first challenged and then changed the way the existing communities on Columbus's West Side perceived their neighborhood spaces. I investigate not only how, in 2001, the trucks crossed the neighborhood's social and cultural boundaries, but also the ways in which the trucks eventually redefined the neighborhood's landscape order.

TRANSGRESSIONS

Since 1990 the number of Latinos arriving from Mexico and Central America to work in Columbus has substantially increased. According to Columbus INFO-base, in 1990 the Greater Hilltop Area had a population of 509 Latinos; in 2000, the population had increased to 3,089 (City of Columbus Planning Division 2004). From my observations as a community planner in the neighborhood from 2004 to 2006, this number must have exploded in only a couple of years.

To verify my observations, in March 2006 I interviewed Santiago Flores, the creator of *La Voz Hispana*, a neighborhood Spanish newspaper. Based on the newspaper's sales and the content of the news, Flores estimates that close to ten thousand Latinos lived in the Greater Hilltop Area in 2006, and most had come from Oaxaca or other parts of southern Mexico, as well as from Central America. The 2010 U.S. Census reports that 44,359 Latinos live in the city of Columbus. In total, 25,973 Columbus residents identify as Mexicans, and a good portion of those Mexicans (roughly 15,000) reside in the Greater Hilltop Area. With the influx of the Latino population arrives an informal food operation to cater to their taste preferences. Latinos are populating Columbus's West Side, and their culinary practices are modifying the existing landscape order.

The American neighborhoods into which Latino immigrants move are almost always deprived environments. They tend to consist of dilapidated buildings covered in graffiti and of streets littered with trash. These aesthetics are often associated with minority groups, the working class, poverty, moderate crime, and illicit drug use. In fact, this describes the Greater Hilltop Area fairly well. Historically, the district was developed as a streetcar suburb, especially the West Gate area closer to downtown Columbus. As one moves westbound along West Broad Street, the landscape typology quickly transitions into car-orientated strip malls and suburban housing tracts. The district, although demographically mixed, is predominately Anglo working class and has a conservative slant. In 2012 a large billboard on West Broad Street exclaimed: "Obama supports gay marriage and abortion. Do you? Vote Republican!"

In 2001, Little Mexico was the first taco truck to appear on Columbus's West Side. After its arrival, at least twenty trucks set up shop in the neighborhood by 2006. Around that time, the taco trucks in Columbus parked primarily along Sullivant Avenue and Georgesville Road, near Columbus's city limits. Some were in Franklin County as well. Taco truck owners would establish relationships with brick-and-mortar businesses of various types and then set up their trucks in what were primarily vacant or underused private parking lots, such as at the side of a convenience store or in front of a laundromat (see plates 17 and 18). They would pay the property owners rent from $200 to $1,000 per month.[2]

The trucks were built very economically. The average outfitting of a truck (mostly salvaged small ramshackle buses or old moving vans) cost $15,000.[3] Most were haphazardly repainted; some had their vintage signage still visible. It was easy to detect where the truck owners had run out of paint or, more likely, out of money. Most often, the trucks only had their names painted across the top, usually names that reflected the places from where their owners hailed, such as Los Potosinos, or after Mexican street foods or Mexican slang—for example, El Huarache Veloz (*huarache* is a typical street food in Mexico City) or Los Chilangos (slang for someone from Mexico City).[4] The interiors of the trucks were assembled with a makeshift kitchen that consisted of a refrigerator, a sink with running water, grease dispensers, and a grill. Irrespective of their decrepit aesthetic and ad hoc assembly, the trucks would quickly—if not immediately—meet the State of Ohio's health code.

The Columbus Public Health Department (CPHD) inspects all the trucks. I spoke with Kelly Dodds, a mobile food inspector. "There are no trucks that we know about that do not comply with the regulations," she stated. She added that the CPHD will work with the owners of any food trucks that do not meet the department's minimal requirements so that the trucks can meet the code.

The CPHD is responsible for checking not only the trucks' kitchen sanitation but also the trucks' mobility. Under current state law, a mobile food-vending vehicle is required to move once every thirty days. The distance of movement is unspecified. Some of the truck owners told me that they would move their truck only a few feet about once a month or drive it to their home for the night. Regardless, mobility did not seem to be enforced, nor did it appear to be a significant issue for Columbus's code enforcement. What mattered most to zoning officials was where and how taco truck owners situated their trucks within parking lots.

Some of the first truck owners in Columbus in the early 2000s had to go through zoning approval. The owners had to draw a site plan to demonstrate that their trucks were not blocking traffic flows in and out of parking lots. This, of course, meant the owners incurred an additional permit fee. Also, the truck owners had to deal with various neighborhood complaints that went through Columbus's Department of Development regarding the trucks' myriad practices. Each truck had different (and seemingly endless) issues to contend with depending on what the owner was doing and where the truck was parked. The Department of Development workers had to check whether the trucks were violating any city code that was brought to their attention. Eventually, zoning regulations for the trucks were relaxed because it became too problematic to regulate the trucks on a truck-by-truck basis. Around 2005, city officials decided that a food truck owner could vend where he or she wished as long as the owner had a business license and met all the CPHD's regulations.

Not surprisingly, taco trucks found spatial and legal loopholes within the established business and zoning practices of Columbus. Informal practices of selling food in semi-public spaces, typically associated with the developing world, had no equivalent in the city. In the absence of regulations for taco-truck-style vending, the trucks quickly overtook the landscape. Obtaining approval to vend tacos from a truck is one matter, but getting the predominant community to accept the practice is quite another.

At first, the community was concerned with the quality of the food. Columbus's chief zoning officer, Chris Presutti, explained when I interviewed him in June 2012:

> My recollection with all the communications and meetings with the community at that time was that there was concern that the quality of the products that were being sold was suspect. But what we learned was that the Health Department indeed inspects them and the very same rules that apply to brick-and-mortar restaurants apply to these uses as well.

Once the community realized that the taco trucks were inspected by the CPHD, the nature of the conversation changed. The discourses became more divisive. They developed from health concerns and aspects of trash, crime, and blight, to whether their immigrant owners were in the country legally and were paying their fair share of taxes. As the dialogues intensified, they became more racist or culturally insensitive. My objective here is not to identify these comments as discriminatory but rather to explore the source of such sentiments. There appears to be a cultural transgression of place reflected in the social morphology of landscape.

When the taco trucks surfaced in the area, the community simply did not know what to make of the trucks from a cultural standpoint. The conventional spatial order the residents were familiar with was unexpectedly unsettled. Most realized that taco trucks were culturally changing the look and function of the landscape, and many believed that this change was deleterious.

Mark Ferenchik (2007) reported for the *Columbus Dispatch* that the taco trucks were "an acquired taste":

> The food wagons are an example of the cultural change sweeping through Columbus neighborhoods: Newcomers bring businesses they knew back home, while residents of a city still relatively inexperienced with large numbers of immigrants wonder how to deal with them. Dave Horn, the Greater Hilltop Area Commission's zoning chairman, said some think they create a "ragtag image" for the neighborhood. Some residents and business owners have complained that customers litter parking lots.
>
>   In Mexico, the wagons are common, said Julia Arbini Carbonell, president of the Ohio [Hispanic] Coalition. She thinks the neighborhood is unfairly targeting Mexican vendors. "The Hilltop is reacting to something not usual to them," said Carbonell, who owns an office building at Sullivant Avenue and Wilson Road. "It

doesn't mean it has no quality and it is no good," she said. "Accept that people have different values and traditions."

The community considered taco truck owners' repurposing of vacant land and parking lots for Latino culinary practices a loss of territory. Greater Hilltop Area residents, of course, had numerous complaints, all of which were associated with a lack of control over their landscape to an uninvited group of people. They felt that taco trucks compromised their cultural dominance.

Bonita Lee, a community planner for the city who has worked with the Greater Hilltop Area, told me in a June 2012 interview that the community's foremost concern was taco trucks' abrupt and exotic impression on the landscape. She noted: "Residents of the area were not accustomed to seeing informal street food vending in the city, let alone within their neighborhood." Lee said many residents simply believed that taco trucks were out of their element. She recollected a number of phone complaints from an individual over the course of a week in 2004: "He did not like the taco trucks being *there*, and did not like the fact that the people were not from *here*" (emphasis added). In this instance, *place* underscores how social practices are understood. An unfamiliar practice in a person's familiar place presents new meanings, which can easily be interpreted as out of place because they deviate from the ways in which things have ordinarily been done. Such sudden social transformations represent the loss of personal connection to place—whether the change is welcomed or not, the essence of place is not the same.

Sibley considers this from a psychological perspective: "Both the self and the world are split into good and bad objects, and the bad self, the self associated with fear and anxiety over the loss of control, is projected onto bad objects. Fear precedes the construction of the bad object, the negative stereotype, but the stereotype - simplified, distorted and at a distance - perpetuates that fear" (Sibley 1996, 15). Drawing from this premise, many community members considered social practices they were not accustomed to as nuisances. Residents tended to focus on undesirable social and cultural differences to validate their point of view. Many times, these differences were rendered down to derogatory ethnic stereotypes.

According to George Mead and Charles Morris (1962), one group of people's cultural assessments used to differentiate them from another social group determines the "generalized Other." Distance has much to do with producing a mental image of the generalized Other. Unlike many states along the border, Ohio is not usually associated with high migration numbers from Latin America. In Ohio, issues of Mexican immigration are culturally distant but politically central. The lands beyond the border exist largely within Ohioans' imaginations. For many of them, distorted stereotypes define the ways Mexicans live. Mexican livelihoods stem from the "third world," a distant place filled with informalities that unnerve many of Columbus's citizens' seemingly pure sensibilities. Seen through this dichotomy, taco trucks are a "third world" practice that defiles Columbus's image as a prominent city in the developed world. It may seem inconsequential to generalize about people in faraway places, but generalizations become culturally problematic when those people begin to move into the neighborhood at a high rate. The foreign quickly becomes the fraught familiar. And at first, unfortunately, prejudices kept many of Columbus's West Side residents from embracing taco trucks.

Beyond stereotypes, there are clear cultural differences between Ohioans and Mexicans. These tangible differences must be assessed because they can cause Ohioans to feel uncomfortable when interacting with Mexican immigrants. Presutti plainly asserts that the community's concerns about taco trucks are "more cultural than anything else." He points out: "They [Mexicans] look different and they speak a different language." In June 2012 I spoke with Koki Garcia, the manager of Koki's Tortillas, about the ways in which perceived cultural differences affect the treatment of Latinos in the city. A bilingual Mexican American born and raised in the United States, Koki discloses to me her personal impression of what it is like to be Mexican in Columbus:

> This is the first place I've ever been where I've had to convince people I can speak English [she laughs]. I've been to different stores and at times I'm waiting at the counter, waiting my turn, I get the 'does anybody know Spanish' before I've even opened my mouth. It's a new experience more than any other city I've lived in. It really shocked me a lot when I moved here. To see that difference in dealing with Mexicans, I've never experienced it. . . . I've not been in a place where I feel resistance to having a different culture involved in the city.

Koki's experiences of being treated differently because she looks different demonstrate that people in the community consider her an outsider. Language, dress, religion, and even skin color are noticeable cultural distinctions that reinforce one's convictions about the generalized Other. Unfortunately, aspects of language and cultural values not only perpetuate stereotypes, they also serve as cultural barriers that only intensify social boundaries.

In sum, many Ohioans unfamiliar and uncomfortable with Mexicans moving into the neighborhood suffered from a severe case of xenophobia. "A taco truck on every corner," they feared, would turn America into Mexico.[5] The overarching worry was that Mexican immigrants would contaminate American society and destroy the country economically. At the neighborhood level in Columbus's West Side, arguments against taco trucks varied greatly, but they were all primarily related to Anglo lower- to lower-middle-class midwestern discernments of Mexican cultural practices. For the Anglo community, Mexican practices belonged in Mexico, not in Columbus. Mexicans were considered not only different but also dirty and disorderly—which could have detrimental and atrophic effects on the residents' landscape and devalue their property. At first, regrettably, most in the community were uninterested in learning about their new neighbors. Instead, attributes of Latino culture were almost always considered trash.

TALKING TRASH

As the West Side neighborhood's landscape seemed to slip into total disarray due to the belief that taco trucks were trash—they looked trashy, attracted trash, and most likely the owners cooked contaminated cuisines—the community decided to reintroduce order, which meant eradicating the trucks. Discourses about the trucks began to make their way across the neighborhood and into community meetings. *Dirt* and *trash* were reoccurring talking points.

While conducting interviews with people who lived in the area, I had several people unwilling or apprehensive to do a formal interview with me. Still, they would tell me offhandedly that "the trucks let the trash blow everywhere" and that they thought the trucks were unsanitary and unsightly. Others told me that they did not care anymore that the trucks were there but wished that the truck owners "would pick up the trash." On occasion, people distrusted my presence and simply walked away. My queries into the matter, especially at the community meeting I attended, seemed to strike a nerve. In fact, I made many people extremely uneasy or anxious, and I sensed that there was a lot of tension regarding the presence of taco trucks in the neighborhood.

Although the community was already gritty and brimming with trash before the taco trucks arrived, the latter seemed to attract more trash and filth. This reinforces the notion that taco trucks were considered out of place. Cresswell (1996) demonstrates that unwelcome transgressions of place are typically associated with "dirt." "Dirt is something in the wrong place or wrong time. Dirt disgusts us because it appears where it shouldn't be. . . . It annoys us in its persistence, in its audacity to keep turning up in places we thought were clean, pure, and pristine." Thus, for Cresswell, things that are out of place or people who transgress, become dirt (38–39). Likewise, Sibley (1995, 24) posits "dirt" to be a negative way in which Anglos dismiss and condemn dark-skinned newcomers and draw group boundaries. Not surprisingly, issues of dirt seem to coincide with preexisting stereotypes about Mexican culture. Mexicans are interlopers in the neighborhood and therefore generate grime. Anglo neighborhood residents perceive taco truck spaces as threatening because they convince themselves that Mexican immigrants are filthy, and perhaps the spicy, contaminated tacos they serve will make them sick if they were to eat one. Dirt and illness suggest a direct link between the taco trucks and the community. Because Mexican immigrants' culinary practices are perceived as unsanitary, taco trucks become a health hazard and therefore need to be eradicated.

Lidia Flores, the owner of the Little Mexico taco truck, divulged in a June 2012 interview: "The people here, they stereotype you. They think, if you are from Mexico, you aren't a good person, you're dirty. I think that it is because we are Latino or Mexican, they think the worst."[6] Most of the people who did not like the trucks associated them with the type of people who owned them, Mexicans, and opinions about the trucks were most often formed first from racial prejudices. Lidia believed her truck was an aesthetic issue: "There were various places, the same establishments around here now . . . they would say that they did not want any Latino establishments near their business. They said we were very dirty, that we did not throw out the trash, that we did not follow the regulations of the food department." These complaints, she noted, threatened her business because these neighbors were determined to shut her down. She had the burden to prove otherwise: "The city thought that putting in this type of business would appear bad for the city's image. . . . Therefore, we had to fight legally against the city in 2001 so that we could put this establishment here." Lidia eventually showed the city that her establishment was clean and that she followed all state and local laws.

In addition to complaints from neighbors and having to battle city officials, Lidia was verbally harassed and her taco truck was vandalized on various occasions. When she first opened for business, people would break windows, throw eggs, and shoot BBs at her truck. Many of the neighbors' perverse perceptions of Mexicans and taco trucks became physical threats. As Sibley (1996, 14) posits, negative stereotypes "play an important part in the configuration of social space because of the importance of distanciation in the behavior of social groups." Because many in the community wanted to distance themselves from Mexicans and taco trucks, some tried badgering them out of the neighborhood.

While discussions of trash were often aspects of discrimination, some legitimate trash issues concerning taco trucks should not be discounted. When several of the trucks first opened, they did not have trash receptacles, nor were they completely in compliance with health code. It did not take more than a year, however, for Mexican immigrants in Columbus to learn the process. After the CPHD inspected the trucks, the owners would invest in running water, gloves, trash receptacles, proper refrigeration, or anything else that needed to be in compliance with the CPHD's health regulations. Some of the trucks associated with trash were in parking lots with illicit drug users and loiters. These parking spaces collected a lot of litter that blew around the taco trucks, but the litter was not actually produced by the trucks. Rather, the trucks' appearance blended in and became part of the problem.

Consequently, there was a gradient of discrimination that ranged from hate crimes to "cultural confusion." I define "cultural confusion" as the ignorance or lack of understanding of another group's practices, which allows one to validate preconceived stereotypes in order to frame an argument around unfounded judgments or to justify persecutions. One's general perceptions of another's culture may have a grain of veracity, but these perceptions are used as an excuse to exclude a people and their practices. This, I posit, is the main issue with taco trucks and trash in the Hilltop community from 2000 to around 2005.

Ohio Hispanic Coalition president Josué Vicente explained why the community refused to accept taco trucks: "The issue with taco trucks at first was realistically an issue of discrimination and racism." He piped up, "You see, most people like Mexican food, but not the people. That's the problem, not the food." However, Vicente did concede that there were some legitimate concerns about the taco trucks' contributing to the trash blowing in the area. When some of the trucks first opened, he noted, they did make some mistakes, especially when working in a foreign language with the health code. "We noticed that some of the vendors, not all of the vendors, forgot to buy a trashcan. And that is where some issues started to come up. Some of the neighbors were starting to say that the trucks were contributing to the trash problem." Vicente asserted that the trucks were not the source of the community's trash problem, however. "When you go and do studies in those particular neighborhoods, even well before the taco trucks arrived . . . it was trashy, [and] it was dirty. So taco trucks have nothing to do with the main problem with trash in those neighborhoods." Although the taco truck owners bought trashcans and worked hard to keep the area around their trucks clean, the residents found other issues with the trucks. Arguments against the trucks escalated from trashy and unsanitary to being illegal in some form or fashion, which could range from a zoning code to the owner's "legal" status. The swirling issues around taco trucks became a regular part of the Greater Hilltop Area Commission meetings. Vicente attended the meetings to represent the Latino community and taco truck owners. Often, he was the only one present at the meetings who could represent the Latino community, as taco truck owners seldom knew about the meetings or the content of the meetings; they also had very little to no understanding of English. In other words, taco truck owners were linguistically excluded from the meeting space that determined their place within the community.

Most of the taco truck issues at the meetings had spiraled to whether or not the trucks were paying taxes, and to the allegation that the trucks were bringing crime and violence to the neighborhood. Negative perceptions about the trucks were worsening. Vicente described his interactions at these meetings:

> The role of the Hilltop Commission is to provide services to anyone who wants to open a business will succeed as a business [*sic*]. They weren't doing that. They were trying to act as police, inspection, private immigration, and IRS. I went to all those meetings and the biggest issue was: "Well, these people aren't paying taxes." I said, "How do you know that? Let's go and open the books [tax records] of these people and let's go and open your books and see who is not paying taxes." They shut up right there. The next meeting I went to, they were complaining that the taco trucks were stealing electricity. I asked them: "When are you available and we will go around and see who is stealing electricity and we will call the police right there." We went to all the trucks in the Hilltop Area and everybody had their books, everybody had their documents, everybody had their own meters and how much they pay.

Vicente argued that, because taco trucks were owned and operated by Mexicans, the Hilltop Area Commission was not doing what they were supposed to do, which is take care of all business owners in the area regardless of the type of establishment they own and operate. The Hilltop Area Commission had excluded the Mexicans from their responsibilities. Vicente believed Latinos enhanced the neighborhood, but to the Hilltop Area Commission, Mexican immigrants were malevolent, and the commission could only focus on false allegations based on stereotypes. He elaborated:

> A lot of the business people there [in the Hilltop Area] are totally ignorant. It's amazing how many opportunities this country will give you, even though you don't have the proper education. And I guess that is what is happening with the people in this association, especially in the Hilltop Area. The Hilltop Area is one of those areas that you're afraid to walk down the street, even before the Mexican community arrives. . . . The arguments against the taco trucks are unfounded. They aren't creating violence; they aren't creating a hassle for anyone. They are selling food, they are promoting their businesses, and they're paying taxes.

The issues surrounding the taco trucks continually shifted around prejudices. Most of the community leaders and several of the businesses in the area in the early 2000s did not recognize Mexicans as their equals. As Bonita Lee put it,

"It would be nice if they [community residents] saw human beings there [at the taco trucks] trying to make a living and just having a business, but it's just beyond that." At the low end of the spectrum, trash described the people at the trucks; at the other end, trash came to depict the trucks themselves. Many in the community believed that the trucks tarnished the neighborhood's image and created unfair competition for brick-and-mortar establishments.

I spoke with Chuck Patterson in June 2014 to discuss the adversities among the trucks and their neighboring brick-and-mortar restaurants. Patterson has been the chair of the Greater Hilltop Area Commission and one of the area's lead real-estate agents. He is a heavyset, light-skinned African American man who has lived in the area all his life. I met up with Patterson on West Broad Street, at the heart of the commercial district of the community.

Patterson gave me an impromptu tour of the street and then slowly began discussing the community issues associated with taco trucks. As we walked the street he pointed out all the vacant, dilapidated buildings and how difficult it is to bring businesses into the area. Although he is not an advocate for the trucks, he tried to take a neutral stance. He is careful not to stereotype the Mexicans who own the trucks, but he does focus on the perceived aesthetics and property issues related to the trucks in the neighborhood. Patterson said that local businesses thought taco trucks had an unfair advantage over brick-and-mortar restaurants because trucks do not have the same overhead and business expenses. He also claimed that the taco trucks' aesthetic induced blight, and that the trucks' shoddy appearance repelled people from investing in property in the area. In Patterson's words:

> It's probably an economic and an aesthetic issue. As we try to bring in other businesses and get this section of West Broad Street revitalized, we've got to even the playing field for the brick-and-mortar and the vending people at the same time. The aesthetics are important. If we are going to get streetlights and new development to spread, you don't want it to encounter something that is not pleasing to look at. . . . And as long as a bright, shiny, new business is surrounded by a neighborhood their customers fear, the businesses [buildings] will not be invested in.

Patterson believed that taco truck owners only wanted to make a quick buck and therefore were not interested in becoming a permanent part of the community: "If they [Mexican taco truck owners] are not investing in a [brick-and-mortar] business, they aren't investing in the community. Rather, they are throwing up the cheapest possible building [a truck], making the largest possible profit, and getting out as quickly as possible. That is not going to help us." As I interviewed

Patterson, it became apparent that he had a narrow understanding of taco truck owners' business practices, their life circumstances, and their long-term goals. From speaking with more than twenty taco truck owners in Columbus, I learned that most would love to have a brick-and-mortar restaurant but did not have the finances or U.S. citizenship to fill out the paperwork needed to open their own restaurants. Yes, taco trucks were circumventing many established business laws, but only because the owners had no alternatives. Taco truck owners ingeniously used their trucks as a spatial strategy to survive economically in a country where they are afforded minimal opportunities as noncitizens.

I asked Patterson if there were any positive cultural attributes of taco trucks the community could embrace. He respectfully disagreed with my assessment of the trucks as a cultural phenomenon. To him, they were not following formal business protocols. He argued that all businesses in the neighborhood had to abide by the existing community's traditional business practices. As far as Patterson was concerned, parking a taco truck in a parking lot and never moving it was counterintuitive and opposed the business practices that the community would condone. Patterson protested:

> For those businesses that do want to be a traditional business in the community, it's difficult for them to jump through all the required hoops, for fire safety, sprinkler systems, parking spaces available, any code issues, grounds maintenance and so forth, when they see a vending truck that never moves. . . . 24 hours a day, seven days a week, 365 days of the year, it sits in the same spot, it's supposed to be moved, it's not supposed to maintain that space. Those are the rules, and we all have to live by the rules, no matter where we're from, what we look like, or what language we speak.

Patterson raised the issue of mobility: taco truck owners were cheating the system by not moving. The trucks appeared to be criminal because they did not fit within preexisting city policies. Therefore, they were not part of the community's time-honored culture.

Another reason the taco trucks looked out of place is because their function did not follow their form. The trucks, which seemed mobile, were stationary. They were not doing what they were designed to do—move on a daily (if not hourly) basis. One could assume that a truck that never moves is broken down. And a broken-down truck is a vehicle not properly invested in. Multiple ramshackle trucks speckled across parking lots taint the streetscape.

Immobile taco trucks look like "trailer trash," and the trucks are subject to the same jokes as those associated with mobile homes. One resident of the Hilltop Area told me that "there are always plenty of trailer jokes to go around." Trailer jokes are associated with something that has been stripped of its mobility. Comedian Jeff Foxworthy, known for his southern sense of humor, tells these sorts of jokes best: "If you own a home that's mobile and 14 cars that aren't, you might be a redneck" (Foxworthy 1993). This notion of immobile mobility associated with "white trash" country folks is easily transferred to the Mexican immigrant population, which has an immobile mobile operation. Immobile mobility can also be understood as the perception of something that should be more mobile than its most basic mobile necessity. The taco trucks represent this mobile but yet immobile condition and become catalysts to chaos. A taco truck that sits in a parking lot and never moves is a metaphor for trash. The temporary aesthetic of the truck cannot be understood without the variable of time and the socioeconomic perceptions of that condition.

Most residents in the neighborhood believe if a truck has wheels and an engine, it should move periodically. For Mexicans, the truck's mobility is one of minimal necessity; the truck is a stepping-stone to acquiring a brick-and-mortar restaurant of their own. In the meantime, a makeshift kitchen on wheels allows them to seek affordable spaces that they can rent to sustain their family and save money to fulfill their "American dream." Immobile mobility is a temporary circumstance within the context of a taco truck owner's life. To the taco truck owners, the truck is a provisional condition as they strive to create their permanency in the United States. And in Columbus, this socioeconomic survival strategy has succeeded.

The Greater Hilltop Area Commission members, no matter how far they tried to stretch their powers, did not have the authority to regulate the trucks to their vision. Nor were they able to persuade city officials to change the rules based on the community's interpretation of what constitutes place-appropriate or traditional business practices. The community may have had the ability at first to develop more stringent regulations against the trucks when it came to public-health matters, but what the trucks did have in the beginning was time—time to become a mainstay in the area and allow people to interact and become familiar with them. For some, the trucks became a welcomed cultural component to the neighborhood. And curiously, whether the trucks were dirty or trashy, often made no difference at all.

INCLUSIVE TACO TRUCK SPACES

Taco truck space in Columbus evolved from serving just Mexicans immigrants to serving the community at large. Traditional taco trucks, which easily could have been excluded from the area, were eventually accepted and in the process became inclusive public spaces. The majority of the residents became enthusiastic about the trucks. Bonita Lee considers them a constructive cultural exchange: "It's good to learn about other cultures and get out of our little world here. . . . It's a good thing. Columbus is very different than what it was twenty years ago. It's been a quick change, a very quick change. But it's been for the better of the community." The trucks have been steadily altering the community's mentality and social structure. This was apparent during my time spent around the trucks over the past ten years.

In 2004, as a community planner, I spent much time talking to taco truck owners; what I witnessed back then was primarily a Latino clientele. Returning to conduct research on the trucks in 2012, I discovered that a diversity of customers frequented the trucks. The trucks were not just catering to Latinos but sought to serve almost everyone who lived in the area. I spoke with the residents patronizing the trucks, and what I heard repeatedly was that the trucks offered extremely good food at a very affordable price. In the Greater Hilltop Area, where most people have little money, the trucks filled an economic niche and captured a part of the demographic that may have been wary of the trucks at first, or perhaps did not have a voice in the conversation to begin with.

I spoke with a middle-aged white woman about eating at the trucks while she was waiting in line at El Huarache Veloz, a taco truck on West Broad Street. She was fairly typical of many of the residents I had seen in the area. She was missing several teeth and dressed in a stained Ohio State sweatshirt, shabby gray sweatpants, and tattered tennis shoes. She told me that she lived a few houses down from the truck and decided one day just to try it because there were always people eating at the truck. "At least a couple hundred people a day!" she exclaimed. "The food is good and it is cheap. I don't know if it is clean, but I guess you just have to take your chances," she surmised. I spoke with many others who had similar viewpoints; they did not think the trucks were sanitary or inspected by the CPHD, but they thought the food was good and, most important, inexpensive. Why would people suddenly embrace the trucks, even if most of them believed that the trucks were filthy?

I interviewed Geoffrey Phillips in June 2012 about the many community discourses about the trucks. Phillips is a local resident and head of economic development for the Greater Hilltop Area Commission. He is also a major proponent of the trucks and has sought to find ways to use the trucks to promote the neighborhood to the rest of the city. I met with Phillips at his home, not far from El Huarache Veloz. His house is situated on a beautiful, tree-lined street, but the street is also punctuated periodically with boarded-up houses and buildings. Phillips's house is a two-story red-brick home with a white picket fence.

He has an American flag flying proudly in the front and a Welsh flag in the back. He whispers to me that many of his neighbors complain about the Welsh flag, and he hints that there are many white supremacists in the area—just as I see a Confederate battle flag furling in his neighbor's yard. Phillips speaks about his impression of taco trucks and why he started to eat at them. He describes his first encounter with the trucks as one of both fascination and admiration:

> When I first moved out here, I had never seen one before. They had a bit of a mystique about them; in some ways they kind of really puzzled me, then one time we had a couple of days without power because a storm blew trees down taking out a lot of transformers. . . . The taco trucks were really the only places that were open where you could buy food. And that is when I discovered something I never realized before. These trucks are places where you can get the same food—actually a more authentic version of the food that you would get at Chipotle—and the price is half of what you would pay there or at any restaurant. I believe that others have found the same thing, there are people I have befriended who say the same thing. . . . They kind of grow on you after a while.

Phillips became fascinated with the taco trucks, but he also explained that not everyone in the community felt the same way. He mentioned that many people in the neighborhood had a "white trash mentality" [thinking like white trash]— that they used the trucks to justify crude stereotypes of Mexican culture and to reaffirm their own white superiority. But some community leaders in the neighborhood conceive the trucks as an economic opportunity that could reinvent the district's streetscapes through culinary practices. Says Phillips:

> As far as the way people perceive them on the West Side, I was thinking part of it has to do with what economic status the neighborhood has, but you're always going to have people that don't like anyone if they are a different race. And the trucks are an excuse to talk down or bad about them. . . . As far as I'm concerned, and the people in my association are concerned, they are a welcome attraction. . . . They are something that draw people to the neighborhood as well as feed people who are already in the neighborhood.

I asked Phillips about the distorted stereotypes. Had negative attitudes toward taco trucks persisted, or had people's perceptions of Mexican street food vending changed? Phillips explained that the neighborhood residents' attitude toward Mexican cultural practices had improved over the past decade:

> I think it took a while, because people are always afraid of something they don't know and it's not something people here are used to being around. . . . But since we have now been together for so many years, I think people now have adapted

to the fact that people of other nationalities are part of the neighborhood. And I believe we need to get to know them, we need to be inclusive to them and get them involved with the affairs in the neighborhood.

Phillips explained that not only were Mexicans welcomed to the neighborhood, but their cultural practices around street food and sports were helping to enliven the landscape; as well, Mexican families were a great asset to the community:

> They've added a lot to our city parks with their soccer games, totally filling up a park—even parks where they aren't playing soccer. It's great, because you have a culture centered on family. And of all the neighborhoods we have in the city, according to the demographics and amount of households that are families, the West Side still has the greatest percentage. It is a family community. So I think everyone fits right in. It's a good cultural exchange.

Moreover, Phillips noted that it was not just Mexican cultural practices that were reanimating the landscape: the Mexican community, including taco truck owners, was also buying dilapidated and abandoned properties and making them nice homes again. Phillips disrupts Patterson's statement that the taco truck owners are not investing into the community. They may not be acquiring brick-and-mortar business establishments yet, but they are investing into the housing stock and providing a home for their family. Phillips describes how one taco truck owner renovated a house a few blocks away from his:

> I have seen beautiful houses being made out of houses that were just sitting there, in some cases just falling apart. There was one house on Valley View Drive. It started out looking like a one-bedroom bungalow, and from all the work they [a Mexican taco truck owner and his family] have done and all the additions they've done, my guess is now probably a five-bedroom home. And the property looks nice. They have a great deal of pride in the community and themselves. And the houses are immaculate on the outside, the landscaping is excellent—never a yard that needs picked up. The more families like this that would move into this area, the happier I would be.

Over the past decade, most Hilltop residents became inured to and even fascinated by taco trucks, while others were just indifferent. People's minds about the trucks were changing. Taco truck spaces were slowly subsumed into the West Side's community. As Chuck Patterson put it, "The general consensus in the beginning was very negative, but like many things, the more you see it, the more it's there, the more used to it you become." There are various reasons why clashing issues about the trucks ceased, but most will agree that people became accustomed to them and even developed a taste for their exotic cuisines.

A secondary spatial transgression took place: spaces that initially seemed to be solely for Latinos were now viewed as all-encompassing. Low-income Ohioans, of all ethnic backgrounds, were now frequenting the trucks (see plate 19). Community space was enveloping the taco trucks' spaces. The roots of these changes, I argue, were due to economics as well as to social interactions, but the cuisine aspect itself is what stimulated the positive cultural exchanges.

Josué Vicente claims that, coinciding with the economic recession in 2008, more residents of the Greater Hilltop Area began to eat at taco trucks because the food was reasonably priced for those living on a tight budget.

> Now the majority of clientele are U.S. citizens, Anglos, African Americans, other communities. So now if you go talk to the taco trucks [owners], many of them will tell you that they are surviving not because of the Mexican community, not because of the Latino community, but because of other communities that are going to eat at the trucks on a regular basis.

Vicente also noted that people in the area would not only go to the trucks to eat, they would also try to speak to the truck owners in Spanish:

> It is amazing. You aren't just changing the way people are eating but changing the culture. You have the opportunity to talk to them [the taqueros] and many times establish a conversation to what realistically the Mexican community is all about. And the Mexican community is about hard work, providing for your family, just like any other single American who has moved to the United States.

Vicente eats at the trucks to find out what is going on in the community—not just the Mexican community associated with the truck but also the general community within which the truck is located. Vicente clarifies, "That gives me the insight on how to work with the community to incorporate the trucks."

The postmodern American metropolis may have produced isolated forms of social interactions, such as "the purely atomic individual" and "carceral archipelagos" (Mitchell 2005; Soja 2000), but it has also laid the foundation for the taco truck. The taco truck has added another layer to the postmodern sociospatial matrix—a socioeconomic dimension that does not contribute to individual isolation. In fact, this layer counteracts social separation through eating together. The informal social practices at taco trucks culturally unfold into communities, fostering inclusive spaces within excluded urban environments.

The social rhythms associated with the taco trucks have spatial boundaries that blend and blur with the existing communities and also transform between and within spaces themselves. While it is still elective to subject oneself to a taco truck experience, a large number of people in the Greater Hilltop Area are not only frequenting the trucks, they are unwittingly using taco truck spaces to help restructure their own sense of community. The taco trucks therefore have become more than just culinary spheres for the Latino population: they have become nodes within the larger community's social network.

The sociospatial organization in taco truck landscapes forces people out of their vehicles and fosters friendly interactions. What I observed in Columbus was a high level of socializing. Regardless of whether individuals were strangers, friends, or acquaintances, people would take the time to say hello to one another or strike up a conversation about the cuisine, where people were from, or what their occupations were. Actually, I witnessed many people meeting and talking for the first time and informally sharing a meal together. Almost always, people would shake hands afterward and introduce themselves before departing. These encounters with one another, as well as with the taqueros, help people better understand the demographic makeup of their community, which in turn amplifies one's sense of belonging. Vicente describes these interactions as a positive injection of Mexican practices to the West Side community:

> It's not only the food, but you start embracing everything that is involved with the food. . . . We used to go to the [dinner] table and eat and talk. Right now we don't do that, and families don't even do that right now in the United States. I think that's the biggest problem we have in society. Whether we are talking about the Mexican community, the American community, or any other community, we don't have enough communication within these communities. But with tacos, you go to the taco trucks with your friends and talk. If you go with your non-Mexican friends, the trucks give you the opportunity to make new relationships. We used to go to the table and eat and talk; now we go to the taco truck.

The taco truck not only augments the social function of the contemporary city, it also complicates the notion of what may be considered *slow food*. Originally a culinary movement from Bra, Italy, slow food strives "to prevent the disappearance of local food cultures and traditions, counteract the rise of fast life, and combat people's dwindling interest in the food they eat" (slowfood.com). At the taco truck, tradition is fast food, and Mexican traditional dishes survive, ironically, because of an industrialized food system. The taco truck is fundamentally designed to prepare and serve foods fast to workers on the go. Taqueros serve mostly processed, industrialized foodstuffs that are quickly prepared and devoured. However, they are also recreating traditional Mexican cuisines that evoke a sense of place. Many people who frequent the trucks—regardless of ethnicity or class—are searching for what they consider genuine

Mexican flavors. Serving classic Mexican street food from a truck, therefore, creates a Mexican cultural atmosphere within an intimate social setting. Taco trucks promote Mexican cuisines and customs. Seen this way, it is the down-to-earth scale of the operation that gives the perception of slow food. Therefore, Mexican food at taco trucks is both fast and slow.

Although people are eating rapidly, they do take the time to socialize. Another aspect of this socialization is that only two or three people, at the most, operate the trucks. In Columbus, they are almost always family related as well as the owners of the business. Because each truck is most likely independently owned and operated, there are small differences from truck to truck that add an individual touch to each taco. Consequently, people who return to the same trucks feel as though they are connecting with the owners. The customers form friendships, make acquaintances, or, at least at some level, share an experience by eating at particular trucks in the neighborhood.

It would seem that the taco truck operators found some sort of stability within the community, but they did not. While the economic downturn attracted Ohioan clientele to the taco trucks, it also reduced the number of Mexican customers. Many of the Mexican immigrants who had previously kept the Columbus taco truck owners' businesses in operation had moved away between 2008 and 2012. They either moved back to Mexico or found work in another city or state. In addition, immigration enforcement had beefed up its patrols, which frightened many Latinos and discouraged them from frequenting the trucks. The traditional taco trucks' existence was now foremost reliant on the community they had transformed.

= = =

Taco trucks in Columbus's West Side, which were first perceived as entropic, were eventually accepted as part of the community's character. What made the community tolerate the trucks? I maintain that there are four fundamental reasons the community was able to accept the taco trucks. First, taco truck owners had unwittingly found a large loophole in the city's ordinances pertaining to mobile food vending. Second, the dominant community did not have the power to persuade the city to close these loopholes. The existing community was able to define taco trucks as out of place but did not have an adequate advantage to do anything about it—in part because the community was also disenfranchised. As a result, taco trucks had time on their side. Third, over the period of a decade the community simply became acculturated to the trucks. Taco trucks had the opportunity to integrate into the community, and food helped ease their entrance. This brings me to my fourth and final point: food practices in prosaic public spaces draw diverse people together to interact and in doing so create new cultural geographies.

While there is no doubt that power struggles over territory shape landscape, I contend that the cultural landscape is not defined solely through contestation. Rather, I posit that cultural differences are also transformed through individual interactions that permeate various levels of social structure. Individuals—regardless of race, gender, and/or economic status—accept or reject certain behavioral patterns based on personal preferences and invested interests, which are often economically driven.

Exposure to new social practices is accepted or rejected, lost, forgotten, or transformed based on whether or not the new cultural customs are beneficial to the individual's life practices, especially to a person's pocketbook. This notion contradicts the argument that the cultural landscape is merely contested through class conflict (Mitchell 1995) and supports the theory that various ethnicities and classes are capable of adopting and adapting behavior through communication and conviviality (Adams 2005, 215). Cultural change can take place through the direct exposure to new social practices; thus, culture can be shared and hybridized.

Culinary practices play a significant role in cultural change. They are capable of introducing new ways in which social boundaries are drawn. This is what makes taco truck space exceptional. Taco truck spaces are social nodes where diverse individuals are brought together through cuisine. The people who frequent taco trucks, their social status, and their potential influence can alter community perceptions—and, ultimately, the taco trucks' perceived place within the neighborhood. For the Greater Hilltop Area, tacos brought people together for economic purposes—monetary exchanges assuaged cultural exchanges. Residents acquired a taste for the tacos served from the trucks, and at the same time, their social perceptions of Mexican immigrants changed as well. Some residents no longer considered Mexican immigrants dirty and disorderly but instead looked at them as hard-working individuals who contributed to the community. In the end, taco trucks had created microcosms of inclusion within a community who, at first, tried to exclude them.

Another factor that eased the acceptance of taco trucks was the advent of the gourmet food truck in 2007. Boutique food trucks in Columbus began to pop up in sizable numbers in 2011. Their novelty made serving cuisine from trucks fashionable. While many working-class residents in Columbus's West Side still focused on the negative attributes of ethnic street food practices to undermine taco trucks, the middle class was attracted to many of the same spontaneous practices. Middle-class residents even began to reverence the street food scene. New boutique food trucks introduced sophistication and creativity. Unlike taco trucks, however, gourmet food trucks cohere to the values and parameters of the dominant society. Nevertheless, the acceptance of food trucks of all types helped many in the community embrace taco trucks as part of this quirky phenomenon. However, taco trucks are inadvertently excluded from many of Columbus's central public spaces in which boutique food trucks are featured. This is the topic that I turn to in chapter 6.

CHAPTER 6

COOKING UP MULTICULTURALISM

Arriving at Port Columbus International Airport, one is greeted at the baggage carousel with posters portraying Columbus as a multicultural metropolis. The images depict the city skyline and display various aspects of the city's array of activities. A little girl plays with an electricity ball at the science center, a ballerina strides across the stage at the preforming arts center, a group of people party at an open-air concert, and a gourmet food truck vends on a street corner. The images are part of a multimillion-dollar branding initiative produced by Columbus Partners to illustrate Columbus as a pulsating place to live.

Columbus economic developers are devising ways to showcase the city as having a sophisticated social scene. And as they struggle to dig up new ways to spice up the city's dull urban vibe, they may have found their remedy through food trucks. The mental image in 2001 of taco trucks as filthy had been flipped: by 2012, they were in vogue. Today, food trucks are endemic to Columbus's landscape. Indeed, the Anglo middle class celebrates the trucks for the profusion of culinary delights they offer. The city's multitude of food trucks has injected its conventional landscape order with a much-needed shot of cultural vivacity.

Vibrant symbols of urban prosperity, Sharon Zukin (1996) argues, stimulate the economy aesthetically. In presenting her argument about the symbolic economy, Zukin proclaims that urban boosters and the private sector are increasingly reconfiguring public places into spaces for consumption practices, such as going shopping or sipping cappuccino. To attract the affluent, urban developers upgrade the urban landscape through employing the right kinds of cultural symbols—stylish shopping malls, chic cafes, gourmet grocery stores, and hip art galleries. Paralleling fashion trends in urban design, food trucks fall in line with these sorts of consumption spaces. But while boutique food trucks fit well into Columbus's symbolic cultural economy, taco trucks do not—at least, not in practice.

Artisanal food trucks frequently park in Columbus's central public spaces and are reverenced by Columbus's Anglo middle-class residents. Meanwhile, traditional taco trucks mostly remain in disenfranchised neighborhoods or tucked into some sort of interstitial space. These differences arise because of the types of clientele the trucks cater to as well as the social practices they represent. Gourmet food trucks easily engulf the city center's consumption spaces because Columbus's middle class is infatuated with them. Conversely, taco truck owners focus on feeding the low-wage workers who maintain consumption spaces or work in landscapes of production, such as factories. These differences add up to substantial differences in the ways in which food trucks as cultural symbols are coded by ethnicity and class.

For the purpose of this chapter, I reconceptualize food truck spaces across Columbus through the perspective of white privilege.[1] White privilege is commonly defined by how Anglos "accrue" opportunities and benefits "simply by the virtue of their whiteness" (Pulido 2000, 13). And because middle-class Anglos almost always cannot perceive their own privileges, they do not realize how their reflexive social practices in spaces can aggravate racial inequalities (Pulido 2000). The performance of middle-class whiteness ascribes a set of privileged meanings to food spaces that can inadvertently lead to the exclusion of people of color (Guthman, 2008; Slocum, 2007). By examining whiteness in social spaces, we illuminate the imperceptible boundaries that nonwhites cannot cross. This alternative framework elucidates the ways in which the Anglo middle class employs the symbols and practices of food truck spaces to their socioeconomic advantage while exonerating themselves from any form of cultural dominance or spatial inequality. To look at Columbus's through this filter, we must take into consideration how all food truck social spaces relate to one another at multiple scales.

"A SMART AND OPEN CITY"

Columbus boosters and economic developers sought to build a brand for the city's bicentennial and have called on city residents to contribute ideas about how the city should portray itself. City officials employed the marketing firm

Ologie to find the best brand to sell Columbus as an exhilarating place to live and work. Their focus has been on an eight-year initiative called Columbus 2020, which was revealed in 2012 (Brand Columbus 2012). The creation of a successful city image—ultimately an agreed-upon sense of place—is a crucial component of economic survival in a global marketplace. *Brand Columbus*, on its webpage, emphasizes that the city's image translates into income generation for the city and its residents.

> The economic implications of attracting business to our region, retaining business, hosting meetings and events, attracting top executives, educators and physicians and encouraging college graduates to remain in the area are significant. This will be the difference between thriving in the next century or, at best, staying status quo. The opportunity to express our essence and story in a consistent manner, speak with one voice and build further collaboration is immeasurable.

Urban boosters and economic developers must demonstrate that Columbus matters as a place. They must advertise an adventurous social scene to the global marketplace in order to more effectively accumulate capital in a world where financial investments are free floating.

Columbus's planners, marketers, and residents have always struggled to define Columbus's social atmosphere. Scripting a sense of place—when not everyone necessarily feels the same way about the city—is challenging and putting feelings about a place into an illustrative package to promote is difficult. The *Brand Columbus* website addressed this issue. "The formation of Mayor Coleman's Bicentennial Committee in 2007 proved to be the spark that ignited critical conversations about Columbus's national image—or lack thereof" (www.brandcolumbus.com). In June 2012 I spoke with Vince Papsidero, Columbus's principal planner, at the planning office in downtown Columbus. He elaborated on the city's effort to reinvent itself.

> Columbus as a community has struggled for a long time trying to establish an identity for itself. People who live here kind of understand what Columbus is all about, but that message is very rarely communicated nationally. And this year, 2012, is the city's bicentennial, so there was an effort that began last year to try and establish a new marketing identity for the city. And a large number of organizations got involved. The local chamber, the regional chamber, the tourism bureau (which is *Experience Columbus*), the city and other entities got together and came up with a new identity, just called COLUMB**US** with "**US**" being a different font color to try to express "**us**" as a community. And they really focused on being "open" and being "smart."

The *Brand Columbus* webpage explains that "open" and "smart" is about creativity through diversity. "Columbus is a smart and open-minded city with a *progressive* attitude, where people are free to go out on a limb. Where *diversity* isn't just a state of being, but *a state of mind*—made real through people, businesses and neighborhoods every day" (emphasis added). The rhetoric of being "open" and "smart" is directed toward the creative class. The "us" aspect of the marketing emphasizes inclusiveness.

My discussion with Papsidero proceeded to the roles that food trucks play in the city's new marketing production. Papsidero noted, "We have been a pretty accepting community in a lot of different ways, whether its based on race, ethnicity, LGBT, you name it; across the board we are a very open, accepting community, so trying to convey that now is the marketing identity of the city. To celebrate who we are by practice, and, interesting enough, food trucks fit into that." Papsidero believes that the community's acceptance of food trucks demonstrates the city's forward-thinking and open-minded embrace of new people and ideas. This certainly is a positive way to promote the city.

I asked Papsidero if he believed that the general acceptance of food trucks nationally had helped the taco truck's image and if the city was now trying to capitalize on that image. He surmised that it had:

> I would think that the national trend does ease acceptance of all food trucks. . . . The community has an interest in food, and I think of Columbus as being a kind of foodie town because of its restaurant industry that's headquartered here, as well as a very diverse ethnic population that results in ethnic restaurants. Certainly for Columbus, food trucks [are] a booming local industry, and there are now a number of taco trucks in a variety of neighborhoods. . . . I would say more than anything the food trucks are embraced. And I would say [it's] an example of how open and diverse the community is, which also fits into its current marketing strategy about being open and smart. And I think food trucks fit that to a T in many respects.

Food trucks were not only popular in California, they were being revered across the country, and places like Columbus, Ohio, were following the lead. Food trucks are not only opportunities for people to start new microbusinesses, they are also emblems of creative diversity.

When I worked for the city of Columbus in 2004, there were only a handful of taco trucks and plenty of complaints. Today, as I drive around town, there are too many food trucks to begin to count, and there is only praise for the cultural diversity the trucks represent. I spoke with Chris Presutti, the chief zoning official, about the recent acceptance of food trucks and the ways that acceptance was affecting the Mexican community. He found the relationship between the two intriguing, because he realized that one was alleviating complications for the other. He clarified:

> As there is greater acceptance of mobile food vending, at least in the Columbus community, we are starting to see a lot of the very same brick-and-mortar establishments that were viewed as being hurt by these uses, they now are having side business where they have trucks. So some of the better-known restaurants in town now have their own trucks and they are making their way throughout the neighborhood. Boutique restaurants, bakeries, and very well-known, long-established restaurants in Columbus *are now doing the very same things that the Mexican food trucks have been doing for the past ten years.* I think it is only helping the Mexicans, because there is greater acceptance in general of mobile food vending (emphasis added).

This statement is revealing because it highlights the role of gourmet food trucks in increasing the local population's acceptance of taco trucks. This exemplifies how white privilege operates: white people approve another ethnic group's behavior based on whether or not that behavior fits within middle-class, Anglo ideals. Since food trucks of all sorts have been subsumed into middle-class, Anglo society, taco trucks now harmonize with Columbus's landscape.

The Columbus tourism bureau, remarkably, now praises the Mexican taco trucks as contributing to the wide-ranging cultures and cuisines the city can offer its visitors. The taco trucks, which were so viciously contested on the West Side of Columbus from 2001 to 2007, are now venerated as contributing to the city's international image. Columbus residents are giddy about the city's growing assortment of food trucks and elated to spotlight traditional taco trucks on its epicurean stage. The *Experience Columbus* website includes a link to the city's culinary offerings. Featured first under the menu of "food trucks" are "taco trucks." The city is proud of its food truck diversity and of growth in the food truck industry in general. Curiously, it presents the global phenomenon of food trucks as a local characteristic that demonstrates how creative and progressive the community is.

The city capitalizes on the visual spectacle of food trucks because they appear eclectic and eccentric, which bolsters the city's image as "smart" and "open." City boosters are encouraging the diversity that the trucks express by contriving spaces for them throughout the city center. Food trucks are a perfect solution to the city's conservative landscape, because while the trucks themselves express multiculturalism, the seemingly spontaneous practice of eating around the trucks animates the urban landscape. The general consensus is that citizens and urban boosters want food trucks everywhere, especially in the city center to help drive downtown development.

If the city is accepting of food trucks, then policy and zoning should be relaxed as well. I asked Papsidero about having taco trucks downtown: if a food truck of any sort were to park on a street corner in the city center, would city officials have any zoning or other issues with that? He explained that food trucks are allowed to park anywhere they like.[2] I offered him a scenario: if a traditional taco truck were to park near the capitol building, would the city take issue with that? He said, "No." Then I pointed out that, in reality, there are no immigrant taco trucks in the city center. He agreed, saying, "No, really there hasn't been! And that is interesting." He added:

> You know, in particular there is one well-regarded food truck, Junior's Tacos in Victorian Village, which is predominately middle-, upper-middle-class, white neighborhood, large gay community, just south of the university and near downtown. And that truck has been in its position and has not moved in at least three years. And we have not heard any complaints at all.

This statement is telling because it indicates that taco trucks are acceptable in a white, middle-class neighborhood. But as Popsidero and I both noted, this neighborhood is an exception. Junior's Tacos opened because the owners wanted to sell tacos to Latino landscapers working in the area, but over time it began to make burritos and American fare for the community it was surrounded by, in particular college students. Its story is unique, and its presence in a white, middle-class neighborhood is unusual. Most taco truck owners are not actively strategizing about how to capture the Anglo market that is increasingly interested in food trucks—a point I return to in the next section.

COLUMBUS COMMONS: A PRIVATIZED PUBLIC SPACE

Developers have reinvented the site of the former City Center Shopping Mall as a seven-acre, landscaped green space called Columbus Commons. The mall was a drab, uninviting, indoor space that was inadequately connected to its surroundings. Its shops shuttered their doors, and the mall was demolished. Urban developers decided to replace the mall with a large public park and "market-driven development," such as shops and apartments, that would unify the downtown area spatially and aesthetically. The Columbus Commons website describes it as "a unique gathering space for the Central Ohio community" and adds, "Columbus Commons supports the ongoing, market-driven development of a truly remarkable and walkable Downtown neighborhood that integrates living spaces with retail, office, and entertainment opportunities" (Columbus Commons 2012). Columbus Commons is a private development that uses entertainment to attract capital and enhance the urban environment. The park hosts regular diversions to promote an image of splendor, and food trucks are an integral part of its programmed activities.

In crafting the city's identity, city boosters work closely with the Columbus Partnership, a 501(c)(3) nonprofit organization led by fifty-two chief executive officers who are part of Columbus's business elite and make decisions about Columbus's economic development. They work closely to help the city establish a corporate-like brand. The Columbus Partnership describes its members as "catalysts for civic improvement" and describes its mission like this: "The Partnership engages in all major projects that need strong civic leadership and intend to enhance the quality of our schools, arts and cultural organizations, or the development of downtown Columbus. The Partnership provides strategic approaches to turn vision into action to achieve the desired results without taking credit for accomplishments." To put it in a different light, the Columbus Partnership strategizes how best to economically develop the city while remaining anonymous in the process. It is a hidden hand of power with tremendous influence over how and for whom Columbus will look and function. It is not only constructing the city's image but also molding the cityscape to bring to life its marketing concept. In this way, the partnership guides how and where resources are allocated.

Columbus's central civic spaces are being transformed through the visions and decisions of the corporate elite in a nebulous manner. Such shifts in power to allow urban boosters to manage public spaces can pose a substantial risk. As Zukin points out, "Handing such spaces over to corporate executives and private investors means giving them carte blanche to remake public culture. It marks the erosion of public space in terms of its two basic principles: public stewardship and open access" (Zukin 1996, 32). Columbus's new private development is camouflaged as a public park. In the context of Columbus's new narrative as a "smart" and "open" city, it is interesting to investigate to what extent this privatized public park is accessible to all. To do this, I evaluate the types of food trucks and people present within its spaces.

The park opened on Columbus's bicentennial year in the summer of 2012. One of the park's first events was the Columbus Food Truck Festival. Papsidero described the event:

> Columbus Commons . . . had a food truck event on a Friday last year, and this was its first attempt, . . . a day-long event. They had seven thousand people

show up, and the lines were too long, and they did not have enough trucks to meet the demand. And if seven thousand people will come in—these are folks predominately from the suburbs, as well as the inner city, a real broad range of folks show up to check out food trucks on a Friday and Friday night—that says something in terms of acceptance within a community.

At the first Food Truck Festival, no immigrant taco trucks were present—but only ten or fifteen trucks were there in total. The following year, 2013, the event hosted forty trucks to better meet demand. Only one, El Taco Tuzo, was a traditional taco truck. In 2014, Dos Hermanos and Los Potosinos participated in the event. Lisa, the owner of Dos Hermanos, told me that she had to apply at least eight months in advance, and organizers accepted only eight new trucks. In other words, food truck owners had to be in the know about the functioning of the event well in advance if they wanted to participate. And even then, participation was limited and favored the gourmet trucks already locked in from the previous year.

Beyond the Food Truck Festival, Columbus Commons hosts about five to ten trucks for lunch on a daily basis. I preformed a windshield survey of the space every day over a two-week period. During this time I never came across a traditional taco truck. I asked Josué Vicente, president of the Ohio Hispanic Coalition, about the lack of participation by taco trucks owners in downtown spaces and at food truck events. He gave me his personal impression of the space's poor incorporation of Latinos:

> For years it has been a problem of having Mexican taco trucks in the city. The city was saying they do not allow it and they would not permit it. Now if you go to downtown and you see all these nice trucks, some try to sell tacos, but they are owned by different ethnic groups. They say they are selling burritos and they are selling tacos, but they have these fancy names and that is when you start thinking, this is realistically discrimination. What is the reason that these people are selling food in downtown with a truck? What makes a difference with these trucks? Why can't a taco truck owner have the same opportunities as well? The taco trucks would love to be downtown, and people would accept them. But the problem is that up until right now, there haven't been any opportunities for the taco truck . . . You hear all these issues that taqueros are having with getting access to selling downtown, and then you go downtown and you see all these boutique trucks. So something is not right.

What Vicente is witnessing is not necessarily any malicious intention to exclude taco trucks. Instead, taco trucks are zoned out due to structural racism. The city and food truck organizations had measures in place that made it extremely difficult for traditional taco trucks to penetrate. For taco trucks owners, most who are struggling to learn English and are not integrated into Columbus's Anglo community, so it is difficult for them to break into featured food truck festivals because they are confused about how to enroll in an event. Anglo gourmet food truck owners, on the contrary, are able to take advantage of such policies as they directly benefit their food truck practices.

In addition, taco trucks simply do not fit as well within white people's practices and taste preferences. Anglo middle-class policies and practices promote gourmet food trucks over taco trucks. The city's top-down approach, in programming multiculturalism by embracing the image of food trucks, is flawed. Columbus is not as diverse as it may appear on the surface. The city cannot duplicate informal practices through marketing multiculturalism. And the city cannot create diversity through gourmet food trucks whose only diversity is in the types of cuisine they offer. The Columbus community may now perceive gourmet food trucks as commonplace and whimsical, but to a perspicacious individual familiar with the nation's street food vending history, they appear as a cultural facsimile.

Taco truck owners I spoke with about parking their trucks downtown knew very little about their ability to do so. Most told me that they did not realize they were allowed to vend downtown. Several truck owners, such as the owners of Las Delicias and Tres Reyes, did not know about vending at Columbus Commons. When I told them about it, they thought it was a good idea, but they also told me that they did not know the process required to participate. In addition, they explained, going about this process in English, serving customers in English, and tailoring their menus to Anglos' taste preferences were not only difficult, such accommodations would completely change the culture of their business. For example, the owners of El Buen Sazón worried about moving their operation for one day to an Anglo area of town because they thought they would lose their Latino customer base. Others explained that if they could afford another truck—and a nicer, and more reliable truck—they would definitely start parking downtown and make foods that would appeal to affluent Anglos. One taco truck owner told me he would love to have a fancy truck to go around the city and cook for white people, because they have more money to spend and he wanted to be more inventive with his recipes. Observed from the taco trucks owners' viewpoints, downtown is off limits because it appears as an austere space for Anglo life.

The neoliberal planning initiatives downtown only strengthen the performance of whiteness. The city is attracting a particular class through its marketing, the so-called creative class. It is theoretically promoting diversity but in reality is just attracting more of the same: middle-class Anglos who can afford to consume the creativity and diversity that the city is selling. Although Columbus Commons is designed and planned to be an all-inclusive space, it is exclusive in practice—not because of any explicit, malevolent policy to exclude, but due to the dominant performances of middle-class whiteness. It is white privilege that exacerbates the spatial differentiation of culture and capital.

WHITEWASHING FOOD TRUCK SPACE

In an effort to capitalize on the food trucks' popularity, some entrepreneurs are designing food truck spaces into the city. There is one space in particular that has set out to enrich the street-food dining experience: Dinin' Hall, a renovated warehouse located near downtown where food trucks can park during lunch hours. It is an old, worn-down industrial site that has been reconfigured as a place of spectacle. The facility is designed for a person to order a plate of food outside and savor it sitting down inside a climate-controlled environment (see plate 21). In addition, a person pays for food inside with cash or credit, and the food-truck proprietors bring the food to the patron's table. On Dinin' Hall's webpage (*Dinin' Hall*), the owners describe how their idea came about:

> Dinin' Hall began as a design idea trying to solve *practical* issues of eating at food trucks and carts. Tim and Eliza love to eat as much as they love to sit, and eating street food while standing has become challenging. So, they started to dream. Dinin' Hall was born, a perfect marriage of street food and casual dining experiences. It features a rotating roster of food trucks and carts and their signature items, promoting their *innovative* menus. It provides a cool dining area of industrial charm with community tables and bar seating. This is going to raise the bar for high quality, *gourmet (yet casual) street food dining, right in Columbus!* (emphasis added).

Tables, chairs, and indoor eating allow people to escape the frigid Ohio winter. When it is cold, food-truck business suffers. This indoor space provides a much-needed place for food trucks to make it through winter. But the entire concept also augments the pattern of aligning street food to middle-class Anglos' dining preferences.[3]

A "street-food dining hall" is an oxymoron. Tim and Eliza are formalizing the informal by putting street food in a contained environment. Street food originated to provide cheap and convenient foods for the proletariat to eat on the go. People are meant to eat foods on the street in impromptu spaces set up in between more permanent places. However, white, middle-class midwesterners enhance ethnic street-food practices to their comfort level. Dinin' Hall seemed to be very successful when it first opened. People appeared to like the hybridity of the space. Tables and chairs elevate street-food-truck space and expand the types of cuisines one can now order from a truck—qualities that are not very traditional to the street-food practice but are indeed more amenable to white, middle-class tastes. By programming proletarian street-food practices to conform to prim, middle-class preferences, Dinin' Hall has reappropriated and redefined food truck space.

While at Dinin' Hall, I noticed mainly white, non-Latinos eating from boutique food trucks. In many respects, it privileges middle-class Anglo customers and gourmet food truck owners. The design of Dinin' Hall's space to emulate ethnic street food in a white, middle-class manner almost guarantees that Mexican immigrant communities will be excluded in practice.

Mexican immigrants are not considered part of the creative class. They are not major consumers; rather, they are laborers, and their socioeconomic position most often places them with the landscapes of production. Mexican immigrants' daily livelihoods do not generally cross over into Anglos consumption spaces unless it is for their labor—such as to make a burrito bowl at Chipotle. Gourmet food truck spaces in many respects represent forbidden territory to many Mexican immigrant taco truck owners because they appear to them as economically unattainable and culturally distinct. It is important to emphasize that this socioeconomic blade slashes space both ways. Anglos may similarly fret going into taco truck spaces because they too seem culturally foreign from their point of view. Fortunately, in Columbus, there are some cultural translators to help non-Latinos tip their toes into taco truck spaces.

WHITE TACO TRUCK SPACE

A tour van voyages across the city of Columbus with a picture of the Italian explorer Christopher Columbus on both its sides. The visual is of Columbus with his arm outstretched, holding a fork, as if pointing toward a new world with troves of culinary treasures just waiting to be unearthed and eaten. Below the images are the words "Columbus Food Adventures. Eat. Drink. Explore." The van operates for the small company Columbus Food Adventures. For $55, a person can buy a seat on the van to discover Columbus's Latino landscapes and explore Mexican taco truck terrains. Molly Willow, a writer for *Columbus Monthly*, describes her journey into taco truck environments as both awkward and rewarding. "I was struck by how silly our van load of white people must look to the cart's Latino patrons. We were tourists in our own city, visiting eateries that helped folks feel as if they were back home. I did not expect eating tacos to be such a cultural experience" (Willow 2011). The notion that in the twenty-first century, Christopher Columbus can figuratively lead white explorers through the city of Columbus to discover ethnic foods from Mesoamerica confirms that human exploration of exotic lands has not ceased, and neither have aspects of colonialism.

Columbus Food Adventures is a business that began from a blog, *Taco Trucks in Columbus Ohio*. The blog is about the novelty of taco trucks in Columbus and the varieties of culture and cuisine they have to offer. It became so successful that the bloggers, Andy Dehus and Bethia Woolf, commenced their own culinary tour operation in 2009. They started with taco trucks but have expanded to offer a variety of food tours in the city, from low-end, ethnic cuisines to high-end, hybrid foods. They advertise their taco truck tour on their webpage by saying: "This van tour will explore the taco trucks of the west side, taking you to some of our favorites and providing you with the best of Mexican food in Columbus. . . . This unique city tour is suitable for those who have never visited a taco truck, as well as those who are looking to explore new trucks and dishes" (http://columbusfoodadventures.com).

The tour operators build a relationship with the taco truck owners before putting a taco truck on the tour's parade of stops. As Dehus explained, "We talk to the restaurants [taco trucks] before we do these tours. It is not something we foist upon them; it is something we agree on with them. We have never brought anyone into a place that did not want us to be there." Of course, taco truck owners benefit from the additional business of a van full of white folks. However, middle-class Anglos' power to assert Eurocentric views about taco truck spaces underlines the social differences between the two groups. This section is not intended to condemn the tour operation, because it does have many positive effects for Latino livelihoods. Instead, it is simply a critique that elucidates the wicked ways in which capital produces uneven relationships and contradictions between socioeconomic groups.

Pierre L. van den Berghe (1994) notes that members of homogeneous societies in the developed world often desire to explore foreign lands with remote cultures, places where peasants' livelihoods appear not yet to have been tainted by the standardizing forces of commercial globalization. Seen in such terms, culture is equated with primitive peoples. With the influx of Mexican immigrants from rural communities to Columbus, its citizens no longer need to travel to the rural jungles of Chiapas, Mexico, to encounter "authenticity." They can now visit exotic taco truck spaces in the concrete jungle within their own urban backyard.

The global forces that once homogenized Columbus's landscape are now ironically contributing to its heterogeneity. The appearance of taco trucks in Columbus is inextricably tied to globalization. The past practices of Spanish colonization continue to this day in the United States in one form or another through neoliberalism, de facto discrimination, and white privilege. Mexicans who bear the brunt of global forces search out new spaces in which to make a living, including the United States, where American Anglos come to conceive of Latino spaces as colorful places to consume. Taco trucks, then, become consumption spaces for both Latino laborers and white, middle-class consumers, albeit to fulfill completely different desires.

White privilege allows Anglos to capitalize on the cultures of ethnic groups arriving from the Global South. As Heldke (2003) maintains, aspects of colonial inequalities are bound up within Anglos' consumption of "exotic" cuisines. For Johnston and Baumann (2009), "this means realizing that a contemporary food adventurer who wanders around exploring 'exotic' cuisines is in some ways like the explorers and conquistadors who preceded colonization" (102). Indeed, the phenomenon of Anglo people visiting taco trucks as part of an expedition conjures up notions of Old World conquests of the Americas, as well as antiquated approaches in anthropology.

Columbus Food Adventures has capitalized on Mexican street-food practices and in the process has helped turn taco trucks into consumption spaces for the Anglo middle class. Heldke's (2003) take on this socioeconomic dynamic is that when middle-class Anglos eat "exotic" meals prepared by immigrants in the Global North, they are contributing to cultural colonialism. Heldke defines cultural colonialism as the manner in which Westerners superficially encounter foreign foods and use the "ethnic Other as a resource" (48). It is important to emphasize that cultural colonialism encompasses both positive and negative attributes of postcolonial relationships. The practice of driving around town to eat at taco trucks benefits taco trucks economically, but the power dynamics between Mexican immigrants and non-Latinos in Columbus allow for these sorts of imposed relationships to occur. You most likely would never witness Mexican immigrants taking a culinary tour of opulent restaurants and chic cafes as part of a cultural outing about how white people like to eat. Thus Anglos act upon Latino spaces in a unilateral direction because they can use Latino culture as a resource. In other words, Anglos can exploit ethnicity, but this relationship could never be inverted.

Dehus and Woolf gave me their take on this peculiar relationship. We discussed what made them interested in the trucks, as well as their socioeconomic relationship with the taco truck owners. They told me that both the food and the novelty of taco trucks in the Midwest attracted them, but that their interest in taco trucks was also about the experience of discovery. Dehus explained, "The trucks kind of spoke for themselves as [to] why we found them so appealing. We felt like we were finding something that almost made no sense in the context of Columbus but was completely wonderful." Woolf elaborated: "It was the food more than anything that made the trucks really fantastic, but it was more than that; it was getting out into parts of town that we never went to. It was really a *sense of exploration* and *fun*, because we really thought *we were discovering things that people did not know about*" (emphasis added). Woolf and Dehus emphasized the experience of exploring new cultural terrains. They felt that they were explorers making new expeditions into uncharted Latin American lands within Columbus. Dehus felt compelled to share his experiences by taking others on taco truck pilgrimages: "At the time we started blogging about the trucks, we thought they were really unique. It's such an atypical thing for a midwestern city, and we love letting other people experience the same surprise we had!"

Their tours teach Columbus's non-Latinos how best to engage taco truck environments. The webpage explains, "This food tour . . . includes tastings at stops, air-conditioned van transportation (to and from downtown Columbus and all stops in-between), and a guide with plenty of local culinary knowledge." An "air-conditioned" van that takes one from the city center to taco trucks evokes a level of comfort and safety while venturing into what may be considered sketchy parts of town. I was invited on one of the tours and noted that some of the customers acted wary of some of the neighborhoods they were heading into. One remarked disquietingly, when handed a map of the taco trucks' locations, "Oh, this is definitely West Side!" I should emphasize that part of the purpose of Woolf and Dehus's tour is to break down some of these negative perspectives by providing a safe and comfortable way for middle-class Anglos to interact with taco truck realms. But at the same time, they are capitalizing on the thrill of voyaging into foreign, and perhaps threatening, ethnic spaces.

Dehus emphasized that a primary component of their business was "providing a point of entry" for people who were unfamiliar with and wary about taco trucks. "There are forty trucks; they are all over town; you can read about all of them; and it still won't completely explain to you how it will be different from a restaurant experience. Anything we can do to ease the process provides a point of entry." The notion that taco truck spaces are culturally distinct from customary Anglo spaces illustrates the social boundaries that mainstream white culture draws between itself and the social other, as well as the spatial implications of those social boundaries. In a review on their blog of one of the taco trucks they'd visited, Woolf and Dehus asserted, "There is also a bit of a *sense of 'turf'* here, so if you are going to visit to appreciate the food and the culture, you may feel that you really stand out from the crowd. Do make sure you know some Spanish if you plan on doing more than ordering food to go" (emphasis added).

Dehus and Woolf define Mexican culture on their blog by pointing out distinct differences in language and culinary practices. They believe that their familiarity with traversing into taco truck environments has helped them acquire a cultural know-how that they can pass on to others. They think it is important to help other non-Latinos understand "taco truck etiquette" to reduce the social apprehensions and tensions that middle-class Americans may have when entering alluring yet intimidating taco truck spaces. Some of the advice they give is how and what to order. For example, they tell their customers that they can order as much as they want and order as they go, and that they will pay for their meal afterward. They also encourage their customers to learn a few words in Spanish so that they can order their food in a mannerly fashion by saying "hola," "por favor," and "gracias."

I asked Woolf and Dehus about their main motivation for starting a guided tour of taco trucks. Were they concerned primarily with making money off the taco truck phenomenon, or was there more to it? Dehus responded:

> It was equal parts a desire to make some money and also taking the next step in terms of taking the people to the trucks. We had kind of become evangelists, but now we were providing the opportunity to, in a sense, handhold; to take people to the trucks who may be concerned about their inability to speak Spanish or not knowing what to order. They want some help with how to approach the trucks; we were able to provide that given our experience.

Woolf and Dehus had become cultural translators. They were explaining to Anglos how Mexicans ate. Woolf added that breaking down preconceived stereotypes about the trucks being dirty or other Mexican stereotypes was also important to her: "An educational component is that we are trying to tell people that these trucks are inspected by the Health Department. We really wanted to help the trucks out, encourage people to go, and share this great experience and the food that we were having with other people." White privilege and capitalism certainly produce incongruities and ambiguities. While Woolf and Dehus take Anglos to taco trucks to try foreign cuisines, they do so by unwittingly taking advantage of an economic position that's higher than that of the taco truck owners. However, through this process, they are teaching the Anglo community that taco trucks are safe places to eat at and that Mexicans are hardworking people who are just trying to make a living in the United States. In this way, Dehus and Woolf are positively contributing to the acceptance of Mexican immigrants and their practices in the Midwest.

Taking a van of well-educated, middle-class non-Latinos to taco trucks to eat "authentic" foods situates Mexican cuisine at the center of the discourse around Mexican immigrants. For middle-class Anglos, eating Mexican immigrant cuisines can elucidate the socioeconomic differences between themselves and the people cooking their food. The taco is a signifier of myriad meanings. The taco originated for the proletariat. People who typically eat tacos and Mexican street food on a regular basis do so because they cannot afford alternatives. When the taco crosses over into a more affluent social sphere, its meanings change. This poses a challenging question about class and ethnicity: why would educated whites be interested in eating a disadvantaged Mexican's street food—especially tacos made from beef intestines, brains, and tongue? Drawing upon contemporary social theories, Johnston and Baumann (2009) suggest, "In the omnivorous era . . . high status is signaled by selectively drawing on multiple forms from across the cultural hierarchy" (35). Sampling "exotic" foods demonstrates one's social status—in this case, one's status as an adventurous Anglo unafraid of eating an immigrant's bizarre, spicy foods.

Willow, in her *Columbus Monthly* article, discusses eating a beef taco made from the head of a cow: "I knew enough Spanish to understand what *cabeza* (head) meant when I was handed a beef taco in a parking lot somewhere on the west side a few weeks ago. . . . I wasn't about to be an unadventurous *gringa* (white woman). As it turns out, cabeza is delicious" (Willow 2011). Here, the taco, which is traditionally associated with the food practices of the Mexican day laborer, is now a marker of an Anglo middle-class individual's willingness to try new things. In eating the taco, she is using her privilege to expand her cultural boundaries. According to bell hooks (1992), such practices of "eating the ethnic Other" make middle-class Anglos more worldly and advance their social status. Of course, the symbolism of middle-class Anglo Americans eating working-class Mexican cuisine extends well beyond the perception of food as a status symbol. To many, it is simply an opportunity to eat good food while learning about the culture of a group of people who contribute to the workings of the city.

I asked Dehus and Woolf if they felt that their tour objectified Latinos instead of helping their clients comprehend the complex circumstances that had driven Mexicans to the United States. Dehus surmised, "From the customer side I don't think it is intellectualized in such a manner." Woolf said that the majority of comments they received from people who participated in the taco truck tour indicated amazement at the ethnic diversity throughout the city. "The one comment I hear the most from our customers, and I hear it the most when we go to the market, is that 'I feel like a tourist in my own town.' Or 'I never knew this was here. . . . ' I feel like people are really interested in learning, and I don't feel like it is an issue with objectifying."

When I observed a tour firsthand, I noticed that the tourists were very respectful and genuinely inquisitive. As Dehus pointed out, the tourists were not interested in "intellectualizing" social relationships. For the most part, they were engrossed in tasting new flavors and enjoying themselves. They learned a little about Mexican food but not much beyond that. Their class privilege allowed them to descend upon taco truck space but only to appreciate it as a novel phenomenon. Willow notes a few things she learned about Mexican culinary culture: "It's one thing to have the vague idea that, according to the 2010 Census, there are 56,000 Latino residents of Franklin County [of which Columbus is the county seat] . . . and entirely another to realize the most I know about their local culture is which Mexican grocery has the hot sauce I like" (Willow 2011). After having been chauffeured between taco trucks, Willow's enhanced understanding of Mexican society in Columbus was limited to a salsa, although she was now more aware of how much more there was for her to learn. While the taco truck tours broke down socioeconomic boundaries, they simultaneously reinforced them.

= = =

On May 5, 2014, "Cinco de Mayo," Columbus Commons had its first taco truck festival. The park featured four or five traditional taco trucks. The event's success was fair. According to taco truck owners, the turnout was small because of inclement weather. This special celebration for taco trucks illustrated the city's commitment to incorporating taco trucks into the city's central consumption spaces. In fact, taco truck owners told me they appreciated the effort but at the same time felt objectified by the Anglo middle class. It is humorous to note that May 5, Cinco de Mayo, is not a holiday celebrated throughout Mexico, except in Puebla. Here again, an Anglo-American perspective frames Mexican culture.

Creating a special event just for taco trucks contributed to the sense that taco trucks were different from other food trucks. Middle-class Anglos define taco trucks simply as trucks selling tacos prepared by Mexicans. Placing all the taco trucks together for a one-day, extraordinary extravaganza reframed taco trucks as singularly foreign. Many taco truck owners divulged to me their sentiments. They said that middle-class white people do not really appreciate them for their cooking skills like they appreciate gourmet food trucks. Instead Anglos like Mexican cuisines for the "authentic" exotic culture Mexicans represent. White privilege allows Anglos to enjoy and appreciate a foreign people and their exotic cuisines and at the same time allows them to reflexively interpret Mexican culture as static, alien, and consequently subsidiary to mainstream white culture.

White privilege is a complicated concept, but by carefully evaluating white spaces as distinct from Latino spaces, we can assess the ways the city uses ethnicity to assert itself. In Columbus, white privilege has minimally benefited taco trucks economically, while the city at large has profited from their image and their doppelgängers—the boutique food trucks. Food trucks in Columbus carry two different symbolic meanings: for whites the trucks are markers for multiculturalism, while for Latino immigrants they are emblematic of a culturally established and economically essential practice.

Gourmet food trucks, which have innocently plagiarized taco truck practices, have swamped Columbus's central consumption spaces. In this assertive way, middle-class Anglos significantly contribute to expressing the city's form through their privilege. In doing so, they bifurcate social space by the ways in which they consume the city's central spaces as well as by moving out to live in affluent suburbs. Latinos are consequently circumscribed by the city's in-between spaces. But this does not mean Latinos do not have agency to shape the city to their desires: while taco trucks may not be omnipresent in Columbus's city center, they are pervasive throughout other parts of the city.

Columbus presents itself as a city that embraces diversity, but the circuits of capital have not enabled the city to realize its noble vision. The notion of a "smart and open city" as a capital-accumulating strategy has produced a conundrum—one in which capitalism continues to segregate spaces. In fact, the contriving of Columbus's central public spaces for consumption practices only aggravates the city's socioeconomic development. Urban priorities are not in favor of immigrants who contribute to the city's economy through their low-wage labor. Rather, the city's boosters prioritize investing in a visual lifestyle designed to accumulate ever more capital while they overlook different ways that these visual effects affect members of the city's different social classes and ethnicities. Of course, one could reason that Columbus's marketing campaign is enabling city boosters to attract additional dollars and create jobs for everyone, including the Latino community. I do not argue against this point: the intent of this chapter was not to denounce this strategy as ineffective but rather to demonstrate the ways in which white privilege influences monetary flows in a city.

This chapter focused on white privilege as an unconventional framework we can use to understand how the ensconced class and capital processes led to the development of two different food truck spaces. In chapter 7, I evaluate taco truck owners' spatial narratives. Middle-class Anglo practices certainly influence where taco trucks typically are not, but there are also many other political and socioeconomic processes throughout the city that influence Latino landscapes and the livelihoods of taco truck owners. It is evident that taco trucks are vacant from many of the city's central public spaces of consumption, but it is important to emphasize that they are still welcomed and included within the city's limits. And while white privilege helped paint part of the picture, we must also consider taco truck owners' life circumstances and spatial practices to draw fuller conclusions about how well taco trucks are integrated into Columbus.

CHAPTER 7

FOOD, FEAR, AND DREAMS

An Immigration and Customs Enforcement (ICE) truck sits outside an apartment building on Columbus's west side. ICE's raison d'être is to round up undocumented residents for deportation. While the ICE truck lurks just outside the complex, many undocumented Latinos remain in their residences. They do not go to work. Their children do not go to school. Another ICE truck lingers around Mexican markets and along streets where several taco trucks usually park. The presence of the ICE trucks puts the livelihoods of taco truck owners in jeopardy. One taco truck owner remarked that because of these random immigration sweeps, "to go out to eat at a taco truck is like playing Russian roulette." While grabbing a few tacos from a truck on a neighborhood sidewalk may seem like a humdrum activity, for undocumented immigrants in Columbus, Ohio, just walking on the sidewalk near taco trucks is a perilous and unnerving practice. Franklin County, with Columbus as the county seat, ranks seventeenth in the United States for the number of deportations of "illegal" immigrants who have not committed any crime within the United States (U.S. Immigration and Customs Enforcement 2012).[1]

Many of these Mexican immigrants yearn to become economically independent and gain U.S. citizenship. However, because there is no pathway to citizenship for these immigrants, the majority of the more than thirty Mexican taco truck owners and customers I interviewed live in a legal and spatial limbo. Their undocumented status is criminalized and their cultural behavior is portrayed by some as suspect. ICE profiles Latino immigrants based on the places they live, the stores where they shop, and the ways in which they move between and within such spaces and places. The fear of deportation mortifies and immobilizes many of the Mexican immigrants. These cat-and-mouse games between ICE and undocumented migrants continuously reshuffle social spaces in these Columbus neighborhoods. Many of the Latino immigrants resettle in various districts throughout the city, and so, too, do traditional taco trucks. The taco trucks' mobility becomes a spatial strategy for responding to the political pressures exerted on the Latino population. As the taco truck owners relocate, their trucks' cultural customs hybridize, incorporating influences from their newfound social spaces while shaping a community's social practices.

In this chapter I evaluate the spatial practices of taco trucks in Columbus by considering the city as psychological space. The chapter is an examination of the power of dreams and fear to shape taco truck owners' spatial decision-making and by extension their social practices and landscape patterns. Aspirations motivate. Fear immobilizes. According to Tuan (2013), fear can affect the way a person experiences a city and, ultimately, the daily decisions a person makes as he or she navigates an urban environment. Similarly, Pile (2005) posits that the city is psychological—that the urban experience extends beyond the tangible to our unconscious, emotional state. Pile suggests that the city is composed of dreams that connect the personal to the social: "Cities are like dreams, then, both because they conceal secret desires and fears and also because they are produced according to hidden rules that are only vaguely discernible in their future appearances" (28). Thus, fear and aspirational dreams act as opposing forces that influence one's actions and routines, which socially structure urban space in imperceptible ways.

ICE: CITY OF FEAR

The recent wave of Mexican immigration to Ohio began in the mid-1990s. In the early 1990s there were no grocery stores or businesses that catered directly to the Mexican community in Columbus. The culinary aspect of Mexican identity first began to develop as an informal commercial practice. Koki Garcia explained how her family started selling foodstuffs on the city's west side: "We actually noticed a big spike in the Mexican population around 1994 and 1995. At the time we lived in Detroit, but we would fill up the van with Mexican food products and come here and sell them. And little by little, stores started popping up and then my dad decided that this is where we wanted to start a tortilla factory." Rather than a capitalist market system shaping cultural consumption patterns, this is an example of the inverse scenario: an informal marketplace responding to cultural culinary demands. This marketplace first began with families driving from Detroit or Chicago with Mexican foodstuffs to peddle their products from the tailgates of trucks in vacant parking lots.

Another family I spoke with in June 2012, the Salazars, who own the largest Mexican market in Columbus—La Plaza Tapatía Supermarket—recounted a similar way of launching their business. Gustavo Salazar once drove a truck loaded with Mexican produce from Columbus to Chicago and back every three days.[2] Eventually he earned enough money to buy a three-ton truck, and then enough to open a store.

In addition to these two major culinary establishments, Mexicans and other Latinos began to make food to sell informally. In fact, several of the taco truck owners I met started saving up for a truck by peddling tamales door-to-door. On any given day at La Plaza Tapatía market, you can find multiple vendors hawking numerous Latin American cuisines, such as tamales, gorditas, and empanadas, from the trunks of their cars. As Mexicans and other Latinos began to make money from informal food vending, they invested in trucks.

I asked Lidia Flores, owner of Little Mexico, how she derived the idea to establish the first taco truck in Columbus. She said that she lived in Los Angeles, California, in the 1990s and when she and her family moved to Columbus in 2001, her husband had the idea of bringing the California taco truck to Columbus. Evidently the concept caught on rapidly among the Latino population.

Almost all of the other taco truck owners seemed befuddled by the question of where their idea to operate a taco truck originated. I realized that the question seemed highly illogical from their way of seeing their own culture. Only a few owners told me they saw other taco trucks and thought it seemed like a good idea; most truck owners revealed that there really was no conscious decision to copy a taco-truck-style operation; it was just something they did intuitively or reflexively.

Many described the process of acquiring a truck as if it were innately ingrained in their human psyche. One of the truck owners, Alejandra Hernandez of the truck San Luis Viejo, whom I interviewed many times from 2012 to 2013, maintained that even if there were no other taco trucks in the city, and she had never seen one before in her life, she still would have come up with the idea on her own. She explained, "I was selling tamales door-to-door and my dream was to have a truck. That is what you do: you sell food until you find a better way to sell food. Even if I'd never seen a food truck before, I would have started one."[3] I asked Alejandra, "You wouldn't just keep selling door-to-door until you could afford a restaurant? And why would it be specifically a truck—why not a push cart?" She hesitated for a moment with a long "hmmmm" and then balked: "No, I would have found a way to start selling my food on a street corner, and a truck would be the logical solution here in the United States."

It is intriguing to note that traditional taco trucks are spatially diffusing eastward from California. In other words, the spread of taco trucks and culinary practices coincides with the eastward migration of Mexicans. Ideas are disseminating, and as Mexicans move east, they are discovering and realizing new spaces of economic opportunity by satisfying cultural and culinary cravings.

Local spatiality underlies the informal practices of these incremental businesses. The taco truck owners first set up shop in parking lots along arterial roads in the Greater Hilltop Area, where there is a high volume of automotive traffic. They also parked near apartment complexes with a large number of Latino residents, money exchanges, and laundromats. These were locations that received a lot of foot traffic—spots that most Mexicans could easily see and walk to. The number of trucks multiplied, especially along West Broad Street, Georgesville Road, and Sullivant Avenue. Based on a windshield survey I conducted, I estimated that there were twenty trucks in this area of city between 2004 and 2006. The trucks began to transform the urban order both physically and socially. Not only were the trucks symbolic of the Mexican population's fluctuating status, they were also activating urban space through the social practices associated with eating at the trucks. The trucks contributed to the creation of Latino social rhythms within the Greater Hilltop Area, which helped demarcate this area of the city as an emerging barrio.

Most of the Mexican and other Latino residents moving to the Greater Hilltop Area did not have their own transportation, at least not at first. In most cases, Latino immigrants relied on their social capital or the city's public transit system to move around the city. Most immigrants in this area depended on relatives or friends to drive them to a construction site, factory, or a landscaping job. Those working daily in the service industry, as dishwashers or housekeepers, for example, often relied on the bus system. When Latinos were not carpooling or taking the bus to or from work, they traversed the neighborhood by foot and bike, usually going to taco trucks to eat and/or socialize. The streetscapes were being transformed through Latino social practices, which came to represent Mexican immigrant culture.

The emergence of taco trucks in the neighborhood influenced the trajectories of people and became associated with such movements. This is to say that taco trucks not only created landscape patterns but also manipulated mobility practices and helped to render them visible. Here, *place* is understood through mobility practices: knowing a place by its social pulse—rhythms punctuated by speed and pauses—rather than just by its locale. As Cresswell (1996) asserts, social practices define place. And so Latino social practices redefined the West Side's cultural landscape.

Cresswell has shown that the manner in which a person moves has political implications: "The way people are enabled or constrained in terms of their mobile practices differs markedly according to their position in social hierarchies" (199). In myriad ways, Mexican immigrants' movements came to define their place in Columbus, which proved problematic when the barrioization of the Greater Hilltop Area became a focus of attention for ICE's sweeps.

The practice of immigrants eating tacos from trucks superimposed over a car-oriented and car-dominant environment is an example of a transposed social order. Latino behavior amid an American-built environment appears odd to the Eurocentric eye. Eating at taco trucks or simply walking and bicycling while brown along a commercial strip becomes suspicious behavior in the eyes of ICE.

The places ICE frequents are not based solely on a list of "known illegals" who live in a particular apartment complex but rather on the presence of Latino practices within what was previously a standard American suburb. Medium- to high-density living spaces associated with dark-skinned Mexicans biking, walking, carpooling, and standing at trucks taking bites of tacos in barren parking lots are not representative of Ohio's established white, middle-class social order. For an undocumented Mexican immigrant innocently cycling down the street for a taco or torta, this performance might be his or her return "ticket" to Mexico.

ICE is not authorized to arrest undocumented workers at its whim; the agency is only empowered to detain undocumented individuals who have a criminal record.[4] However, the stories I heard within the Mexican community suggest that ICE's practices may stretch beyond their official mandate. If nothing else, their intimidating presence plays an unshakeable role in how immigrants view the viability of occupying public and semi-public spaces on a regular basis. When I spoke with Ricardo Diaz, the owner of Tacos Ricos taco truck, in September 2012, he pointed to an ICE truck prowling through the neighborhood as I interviewed him. He remarked, "Fucking ICE, scaring my customers away."[5] When I asked whether they drove by regularly, Ricardo exclaimed: "They drive up and down the street all the time. This is the third time I've seen them today." I then asked him what exactly they were doing. He joked, "Well, they aren't bringing me any ice to my taco truck." I asked if ICE agents had ever stopped at his truck. He conceded that they had not, but he said that their constant presence was sufficient to deter Mexicans from frequenting his truck, and it was hindering his business.

As I conversed with Mexican immigrants in the city of Columbus, the issue of ICE quickly became a reoccurring theme. Mexicans refer to ICE officers in Spanish as *el hielo*, the Spanish word for "ice." Lauren Hines (2013), who wrote her geography master's thesis from Ohio State University on ICE's controversial practices, reported similar stories:

> ICE agents present an unpredictable and impending threat; they may suddenly appear to question migrants and confirm their right to exist in the country. In southwest Columbus, this possibility has discouraged migrant parents from opening their front door to let their children catch the school bus. Foreseeable interaction with law enforcement also causes anxiety-based insecurity in Columbus migrant communities. (42)

These are the types of stories I heard all too frequently. Many narratives involved an ICE truck sitting and agents waiting outside apartment complexes, thereby terrifying people and preventing them from leaving their residences for weeks on end. Other stories were about ICE patrolling taco trucks and Mexican markets. ICE was an immobilizer of Latino space, figuratively freezing their spatial practices for days and weeks at a time. Koki Garcia described how ICE's routine patrols affected her business: "Right now we sell [tortillas] to restaurants and stores. Now if there are any rumors at all that immigration [ICE] has been to any of the Mexican stores, the sales do drop. They drop drastically! I'd say at least a week [passes] before the rumors die down and people start going out again to the stores."

Alejandra Hernandez, owner of San Luis Viejo taco truck, recalled one such terrifying experience she had while shopping in the West Side neighborhood:

> I was parked at Tapatía Mexican Market. Thank God, and I don't know why they [ICE] did not capture me. They came from behind me and closed in. I saw them come out from two streets. They tried to herd us all together. One hand just missed my back. I went to another parking lot with my legs completely trembling. I called my daughter to come get me because I couldn't drive because I was so scared!

After this close call, Alejandra became too petrified to continue living and operating her taco truck on Columbus's west side, so she moved—along with her truck—to an all-black neighborhood just east of downtown.

The threat of ICE drove Mexican immigrants in general, and taco truck owners in particular, to modify their movements in order to evade ICE's looming presence. Mexican immigrants had to learn how to outmaneuver ICE while at the same time continuing to interact with other Mexican immigrants for socioeconomic purposes. The ingenuity of the taco truck is that due to its inherent mobility, it can socially reconfigure space as needed. When ICE beefed up their presence in the Greater Hilltop Area, Latinos began to disperse throughout the city, and so did the taco trucks. Alejandra Hernandez's habitual movements, even though she is now located on the east side, are still deeply affected by ICE's slinking around the West Side: "In order to buy my things, I still have to go to the west side of town because that's where all the Mexican stores are. But I try to go as little as possible. For example I needed lots of groceries today, but because of my experience with ICE, I prefer to be missing lots of things before I go to the store, and not go all the time."

Taco truck owners—desperate to keep their businesses afloat—drove to different locales, reconfigured their positions in parking lots, modified their menus, or combined several of these actions. Seen in this way, Columbus's social spaces and political pressures influenced mobility and culinary practices. This is made evident by the ways in which taco truck owners altered their traditional Mexican recipes to appease people in their newfound neighborhoods.

TASTE, SPACE, AND THE TACO TRUCK

> In Mexico, food varies from one state to another. You have people coming from the North and South of Mexico to Columbus. So the taco trucks are not only educating Americans but also Mexicans about various regions of Mexican foods. People from Oaxaca who have never visited Michoacán now can go to a taco truck from Michoacán and experience food from Michoacán and talk with *michoacanos*. When you go around to different taco trucks, one thing is you go around to identify with people from your community, second of all, it's like you're visiting different states of Mexico, here in Columbus.
>
> —Josué Vicente, president of the Ohio Hispanic Coalition

In Mexico, the practice of cooking and eating street tacos blends in with the traffic congestion, air pollution, and the rhythms of the industrial city. The traditional taco that is often associated with taco trucks in the United States is still a prevalent culinary item in industrial regions throughout Mexico, especially Mexico City. The cuisines served at taco trucks operated by Latino immigrants in U.S. cities reflect regional migration patterns. Most taco trucks in California and Texas—states associated with migration from northern and central Mexican industrial states—primarily serve tacos and the occasional San Francisco Mission–style burrito. In contrast, many of the trucks' owners in Columbus serve cuisines that reflect more recent migration patterns, which are not always associated with urban industrial populations but also include rural populations with more traditional livelihoods. In addition, even the taco trucks that sell the food of industrial areas, such as Mexico City, reflect more recent working-class culinary practices in Mexico. Consequently, in Columbus, taco truck owners seldom serve just tacos.

The taco trucks in Columbus sell a wider assortment of Mexican foods than the trucks in any other city in the United States that I have come across. I estimate that the trucks in Columbus represent cuisines from at least fifteen states in Mexico. Further, there are several trucks from the same state but different cities, as well as from distinctive districts within Mexico City. There are also many taco truck owners who serve regional specialties from more than one city or state in Mexico.

Taco truck space takes on a diversity of configurations of places and times. There are two levels of mobility embedded in the trucks. The first level is migration across geographic distance: taco truck owners have migrated more than two thousand miles from Mexico. The second level of mobility consists of the truck's wheels, which allow them to shift spaces socially and thus create places. And although the trucks exude robust mobility, most remain parked in a single spot for several years before moving without notice to another location. There is no single reason a taco truck owner will move, but remaining in business is the primary motive.[6]

The truck owners' place of origin is almost always represented in the cuisine. Although the foods that the taqueros serve are often predictable and reflect a particular culinary region of Mexico, the truck owners will modify the menu to accommodate variations in taste preferences from one neighborhood to another. To be sure, taco truck owners learn to adapt their foods to any given community across an urban environment (Lemon 2016). Various scales of space, relationships with places, and aspects of mobility are found in Columbus's taco truck network—the trucks' menus continuously reflect these entangled topological webs.

In this section I examine the ways in which taco trucks' cuisine changes, depending on the social spaces within which they park (see plate 22). Not only do the taco trucks' menus represent diverse culinary regions of Mexico, but the trucks' social spheres also intersect with various cultural and political processes in Columbus to create new food geographies. Each truck has a unique story behind its evolving culinary practices. Aspects of immigration, entrepreneurship, and gender all affect the ways in which taqueros cook. This section highlights not only how taco truck spaces reconnect immigrants to Mexico through taste but also how they develop and retrofit themselves into Columbus's diverse communities.

Taco trucks' menus most often reflect a place of origin in order to evoke a sense of place among the Mexican immigrant clientele. Mostly notably, the taco trucks are often named after places in Mexico. The Los Chilangos truck (see plate 23) is an example of this type of geographic referencing. *Chilangos* is a colloquial term used to denote a person from Mexico City. Not surprisingly, Juan Soto Cabrera, the owner of the truck, offers Mexico City–style tortas.

Juan's truck is primarily known for its tortas, and his menu includes twenty-two different types of tortas. For example, customers can purchase a DF torta, which comes with "milanesa, pierna y chuleta" (thin layers of steak, pork leg, and pork chop). Each combination has its own name, and the combinations and names continuously change to reflect the current culinary trends in Mexico City. By adopting this dynamic approach to making Mexican food, Juan ensures that his menu bridges the distance between his truck and Mexico City. This is a critical aspect of his operation.

The names and combinations of tortas are constantly evolving in Mexico City, and Juan modifies his menu on a monthly basis to reflect the city's culinary changes. Juan calls his family in Colonia Tacuba once a month to find out about new torta adaptations and their names. He explained that while several types of sandwiches are staples, such as the DF and the Cubana, people who make tortas are frequently experimenting and trying new variations. He noted that the assortment of tortas at any given time in Mexico City is never the same. If there is a new type of torta in Mexico City, Juan adds it to his menu. I asked him whether it matters that his menu reflects Mexico City's torta scene since he is so far away from Mexico City and its culinary practices. He emphasized that it is important because people from Mexico City, who now reside in Columbus, want to feel like they are still culturally connected to Mexico City, and they can maintain this link by trying a flavor combination that has recently become popular in Mexico City. For Mexicans eating their tortas at Los Chilangos, the recurring modifications to the menu make them feel as if they are still partaking in an urban environment from which they are two thousand miles removed. Taco truck spaces not only inspire memories of Mexico, they also create a current and dynamic link to Mexico City's cultural milieu.

Juan and his food truck are still very much connected to Mexico City's torta enterprise. In fact, most torta truck owners I encountered across the country offered similar renditions of Juan's story. They said that they frequently call family in Mexico City to track the city's torta trends. Culinary practices as they relate to places of origin are integral to the ways in which taco truck spaces function socially.

Gender practices are yet another example of how place-based practices from Mexico are transferred to Columbus. Based on my observations, taco truck owners are 60 percent male and 40 percent female. Women who own and operate a taco truck gained their knowledge of culinary customs in their childhoods while cooking with family members, mostly their mothers. For men, learning to cook had occurred primarily in work-related contexts. Mexican men operating food trucks had either learned to cook from their fathers and/or uncles in Mexico while serving street tacos, or from working in the food industry in Columbus. The culinary spaces associated with gendered practices vary. Men traditionally make tacos, tortas, and other Mexican-style street food, while women typically prepare foods that are served on a plate, such as tamales, enchiladas, or chiles rellenos. These gender differences in cooking often become more evident in taco truck spaces.

Several of the trucks in Columbus are owned and operated by married couples. Most of these couples met in the United States and are from different regions of Mexico. Many are not legally married but refer to each other as husband and wife. The couples use their personal knowledge of cuisines from Mexico to contribute to the diversity and uniqueness of the menu. These relationships typically lead to the fusion of two divergent Mexican culinary regions and/or traditions. I explore two particular taco trucks owned and operated by Mexican immigrant couples, El Tizoncito and El Buen Sazón (see plates 24 and 25).

El Tizoncito is a popular al pastor truck located on the northeast side of Columbus.[7] Roberto Torres and his wife, Martina Rojas, operate the truck. Roberto once worked in Colonia Condesa at the brick-and-mortar restaurant El Tizoncito, where he learned to make the original tacos al pastor. His wife adds regional variation to the menu by offering her family recipes. Martina told me that she makes Puebla-style tamales (tamales poblanos) during the winter. Puebla-style tamales are made with poblano peppers and a dark, tart, chocolate mole that coats the inside of the masa (dough). Martina then stuffs them with pulled pork. This particular combination distinguishes Puebla-style tamales from other cornhusk tamales throughout Mexico. Martina also makes pozole, a pre-Columbian Aztec stew common throughout central Mexico. Additionally, she makes sopes and menudo, two other items not typically served at taco trucks.

In Mexico City, it is common for men to make and sell tacos on the street and for women to sell family-style plates in kitchen spaces within markets or to prepare foods at home and then sell them from a basket. Of course this is not always the case, but this division does tend to define gendered culinary practices throughout Mexico City. Having access to a kitchen allows a vendor to make more diverse cuisines than operating from a comal on the street.[8] Interestingly, taco truck space seems to be able to accommodate both practices.

Salvador Navarro and his wife are from Mexico City and operate a taco truck called El Buen Sazón. Salvador proudly told me that he was originally a street food vendor in Mexico City, where he had his own taco pushcart equipped with a comal. He used to make and sell Jalisco-style birria tacos at the Montezuma and Tacubaya Metro stops. He explained that he set up shop on the sidewalks just outside the exits to these stations. Birria is traditionally a goat or lamb stew. It originated in Guadalajara, Jalisco, but is also popular throughout a few districts in Mexico City that are home to large groups of migrants from Guadalajara. Thus, birria is an established culinary practice in both cities. Salvador explained that he normally serves birria tacos, but he also learned to branch out and make other types, such as steak and pork tacos, while in Mexico City.

Salvador cooks street-style foods, and his wife prepares more traditional sit-down fare that is often found in Mexico City markets. He explained that his mother-in-law had a kitchen stall in a market in Mexico City, where his wife worked growing up. There she learned to cook family specialties such as enchiladas infused with habanero sauce, sopes, gorditas, bistec, and chiles rellenos. A few of these items are offered at the couple's truck. Salvador and his wife work well together, each preparing their own specialties. Because they offer both street and market foods, they have augmented the truck with a bar and added barstools. Their taco truck space marries aspects of both street and market culinary practices through a male-female relationship.

Men who did not acquire cooking skills in Mexico learned while working in the restaurant industry in Columbus. Ricardo, the owner of Tacos Ricos, has lived in Ohio for the past twelve years. He migrated to Ohio from Oaxaca, Oaxaca, via Mexico City. When he arrived in Columbus, he first worked as a dishwasher and then a line cook at corporate restaurant chains, such as Red Lobster, Romano's Macaroni Grill, and Olive Garden. He mostly learned to cook American-Italian food for chain restaurants and found he really enjoyed cooking. He divulged that his aspiration as a line cook was to become his own boss. So he saved $12,500 and renovated a truck with a kitchen and grill. He has been operating the truck for eight years. For the better part of this time he has been serving tacos. Recently he has begun to branch out and offer more traditional specialties, such a tlayudas and Oaxacan ice cream. I asked Ricardo how he began creating traditional Mexican cuisines. He explained that because he did not cook when he lived in Mexico, he had to call his mother and grandmother in Oaxaca and ask them how to prepare certain culinary delights such as the tlayudas. For most foods, however, he researched recipes on the internet. He added that he liked to be creative and invent his own dishes by experimenting with ingredients. He often combines techniques he learned from cooking at chain restaurants with his online research and his mother's recipes. His flavors are Mexican inspired, but Ricardo said he works on crafting meals that will attract a variety of people to his truck, Mexicans and Americans alike.

Location and visibility affect taco truck space in unanticipated ways. Unlike El Tizoncito and El Buen Sazón, which are located in the northeast part of the city, Tacos Ricos remains parked on Columbus's west side, where ICE continually roams. Because of his location, Ricardo has felt pressured to make more "Americanized meals," as he must rely on Anglo clientele since many Mexican immigrants have moved away from the area or are simply too frightened to frequent his truck.

Ricardo realized that most Americans ask for sour cream, lettuce, tomato, and cheese, and that they do not like their tacos with just onion and cilantro. To appease the American Anglo palate, he added "American Style" (or "Taco Bell Style" as he calls it) to his menu as a "gringo" option. "As long as the person pays me, I'll make it any way they want it," he exclaimed. In addition to offering two types of tacos, he added other items, such as seafood lasagna. Ricardo acknowledged that he would like to offer more Italian dishes as well as seafood plates, because he had observed that both Americans and Mexicans like these sorts of cuisines. Over the two years I visited Tacos Ricos, many Italian and seafood items came and went. For example, the seafood lasagna was a short-lived offering; it was too difficult to make on a regular basis, and not enough people were ordering it. Regardless, there is almost always a novelty dish on the menu. Unlike the truck owners on the East Side who reflexively reiterate traditional culinary practices, Ricardo must actively modify his menu to maintain a clientele. His only other option would be to move his truck to another neighborhood. Tacos Ricos and the other aforementioned traditional taco trucks in Columbus are predominantly sedentary, and the areas of the city in which they parked proved to inspire their menu in unexpected ways. In addition, continuous mobility between the divergent districts of Columbus has a significant impact on space, cuisine, and culture, because a truck's social sphere must continually merge into the city's diverse demographics.

Lisa and Luis Gutiérrez are a mixed-race couple who own a traditional taco truck, Dos Hermanos. Lisa is a black woman from Boston, and her husband is from Benito Juárez, Oaxaca.[9] Of all the trucks I studied, their truck epitomizes the most dynamic relationship between mobility and culinary practices. For

Lisa and Luis, mobility is at the heart of their business model. The truck has a permanent evening location in northeast Columbus, from 4:00 P.M. until midnight. During the day, the truck moves throughout the city to more affluent Anglo spaces, such as the designated food truck dining hall, Columbus Commons, and food truck events.

Lisa said in a May 2013 interview that to increase sales, she had to be mobile.[10] She explained that during the day the operation must move to take advantage of other avenues of capital (see plate 26). There were not enough Latinos frequenting the truck in the Latino district where they were trying to base the business. In addition, she needed to find places to park the truck where people could eat inside during inclement weather. In order to do this, she started participating in the Columbus Dinin' Hall and food truck festivals. The food truck events and spaces are located throughout more affluent areas of the city.

Lisa emphasized that her heightened mobility (relative to other traditional taco trucks) is possible because of her American citizenship, her fluency in English, and her inherent familiarity with American customs. Because of her knowledge of how American social spaces flow, she is better able to navigate Columbus's urban landscape, which gives her a spatial advantage over her competition. Lisa clarified,

> I think having American citizenship status is critical in this business as far as being mobile. That is why a lot of taquerías [taco trucks] are not mobile. I think maybe not having a valid driver's license, the fear of being on the road with your entire business with you and possibly being pulled over, or deported, and things that come with that situation puts *fear* in people. And I think that's why in the food trucking you don't see a lot of traditional taquerías [taco trucks] moving. That's why they are just sitting on private lots and building a customer base that way.

For Mexican migrants, minimal mobility becomes comfortable as they build familiarity with particular places in Columbus. Likewise, heightened mobility and unfamiliar spaces become associated with worry and discomfort. Ironically, it is the economic hardships of one's place in Mexico that impel one to search for prosperity in the United States. But once in the United States, the scale, type, and experience of mobility is constrained by the reality of life as an undocumented worker in an American city. The truck's mobility is therefore reliant on Lisa's citizenship, her knowledge of Columbus, and her ability to speak English. Lisa elaborated on how fluency in English eases a person's navigation of Columbus's cultural terrain.

> I think the language is huge. It is going to the banks to prepare for the day. You have got to be business-minded to be on the road. There are some things that

occur. I mean, we showed up here with a broken gas line before. You have got to be able to run out and get that fixed. And get ready to serve people. You have got to be comfortable. And I think that not knowing the language, that comfort level isn't there.

Lisa also confided that being a black woman operating a traditional taco truck could be problematic because of the social and culinary context. She noted that the sight of a black woman working at the truck might have actually deterred Mexicans from eating at her establishment: "I would see Mexicans pull up and see me at the window, and they would drive away. Perhaps they thought that a black woman operating a truck meant that the food was not truly Mexican. And being authentic is very important to our operation." Because of this, Lisa works the truck during the day in the city center and her husband operates the truck at night for their Mexican clientele. Their experience shows that race and ethnicity contribute to the ways in which patrons perceive food practices.

Cultural knowledge of culinary practices and taste preferences is essential for Lisa's economic survival. Lisa has come to understand that Anglos and Mexican immigrants have distinctive palates and thus taste preferences. As a business-savvy woman, Lisa has learned to modify her menu to cater to the various cultural predilections found throughout Columbus. In other words, Lisa understands that culinary practices are sociospatially contingent.

Lisa showed me a calendar that lists where she will move for lunch during the day (see plate 27). The calendar is a map—each day is a different place, a different space that she must socially maneuver with her truck. The truck's menu must be modified to its locale. When the truck is downtown, it operates with an English menu and serves more Americanized cuisines. The prices are also a bit more expensive due to the extra costs of paying for fuel and the commissary fees. During the evenings, the truck posts its menu in Spanish and serves more traditional Mexican regional specialties. Lisa explained:

> We want to be competitive with the other trucks, so we often have different specials at night for our Mexican clientele. But during the day when selling around the city center to primarily white people, I make sure I have more sour cream, cheese, lettuce, and tomato on hand because when we do get out during the day, that's what people are looking for. They are a little bit reluctant about the traditional onion and cilantro. They are looking for what they would perceive as a taco, with lettuce, tomato, cheese, and sour cream.

Lisa and Luis have struck a balance of marketing cuisines to Mexicans and Americans through spatial versatility—that is, the truck's movements are based on particular social behaviors at certain times throughout the city. The truck's mobility allows Lisa and Luis to navigate multiple social spaces, which contributes to the truck's cultural practice. Moreover, the couple's divergent origins of place are integrated into the truck's mobility. Having a duality of cultural regions embodied in a singular vessel not only eases the truck's mobility but also makes mobility a necessity. The truck's economic survival becomes reliant on crossing the boundaries of cultural practices that are contingent not on perimeters but on performances.

Culinary practices, when examined in the context of mobility and social space, certainly paint a complex picture. However, these involved and idiosyncratic processes highlight the ways in which cuisine culture is intricately interwoven within social spaces. In addition, these culinary spatial processes underscore the ways in which cuisines evolve and are continually socially constructed. In the next section, by examining the ways in which an African American community reacts to a taco truck parked in their district, I further explore how a taco truck's culinary space culturally unfolds into a neighborhood. In so doing, I argue that through culinary practices, taco trucks can become almost sacred spaces to communities other than Mexican.

BLACK TACO TRUCK SPACE

The San Luis Viejo truck is named after San Luis Potosí, Mexico. Alejandra Hernandez, the owner of the truck, said that she opened the truck because she wanted to create comfort food for Mexicans who had migrated from her hometown. The dish that she finds best expresses the flavors of San Luis Potosí is tacos rojos potosinos, made by taking a corn tortilla, bathing it in a red salsa made with chile de árbol, frying the tortilla, and then filling it with shredded goat cheese and diced onion. Often the tacos are served on a plate covered with sour cream and lettuce and then topped with cooked carrots and fried potatoes. Alejandra proudly described how her tacos served as an emotional trigger for her Mexican clientele.

> When I put my taco shop here, San Luis Viejo, people [from San Luis Potosí] arrived and started eating the tacos. Some started crying and saying the tacos are made just like my mother's. It's like it transports you back to your place of origin. It's a medium to transport you. Mentally, you start to eat and your mind goes years back, to the corner of the kitchen in your house, with your siblings, with your family. Mexican food is very powerful.

I asked Alejandra how she had become involved in the informal commerce of selling food on the street. She said she used to sell enchiladas potosinas and tamales potosinos[11] door-to-door with her mother and sister in Mexico for extra money. According to her, in Mexico it is not uncommon for people to sell tacos and tamales door-to-door or to the neighbors: "Your neighbors in Mexico know who can cook what. So if they want tamales for a special occasion, they will call you up." When she moved to Columbus, she started the same practice on the West Side. Alejandra reported that she loves to cook and wanted to be able to make a business doing what she was good at and enjoyed. Her husband Diego also likes to cook. Diego is from Oaxaca and acquired his cooking skills working on the line at Red Lobster, Texas Roadhouse, and Bob Evans. One culinary advantage that Diego has is that his mother migrated to Columbus with him. When Diego began cooking at restaurants, he also started making meals at home, something he had not done when he lived in Mexico. He actually admitted that he was too macho to cook at home when he lived in Mexico, but circumstances had changed. Now he often borrows his mother's recipes or cooks with her. Because Alejandra and Diego both love cooking, their long-term goal is to open a restaurant. In the interim, they saved $40,000 and used the money to buy an old moving van and equip it with a full kitchen.

When Alejandra opened the truck on the west side of Columbus in 2009, she catered to Mexicans from all corners of Mexico, but her foremost features were traditional delights from San Luis Potosí. Alejandra is very proud of her cooking and her hometown, and she truly wants others to savor the flavors of San Luis Potosí. Her business did well at first and even received a special mention in *Columbus Monthly* as a treasured taco truck destination. However, problems related to ICE's sweeps, fewer Mexican customers due to more deportations, and an economic recession from 2008 into the early 2010s created instability for Alejandra's business. Her Mexican clientele was dwindling, and it was becoming much more difficult to pay the $900 monthly rent for her parking spot. Finally she decided that she had to move the truck elsewhere.

Abigail Mack, who worked at Home Port, a housing advisory center for Housing and Urban Development (HUD), had eaten at Alejandra's truck several times and became aware that Alejandra was looking for a new location. Mack spoke with John Waddy, a civil-rights attorney, community advocate, and local real estate investor. He offered Alejandra the opportunity to park her truck on the street corner of one his vacant properties at no charge. The lot is located in the center of a mostly black, underserved neighborhood. John had been looking for a food truck. His vision for the area was to use food to create a social node on the street in order to produce a positive sense of community and put "eyes on the street."[12] Moreover, John knew that there was nowhere for people to eat in the vicinity. He wanted not only to install a physical presence on the street corner but also to have a place that served quality food at an affordable price. John conveyed his desire to have a taco truck in the community this way:

> The taco truck seems to be an oddity in an all-black community, but it's more than just that. What we have decided is that we need to bring everyone into the community, to help build the community, and I think a contribution by all is extremely important. And one of the things that this community has missed greatly is a place to eat. And this taco truck is one of those places we can now eat at.

Remarkably, the *San Luis Viejo* taco truck and the African American district developed a symbiotic relationship.

The district is an underprivileged African American community that was separated from the rest of Columbus by the construction of Interstate 71 in the 1950s. To make way for the freeway, houses were leveled, families were displaced, and the community was left socially splintered. From that point on, the neighborhood was geographically excluded from the city's resources and ultimately experienced a downward economic spiral. The socioeconomic impact on the community is still apparent today. There are no affordable markets selling fruit and vegetables in the district. A few grocery stores have come and gone, and their failures have created a bleak outlook on food access and economic opportunities throughout the area.

In this disenfranchised district, the community's well-being has suffered. The neighborhood is now overrun with convenience stores selling, for the most part, liquor, cigarettes, chips, and candy bars. John described the economic issues with food access as a grave health problem. He critically observed, "The basic things that the stores in our community sell is sugar, salt, cigarettes, and beer—the four things that have plagued the black community as far as health is concerned." Because of the lack of access to healthy foods due to the neighborhood's socioeconomic position within Columbus, the area can be considered a "food desert." Shaw (2006) defines a "food desert" as a low-income area of a city with limited opportunities for residents to purchase healthy produce at reasonable prices. Although there were a few fast food chains in the vicinity, the neighborhood residents desired an array of high-quality cuisines. Moreover, many wished for an affordable dining establishment that they could embrace as part of the community. As one of the residents told me, while munching on his tacos:

> You know, I just bought these tacos for $1.50 apiece, three of them. A lot of people in this neighborhood don't have a lot of money to spend. Now you've got good fresh food right here! You can come here as a high school or as an elementary

school student in the summertime and get a taco, and that's better than going to McDonalds and getting a double cheeseburger. I really think it's helping out this economy and this neighborhood a lot. When you come here with a food truck, making an honest living, feeding your family off the money that you make, I think black people are accepting to that. I know that I am, and I think I can speak for other black people when I say that it is easier for people coming in trying to enhance our society as opposed to people coming in trying to tear it down by robbing, stealing, and killing.

The unique aspect of San Luis Viejo is that although the truck stems from a Mexican heritage, it has been embraced as part of the black community. Alejandra had even established a reputation with some of the houseless people in the neighborhood. She often provides them with free food. She told me that she felt sorry for many of the people in the neighborhood and found it depressing that so many people in a country with as much monetary wealth as the United States could not afford to eat. I witnessed Alejandra giving tacos at no cost to many houseless folks. Indeed, a few people told me that she would often only charge people what they could pay. One man witnessed her generosity: "She knows that times are tough around here. There are people living down here on the street corner. She will give them food even though they don't have any money, she still will look out for them. You know, that's a blessing. You don't got a lot of people like that. That's a blessing. And not only that, [the food is] as good as hell."

James Johnson, an elderly houseless man who goes by the nickname "Pickle" and lives in a van on a vacant lot down the street from Alejandra's truck, commented on the social benefits the taco truck brought to the community: "Actually [the taco truck] is needed, if you notice there is no place to go and eat hot food. No place to sit down, converse, and enjoy yourself for a minute. This is needed, totally needed. It is a very good asset that we have something like that for the community, where people can get together and have better communication amongst all races." Pickle's statement reveals that the taco truck not only provides a disadvantaged neighborhood with a place to eat inexpensive meals, but it also bridges cultural backgrounds through culinary practices and conviviality.

Because of the unique location of this truck and the Mexican cuisines that the truck represents, I spent several weeks interacting with the people who work at the truck and the residents who frequent the truck on a regular basis. I noticed that the truck's original menu had been covered with a new, simpler menu written on a sheet of paper. The old menu contained many more traditional items and regional specialties, such as tacos rojos potosinos, enchiladas potosinas, chicharrones (fried pig skin), chorizo, and alambres. The new menu was smaller and featured primarily grilled chicken, smoked pork chops, pan-fried tilapia, burritos, and tacos. Alejandra had modified the menu for two reasons: first, she wanted to focus on flavors that were a bit more familiar to the community's palate. Second, because Alejandra now lived and worked on the east side of town, it was a challenge to go to the west side of the city, where both the Mexican markets and Restaurant Depot are located. Before she altered the menu, I asked one of the customers to tell me what she thought of the items the truck offered. She began to read the menu out loud: "Chorizo, I don't know what that is. . . ." While pointing to the menu at "chicharrón en salsa rojo," she said: "Chicken-chara-don, whatever that is, in salsa in ro-ho, I'm not real sure what that is. It's *definitely* diverse!" Clearly, the traditional menu was confusing to many African American residents.

I asked Alejandra about the changes to the menu. She responded that because more black people were ordering and eating grilled chicken, fried fish, and smoked pork chops, she had to revise the menu. She also said that certain foods would go to waste and at other times she did not want to go to the west side of the city because she was afraid of confronting ICE. Many times, I noticed that the only things she was able to make were burritos and quesadillas. Alejandra's customers were at times frustrated with her because she did not have most of the items on the menu readily available; at certain times she could not even prepare tacos because she did not have tortillas, and often she would just remain closed. To complicate matters, Alejandra's family only had one car, and during the day her husband always took the car for his landscaping job. There were many days when Alejandra was stranded at the truck with only a few items to offer.

I asked Alejandra if the changes to her menu meant that the foods she offered were any less Mexican. She looked at me, baffled. I tried to clarify my reason for asking, "Well, these dishes that you are offering now are not what you would necessarily consider traditional foods that represent San Luis Potosí. For example, grilled chicken and rice could also easily be considered American as well; do you believe it is losing its Mexican origin when there are more similarities than differences?" She was frustrated that I had asked such a preposterous question, which she interpreted as calling out her cooking as not truly Mexican. She exclaimed, "There are special seasonings in my cooking that make it Mexican, because the marinade I use is passed down from my father's side for generations." When I asked her about the special seasonings, she quipped, "It's a secret." I then asked, "What would you consider to be the key ingredient that makes Mexican food, well, Mexican?" This stumped her for a good while. She eventually responded:

> Freshness. The food has to be fresh. You have to use fresh ingredients and know how to prepare them by hand in the kitchen. Also, love and sweat. I put my life into my food because this is what I enjoy doing. I want people to enjoy the way I make food and to know that I represent my country, my state, and my city, San Luis Potosí. I want people to eat my food and love it because that is who I am, and that's what makes Mexican food Mexican.

I was trying to figure out how Mexicans themselves defined their own foods, not how an outsider would describe the food. Mexicans define their food by the emotions that the cook puts into it, much like Tita filled her tamales with her own tears in *Like Water for Chocolate*, but in this case it's more like water for taco trucks. Cuisine is changed through social exchanges and by how a person perceives a place. Alejandra could modify her menu to fit within the social framework of the black community and yet still consider her cuisine Mexican. It was her passion for cooking and the community that made her food truly Mexican.

A grilled chicken plate served with rice, beans, and white corn tortillas eventually became Alejandra's specialty for the community. Every weekend, she and her husband would grill two or three dozen chickens for the week, and the grilled chickens were always a great success. Speaking with a group of black men from the district who were all eating chicken dinners, I asked them what they thought of their meals. They perceived the taco truck parked in an almost all black neighborhood as almost surreal: "The food is great. Can't believe we are in the middle of the hood." Another friend chimed in, "It seems like we are in Mexico to me! The food is that good! It's like we are in Mexico!"

Alejandra's taco truck had become a social node where people were not just eating Mexican cuisine but were conversing about local issues and getting to know more about Alejandra and her culinary practices. San Luis Viejo became a convivial place with a vibrant social atmosphere (see plate 28). I spoke with two women who work at the King Arts Complex, an African American art education center in the area. Demetries Neely, the center's director, exclaimed, "This community is a traditional East Side African American community, so this truck here helps us learn about our brethren from Mexico. And on Cinco de Mayo Day, I think we should turn this whole neighborhood into Cinco de Mayo Day!" Bettye Stull, curator of the King Arts Complex, added: "I think this is a wonderful opportunity for people in the community to stop here and have authentic Mexican food. Not only do they have authentic Mexican food, they have also added a touch of soul."

On another day at the truck I met a young African American family—a mother and her two sons—speaking with Alejandra as they ate. The mother asserted that the taco truck was a great place for her boys to learn Spanish. She pointed to her youngest son who was about eight years old, and said, "He's in Spanish immersion at school, and so he is learning Spanish. And I was saying to him that it would be helpful if he comes and speaks with Alejandra and works on his Spanish and she can talk to him and work on her English. They can help each other." Alejandra nodded in agreement.

Alejandra and her husband were savvy enough to find flavors and ingredients that the Mexican and African American palates had in common. Once she had identified a common denominator, she was able to reintroduce certain Mexican flavors and traditional cuisines to the menu. And over time, black people in the neighborhood began to try new dishes. For example, flautas were often ordered by people willing to try new things. Alejandra explained that although it would take time, she would eventually add her traditional items again and return to operating from her original menu.

On one occasion at the truck, I sat with John, Pickle, and John's friend Lawrence. The three men discussed the different plates they had ordered. Alejandra came out of the truck to hand them their dishes and then sat down at the table. Pickle was excited that they had smoked pork chops and was eagerly applying salsa. John asked Lawrence if he had tried his flautas yet. Lawrence answered that he had and they were delicious. Alejandra struggled with English as she told Lawrence a little bit more about the specialty: "These are flautas potosinas, from my place I lived in Mexico, we make this." He exclaimed, "Oh man! Take me back to Mexico with you, knowing what this is like!" The San Luis Viejo truck had once carved out a space that connected Mexicans to Mexico through cuisine. Now, it creates a place where low-income African Americans in the inner city can experience Mexico through taste and social space. On occasion, when business is steady, Alejandra offers more traditional cuisines, such as tacos rojos potosinos and enchiladas potosinas. She marveled:

> We are all the same around here because we are all eating tacos rojos potosinos and enchiladas potosinas. That's what's uniting us all around here. And the community loves it. And it doesn't matter to them to eat in the street standing up. Why? Because the food is delicious and that [is] part of our culture. The community is uniting around our culture. They love our culture!

Alejandra's move to the East Side has been extremely beneficial not only for the community but for her as well. I asked John about this budding relationship with Alejandra. He first pointed out that the district used to be part of the

Underground Railroad. Then he elaborated on how the area had always been a place to help others:

> As a historian and studying what the slaves went through, I think about the slaves that ran away. And all of the people in the community knew that it was a runaway slave, they did everything they could to feed that person, to clothe that person, raise the spirits of that person, and more importantly help them learn to read and write. And give them safe passage.... So I don't see Alejandra being much different than that.

John has helped Alejandra tremendously with several aspects of her business and her family life. Not only does John allow her to park her truck for free, but he also helped her deal with a city citation.

Alejandra had been pouring mop water into the storm sewer; someone had seen her and reported that she was pouring grease into the storm sewer. Representatives from CPHD arrived, along with someone from the sheriff's office, with the intent to shut down her operation. She was not able to understand them very well and did not fully realize why she was in trouble. She had to close the truck temporarily, but John was able to help her by calling several city offices and talking with various officials about the situation. Eventually the court sent her paperwork, and John talked to Alejandra about the proceedings. He explained that she was not allowed to put anything but rainwater into the storm sewer. She would have to review basic sanitation rules related to operating a commercial kitchen and give the court a written response explaining how she would change her practices. John offered to help her with the response, explaining that they would write that they would properly dispose of all the gray water and assure the court that no incident of putting gray water in the storm sewer would ever happen again.

John was able to help Alejandra maintain her business; without his help, the city and state would almost certainly have closed down her truck. In addition to assisting Alejandra with this particular issue, John has also worked with Abigail Mack to find small grants for neighborhood improvements. In fact, the two were able to secure a small grant to purchase potted plants, picnic tables, and chairs to put out around the truck. In addition, John has advised Alejandra on other legal matters, such as contacting a lawyer who could help Alejandra's children apply for the DREAM Act and provide her with information about her own dream of being sworn in as an American citizen.

Alejandra's taco truck has truly created a place for positive cultural exchanges. I believe John put it best: "This truck has introduced me absolutely to a new culture that I have personally taken for granted because I did not interact [with anyone from that culture]. Now I'm interacting and I'm learning that beyond the faces there are families; there are businesses; there are people that have needs, desires, wants. And it's powerful. All from a taco."

= = =

Columbus's diverse taco trucks illustrate the dramatic impact social spaces have on culinary practices and the ways in which culinary practices act upon social spaces. The social topologies and political forces embedded in Columbus's landscape, such as ICE's discriminatory practices, comingle with cuisine culture to engender peculiar and powerful social practices and patterns. For example, taco trucks moving across the city to Columbus's East Side represents the desire of many Mexicans not to reside next to each other on the West Side due to fear of deportation. The immigrant Mexican population was learning to diffuse throughout the city as a survival strategy because living in the same area of the city attracted unwanted attention.[13] Some taco truck owners ensconced themselves in new neighborhoods, others opened in the northeast of the city to cater to the burgeoning Mexican immigrant population, while some remained on the west side and simply modified their menus for Anglos' palates.

Food served in public spaces also allows people to appreciate cultural differences through conviviality. It is through such social interactions that relationships develop and foods become hybridized. San Luis Viejo is a perfect example of this process. The truck's curious placement in an all-black neighborhood has created a social node along the street in which cultural exchanges have been initiated. The truck has become a permanent feature of an all-black district because the food the truck owner served filled a socioeconomic demand. In turn, the community embraced San Luis Viejo and its owner as one of their own. In this reciprocal way, cuisine bridges social differences to redraw cultural boundaries and to forge a new culture. This is what it means to say that the taco truck is an evolving American space.

AN EVOLVING AMERICAN SPACE

Many mornings I leave my house in South Austin and walk a few blocks to El Primo, one of my neighborhood's taco trailers (see plate 29).[1] I order a couple of breakfast tacos from the taquero, José, and chat with him in Spanish about the weather or his family in Michoacán. I then hang around and watch other customers as they place their orders. Standing around the trailer is a good mix of people who individually come together to eat tacos and tortas. Most are day laborers—Mexican gardeners and housekeepers. Many hipsters are also attracted to the truck—this trailer is parked just outside a popular coffee shop that is well known for its locally roasted blends. I overhear Mexicans conversing in Spanish with José, while hipsters speak of the "right ways" to eat tacos in Mexico. Mexicans eat tacos "with only onion and cilantro," some say. Others tell their friends, "Order corn tortillas, not flour. They don't eat flour tortillas in Mexico!"[2] Hipsters have a notion that this truck is the truly "authentic" kind—one that arrived in South Austin from Mexico with its trailer and its recipes untainted by American tastes. Little do they know that José has been adapting his foods for Austinites since he started his business in 2009. He has added breakfast tacos and burritos and has even made his savory serrano salsa not so spicy. In fact, he continues to adjust his menu to the neighborhood's changing demographics. Much like all the other taco trucks featured throughout this text, El Primo taco trailer is a continually socially shifting space, no matter how unadulterated it may appear.

Austin is a fairly laid-back city that has a laissez-faire relationship with all food trucks. Food truck owners find their most socially appropriate spaces to park throughout the city, with hardly any harsh policies or cultural conflicts dictating what the trucks can and cannot do. With this open approach to food truck vending, Austin city officials allow truck and trailer owners to create their own uninhibited spatial order. I am happy to have three traditional taco trailers within three blocks of my house and several others in the vicinity. Each truck has taken on influences from its neighborhood and in turn has affected the residents' relationship to the street.

Prosaic public places are profoundly poetic. Tacos trucks subtly but yet powerfully express not only Mexican cultural identity but also the socioeconomic and political influences that act upon them. They are ingenious spaces because they meet the demands of Latino immigrants while navigating urban policies and negotiating socioeconomic forces. For sure, taco trucks are evolving spaces, but so too are the American cities, neighborhoods, and communities within which the trucks park. Taco truck spaces culturally unfold onto the streets, and as citizens consume their tacos, the city socially and politically subsumes the trucks. In the context of this relationship between the city and its taco trucks, Mexican immigrants assimilate and contribute to American culture and the making of the American cultural landscape.

I hope to have shown in this text that there is much more to taco trucks than tacos. Taco trucks express myriad socioeconomic phenomenon. They are mentally slippery spaces because they are experientially located somewhere between the United States and Mexico but are also physical spaces that change the character of a city, its neighborhoods, and its streets. Taco trucks are places where the act of eating strengthens one's cultural identity, and they are also socially charged, symbolic spaces that take on a multitude of meanings and are capable of responding to the social and political demands of a city. By examining taco truck space, where a cultural practice is entrenched in a truck's mobility, I have tried to illuminate just how dynamic culture can be, especially culinary culture along American city streets.

In addition, I aimed to make clear how social practices shape landscape. That landscape is actively being made and remade by iterant practices and ordinary routines that we all too often take for granted. But it is in the mundane, the everyday, and the idiosyncrasies of daily life that the city asserts itself and renders its underlying social structure, albeit often in a spatially cloaked logic. In everyday encounters along the prosaic public street, social practices add experiential layers of life to the urban landscape to create a palimpsest of cultural patterns. These patterns are often indiscernible to us because we are unwittingly complicit in their making. And because they are unconsciously in-scribed into our spatial memory, they tend to cloud our view and understanding of our own personal surroundings. It is consequently challenging for us to see our own culture and what it signifies. But for those who know how to decipher the ensconced social codes assembled and embedded in landscape, the city's form and social organization begin to make some sense. There certainly are strong social structures in cities that appear to be utter chaos: as I have argued throughout this text, there is order within disorder. Cities are always socially reorganizing themselves in ways that urban planners and designers seldom understand and could never foresee or imagine. Low-income Latinos employ their agency to carve out cultural pockets of space in cities as they go through their everyday routines. Taco truck space is just one of many examples that ex-press the unplanned character of cities. I hope that by deciphering taco trucks' spatial arrangements throughout the Bay Area, Sacramento, and Columbus, this book has elucidated how these cities operate socially and politically.

Let us return to Katie W., the Yelp reviewer at the beginning of the book. She innocently crossed into taco truck space to taste a taco. Her genuine keenness to try new foods in an unfamiliar environment is a prime example of how cultural boundaries get broken down without ulterior motives. Gradually, conviviality between divergent social groups eases cultural integration. However, in the neoliberal city, ethnic cuisines are a sought-after commodity. Pursuit of that commodity can frequently lead to friction between those who hold economic supremacy and those who are at their mercy, underscoring this dichotomy in the urban economy.

Along with the economic friction, the social power of food is undeniable. Food is fashionable. Culinary spaces are increasingly becoming entertainment places. The question becomes: For whom do these spaces operate, and why? Are these spaces to entertain the middle and upper middle class on an exotic food quest? Or are they spaces that sustain low-wage laborers' livelihoods? Be-cause the neoliberal economy works to culturally recreate spaces to accumulate capital, it jeopardizes immigrant identity. Foodways, which were traditionally sluggish processes of social integration, are quickly becoming ways to sell a city as a multicultural playground. Now that urban developers and city councils select culinary narratives to sell their communities, city planners and elected officials must be mindful about whom these narratives benefit. These economic and social hierarchies that arise around food have the power to substantially remold the cultural contours of cities. That is a power that must be fully vetted and analyzed in order to minimize the potential sociospatial injustices that could arise from this remolding.

Because food is becoming a catalyst for gentrifying neighborhoods and even entire cities, this raises multilayered questions for urban planning, which thus far seems to generate mostly problematic responses. For instance, to what extent should privileged social groups respect the food identities of immigrant cultures? How do urban boosters include a group's foodways and food practices while not excluding the social group of the people who brought them? More formidable groups must consider these sorts of questions when they are directly marketing and branding other peoples' culinary identities.

Food performances also play a significant political part in how the image of a city is produced. Culinary philosophies are reflected in the urban spaces themselves. What a city looks like is often defined by its cuisine culture. The meanings of food as tied to the symbology of landscape have influential implications. Culinary performances are critical for geographers and food scholars to continue to evaluate. These complex relationships must be further scrutinized in future studies of food and urban space to draw fuller conclusions about how taste preferences profoundly shape social relationships and urban space. Food performances as an integral part of the urban landscape shed light on social justice issues of not just who eats what where, but who gets to eat; this, in turn, influences how underprivileged social groups claim their right to the city.

Mexicans claim their right to the city by taking and remaking city streets for their culinary practices. Serving tacos from trucks mixes and blurs the social function and meanings of private and public spaces, and this mixing and blurring confounds city officials' perceptions of this practice as it relates to the design intent of the street. The taco trucks' tactics have flipped the function of the modernist streetscape. The spatial dimensions of streets in the United States are prominently designed to maximize vehicle efficiency (Berman 1988; Harvey 1991; Fyfe 1998). Modern architects and engineers have incorporated the mentality of "the system" to make the city's street network a more efficient capital-producing and capital-accumulating machine (Berman 1988; Harvey 1989a, 1989b, 1991, 2003; Lefebvre 1991). But the taco truck inverts the very nature of the modernist street and the parking lot by socially shifting space and informally providing ephemeral public places for people. In so doing, it reorganizes urban spaces by making places that are meaningful, especially to Mexicans. It is serving up a cultural dish of identity to a disadvantaged group of people who are all too often forgotten in top-down planning and policy initiatives.

Taco trucks merge past Mexican street food practices with present-day modern American streetscapes in a surreal manner (see plate 30). Taco trucks are establishing a new social structure within cities that seem to be in the process of being pulled apart at their social seams by the automobile. This aspect of the truck is especially innovative as the postmodern city becomes more "fragmented," "restless," and "kaleidoscopic" (Soja 1989: 187). Seen in this upended way, the taco truck is spatially stitching together fragmented, fixed places and using cultural practices to forge a new flow of capital accumulation for the working classes. And it does so by wresting the street away from the urban planner and the engineer and reclaiming it for the pedestrian. The taco truck redefines the street not with some predetermined goal of activating urban space but under its own social and cultural guise. The taco truck's spontaneity makes the street a serendipitous urban landscape that harks back to the ways city streets originally functioned, before the advent of the car. The street becomes pedestrian again, ironically through the sociospatial practices of a motorized truck. But the taco truck's nonconforming uses, its unpredictable qualities, and the chaos it supposedly induces disrupt, disturb, and challenge the contemporary conformist concepts of the street and to whom the street belongs.

As taco trucks owners take and remake leftover spaces in the city from the bottom up, city officials try to regulate the trucks' peculiar practices from the top down. These clashing cultural forces create a tension between what the truck owners *desire* to do and what city officials *require* the truck owners to do. This tension makes for interesting and distinct taco truck mosaics within cities. Each mosaic speaks spatially about this uneasy relationship between cities (as city officials and citizens conceive the cityscape) and truck owners (as they personally perceive urban space as they live and work along its streets day by day). Who the city is programmed for and how it is inhabited are often at irreconcilable odds. Taco trucks may appear unsightly to some, but perhaps there is no truer or more genuine expression of an unfinished city than immigrants informally vending traditional foods along streets.

For Emilia Otero in Oakland, taking to the streets and sidewalks to sell street food is asserting one's right to the city. However, for Oakland officials, serving and savoring tacos or tamales on the street is not a public right but a private practice. It is a perverse practice that must be regulated in culturally appropriate ways. A new, insidious form of "redlining" is developing that defines Latinos' place in the city by their social practices. This means allowing Latinos to vend along the streets and sidewalks in East Oakland, but not elsewhere. For Oakland officials, Latino street food vending is magnificent to have in the city—as long as it remains in its proper place, the barrio. Outside of this area, it is considered by some city officials and citizens to be a malevolent practice. And now that Governor Brown signed the Safe Sidewalk Vending Act (SB 946 Sidewalk Vendors) in September 2018, legalizing street food vending throughout

California's cities, it will be interesting to see how Oakland city planners will work with Latino sidewalk food vendors in 2019.

Meanwhile in San Francisco, taking the street is not strictly forbidden, but it is extremely difficult to get approval from city officials. There, Matt Cohen learned to use social time to interpret San Francisco's public streets. He organizes gourmet food truck events so that he can reprogram a streetscape within the city's socially acceptable time-manner-place parameters. Unfortunately, most traditional taco trucks cannot conform to such scripted spaces. This is partly why only a few traditional taco trucks are parked on San Francisco's streets and most are found in the East Bay.

City officials in both Sacramento and Columbus envision the symbology of their public streets as contributing to the marketing image of the city. Curiously, they both have totally opposite approaches to regulating streetscapes for food truck vending. In Columbus, food trucks are allowed to park on private lots and seldom move. This had also been the case for public streets, but this aspect of food vending had not challenged the city until gourmet food trucks came along. From 2012 to 2014 Columbus planners addressed concerns about vending on public streets and agreed to permit food trucks to park anywhere their owners would like. In Columbus, city boosters and citizens concluded that food trucks strung along streets and scattered about the urban landscape positively contributed to the city's progressive identity. For them the trucks are cultural capital that attracts dollars to the city. In Sacramento, on the other hand, vending foods from trucks is a pernicious practice that tarnishes the cityscape's pristine appearance and marketing narrative as the "Farm-to-Fork Capital of America." In Sacramento, the trucks compete with the city's sidewalk cafe aesthetic and cut into restaurateurs' profit margins. From 2002 to 2015 most Sacramento officials were against trucks parking on private property adjacent to the street and never moving. Although food truck vending laws since 2015 in Sacramento are steadily progressing in favor of the trucks, it does appear, for the most part, that city officials and restaurateurs would still like to see food trucks conform to a land use away from restaurants and the downtown area, or at the very least, remain in motion.

Taco trucks, unlike so many gourmet food trucks, rarely move. Strict regulations ordering them to keep their wheels rolling simply cause trucks to relocate. While it is perfectly acceptable for trucks to remain parked in industrial and commercial corridors in Oakland, a few trucks do not have licenses or health permits. A couple of trucks use their mobility to evade regulations. In Sacramento prior to 2015, most of the trucks that were not grandfathered into code scampered to the edges of town, just across the city limits. One truck was able to conform to the previous strict mobility regulations of the city. Its owner

learned to negotiate the social terrain by creating a fixed route: he served burritos at various locations throughout the city center at designated times during
the day. And in Columbus, taco truck owners use their mobility to elude ICE.
They disperse to other parts of the city where they feel they can catch Latinos'
ebbs and flows but not be disturbed too frequently by ICE's perilous patrols. Taco
trucks' mobility empowers taco truck owners to reinvent space when things are
not working in their favor. Taco truck owners can always find a spatial solution.

A taco truck's mobility is a fascinating feature of the capitalist city because
taco trucks cannot be completely eradicated by any zoning law or policy; they
can only be ceaselessly displaced. Because cities cannot obliterate taco trucks,
they must envelop them. Taco truck owners have creatively devised a way to
assert their agency in the making of the unfinished city. If the very nature of
capitalism, as Harvey (1991) argues, is to reinvent itself by destroying what it
has created in order to build things anew, then it must favor flexible spaces and
mobility. The ability to spatially respond, physically adapt, and socially adjust
to the forever-transforming built environment, social streams, and monetary
flows of a city is perhaps the ultimate capital-accumulating strategy for the urban poor who are most threatened by socioeconomic segregation, gentrification,
and urban renewal. The taco truck's inherent mobility allows it to adapt spatially
to avoid capital annihilation. Ironically, through this process of adaptation, it
also socially reshuffles urban space. As taco trucks move around cities, they
engage their newfound environments to create new sorts of social spheres. In
myriad ways, a taco truck's mobility practices spatially recalibrate cities to be
more socially just.

As taco trucks redraw sociospatial and cultural boundaries, they create and
accentuate paradoxes in the definitions and functions of inclusive and exclusive
spaces. Because taco trucks are located along streets, they are socioeconomically
connected to the area of the city where they are parked. Streets are conduits for
socioeconomic exchange. If a taco truck is parked along a street, it can infiltrate
a city's sociospatial network. Seen at the scale of the city, taco trucks are even included within urban environments where city officials work tirelessly to exclude
them. But zooming into the microcosms of taco truck spaces sheds a different
light on inclusion. Streets, regardless of where they are in a city, are public. Trying to push taco trucks out of the city limits or circumscribe them to one area of
the city—as was done in Sacramento and Oakland—is exclusionary in practice,
regardless of city officials' motives. In Columbus these paradoxes are especially
apparent at the scale of the neighborhood and the street. There, city officials and
most citizens work to embrace taco trucks, but the practices of middle-class, Anglo residents and the threat of ICE inadvertently shove taco trucks into interstitial
spaces, many of which are dilapidated neighborhoods where taco trucks may or

may not be welcomed by the immediate community. Surprisingly, regardless of a community's demographic context, taco trucks' practices almost always make inclusive spaces out of exclusive spaces as they tap into the conviviality and monetary flow of the public street. In the process of converting exclusive spaces into inclusive spaces, taco trucks redraw social boundaries and redefine culture. In other words, taco truck spaces are able to erode exclusionary circumstances as taco truck culture unfolds onto the streets and into the city. And unexpectedly, taco trucks typically do this in neighborhoods that have been historically excluded and in communities that do not initially welcome the trucks' newly established presence. They create microcosms of socioeconomic opportunity not just for themselves but also for neighborhood residents.

Taco trucks adhere to fragmented and tumultuous urban topographies by being ongoing, flexible, socially malleable spaces. A taco truck actively reshapes landscape through its spatial versatility. In this sense, the taco truck is amorphous. It is a free floating form, a fluid space that picks up social influences and responds to political pressures as it motors about town. Taco truck culture and city politics flow together to become one. And when a taco truck parks within new surroundings, it highlights the space by calling attention to it. The taco truck makes us look again at what once was a void space by claiming the space and abstracting its qualities. By creating ambiguities, the taco truck makes us see the urban landscape in a way that we had not and could not before. At the same time, it tells us what we always knew about that space but weren't capable of clearly conceiving. Seen through this paradoxical lens, the taco truck changes the city while indicating to community members, in many subtle ways, who they are, who they are becoming, and, really, who they have been all along. It is an ongoing conversation between city and truck. In this revolutionary way, the taco truck continuously challenges us to reconsider and reconceptualize how our everyday, commonplace environment is actually quite remarkable.

The taco truck that I believe most positively expresses a truck's surreal qualities and sociospatial dynamics is San Luis Viejo, which is parked in an African American neighborhood in Columbus, Ohio. Alejandra's truck is revered as alleviating many of the community's distressing food issues. Through a mutual relationship between a black community and a Mexican-immigrant-owned taco truck, people mingle and foods mix. A virtuous cultural exchange takes place, all while Alejandra alters her cooking practices to meet the taste preferences of the African American community. The community and the truck's social spaces are symbiotically created.

In many ways, taco trucks have taught us how taste relates to space. Taco truck owners cook what they know and intend to recreate flavors from Mexico in their new locale, but operating a taco truck is a business, and remaining in business is a truck owner's primary motive. Taco truck owners learn about their newfound community by cooking. They add items to the menu and alter flavors to entice more people to come to the truck. In this way, society is actively defining and redefining what is considered to be Mexican cuisine. Social practices influence culinary practices. By examining cuisine in relationship to mobility, space, and place, I have tried to show that culinary meanings are continually reinterpreted and that foods are ever evolving.

Kogi Korean taco truck in Los Angeles is another excellent example of the dynamic relationship between cuisine and space. This taco truck was fashioned in Korea Town in Los Angeles. This area of L.A. has a large Korean community, but its population is prominently Latino. Korean cooking integrated into a taco truck to create the Korean taco. Thus the taco truck has influenced cuisines beyond Mexican. In fact, the Kogi Korean taco truck sparked the gourmet food truck movement that swept the nation. Kogi uses social media to its advantage, a distinct practice of the gourmet food truck that sets it apart from a traditional taco truck. The artisanal food truck, a reinterpretation of the taco truck, has further hybridized foods and continues to produce new hyperreal spaces. In the film *Chef*, a gourmet chef quits his job at an upscale Los Angeles restaurant, buys an old taco truck, and refashions it for his artisanal Cuban sandwiches. In one scene, he gives the truck a facelift by painting over the taco truck's name and menu. This scene depicts the erasure and hijacking of one cultural way of life by another. This part of the movie is a perfect metaphor for how middle-class Anglos stripped Mexicans of their food truck identity. We only have to tune our televisions to one of the food networks to note that the only food trucks featured on their shows are the boutique variety. The gourmet food truck has eclipsed the taco truck, and in the process, American middle-class Anglos seem once again to have overlooked and subconsciously dismissed their immigrant roots and ethnic influences.

Unfortunately, new boutique food trucks have created new challenges for taco truck owners. Boutique food trucks are often able to overtake the most affluent spaces in cities and also cause city departments to hike the cost of food truck vending licenses. While most traditional taco truck vendors have remained resilient and continue to focus on Latinos as their main clientele, others have decided to redefine their practice. Those who speak English fluently and have American citizenship are able to make the leap from a taco truck to an artisanal food truck. For example, George Azar, who fought the good fight for so long against the City of Sacramento, eventually decided to go gourmet. He updated his truck, gave it a fresh new look, and now travels to almost all the food truck festivals across Northern California. His business could not be better.

When I first started working with taqueros and writing about their social struggles in 2004, the gourmet food truck movement was yet to commence. Today artisanal food trucks are popping up on city streets around the world. They are popular in Berlin, Copenhagen, and Bogotá, just to name a few international capitals. Recently I was invited to speak at La Sabana University in Bogotá about the evolution of traditional taco trucks. At the end of my talk one of the audience members told me he simply could not imagine Mexican food sold from trucks to day laborers. He explained that in Colombia the trucks are about gourmet cuisine. "They are for hipsters and the wealthy, who like to try different foods, not for underprivileged workers," he exclaimed. The idea that food trucks were originally intended for the proletariat appears as a foreign concept to many members of the middle and upper middle classes across the globe. The ersatz image of the American gourmet food truck has certainly been exported. Food trucks of all sorts are now substantially shifting urban spaces around our planet in unanticipated ways.

But back to South Austin, where the taco truck is more than just a street food novelty. In South Austin, the taqueros at El Paisa (The Countryman) serve tacos and tortas to a clientele made up mostly of Mexican immigrants. The truck is parked adjacent to Meliana #1, a Mexican convenient store along South Congress Avenue, a major thoroughfare. The store has a small Mexican food counter, offers money exchanges, and sells bus tickets to Mexico. One night, around midnight, I decided to try the truck's tacos. As I waited for my order I heard a loud vehicle pull up. I turned to see a large bus stopping alongside the taco truck. The name on the side of the bus read, "Omnibus Mexicanos." The lit sign at the front of the bus pulsed in red letters, "Monterrey—Salida 12:15." Several Mexicans, who had been standing there waiting with their suitcases, satchels, and new flat-screen televisions, began to load their belongings. The conductor took their tickets, and they took their seats. The bus ride from Austin to Monterrey is approximately ten hours.[3] The people already appeared fatigued; many had probably commenced their journey elsewhere early in the day. Their long bus ride ahead seemed daunting. Many of them would make bus connections in Monterrey to other parts of Mexico. I overheard several of them talking about traveling on to Mexico City or Guanajuato. This particular taco truck space is tied to many places throughout Mexico through Mexican transnational mobility practices. This taco truck is not only a transformative space where one can experientially reemerge in Mexico, but it is also a portal on the public street from which one can literally take the road back home. And so, taco truck space goes on unfolding into the frontier.

NOTES

Introduction

1. Carey McWilliams (McWilliams and Sackman 2000) uses the phrase "factories in the field" to discuss the exploitation of Mexican laborers in California's agricultural system.

2. Neoliberal cities promote the privatization of civic life and often use marketing techniques to attract dollars to the city.

3. I use the terms brown, white, and black not strictly as the census defines them but to denote skin color. I do this not to stereotype ethnicity or generalize about racial differences but to make evident some of the logic of racial undertones that often dominate the ways that various ethnicities, races, and cultural groups come to perceive the spatial practices of people unlike themselves.

4. Pulque is an alcoholic beverage made from the sap of the agave plant. It is similar to tequila but produced in a different region.

5. A *tamale* is most notably recognized as a corn husk wrapped around a cornmeal stuffing with various other ingredients, such as *nopales* and turkey. During Spanish colonialization and the Columbian Exchange, the tamale was adapted to European tastes. Pork fat was often added, and various Old World animal proteins were incorporated (Pilcher 1998).

6. Mexican-style chili has mostly faded from modern Mexican cooking. Ironically, chili has now become associated with Anglo-Texans. For more on chili and the chili queens, see Jeffrey Pilcher's book *Planet Taco: A Global History of Mexican Food* (2012).

7. Bell was trying to make a fast food even faster, which is ironic because using the drive-through at Taco Bell is typically much slower than ordering and eating from a taco truck or any taquero on the street.

8. I conducted interviews with taco truck owners in both English and Spanish, depending on which language the taco truck owner preferred. A footnote appears after the first quotation from an interviewee if his or her interview was conducted in Spanish and translated into English.

9. Immigration and Customs Enforcement (ICE) is quite aware that many of the Mexicans immigrants who own taco trucks are without their papers. In fact, in some cities ICE officers frequently patrol around the taco trucks. Nevertheless, I have changed the names of undocumented immigrant taco truck owners and their trucks throughout this book if I identify them as undocumented. I also do not divulge the specific locations where their trucks park or show images of them or their trucks.

10. This is taken from my personal encounters with taco trucks as well as from an online search for taco trucks in each state. There are probably taco trucks located in others states not listed.

11. *Lonchera* means "lunch box" in Spanish, and the word *lonche* is an English loanword in Spanish for *lunch*.

12. Cinco de Mayo, 1862, is the infamous day the Mexican Army pushed the French Army out of Mexico at the battle of Puebla.

13. Issues concerning taco trucks in East Los Angeles do not represent typical cultural transgressions. Taco trucks have been in East Los Angeles since the 1970s. They are a prominent Mexican part of the city, and often the people who do not want taco trucks are Mexican restaurateurs (Hernández-López 2010). And the Anglo side of the debate over taco trucks is split. Anglo Angelenos throughout the city either find the trucks out of place in the United States or love them for their ethnic foods (Hernández-López 2010).

14. Italian elites also used iconography for this purpose in forming the architectural design principles of the time.

15. Sharon Zukin, although an urban sociologist and not a geographer, has engaged with much geographic material on landscape and urban studies.

16. See also: Cosgrove and Daniels 1992; Duncan 2005; Duncan and Ley 1997; Mitchell 2003, 2008.

17. There are more many more social kinds of geography, simply too many to mention here. Instead, I cite works of social geography that are relevant to the topic of this book.

Chapter 1. Remaking Oakland's Streets

1. Interview with Emilia Otero.

2. Interview with Emilia Otero at La Placita.

3. The name of the truck derives from the town of El Grullo in the Mexican state of Jalisco; *El Grullense* has become a colloquial Spanish term in Mexico as a place for peasant food.

4. The number of reported taco trucks varies. There is no accurate count by the city. I have heard from Emilia Otero that there are as many as 120 traditional taco trucks

throughout Oakland. And I have heard several accounts for fifty to eighty by taco truck owners. I did not try to figure out the number of trucks in the city beyond general estimates. I counted upward of thirty-five once. Windshield surveys are incredibly difficult in the area because you literally have to comb every street. And times of day and days of the week are also important because some trucks come and go constantly. However, I would estimate that there are at least seventy in southeast Oakland and probably one hundred in the city.

5. I have not been able to find a consistent report on the number of nonpermitted (city or health) taco trucks in Oakland; it appears that many truck owners, if not most, are operating without a city permit, some even without a health permit.

6. Certeau (1984) also notes that cities are not understood as planned areas but are perceived through lived space.

7. Trucks, food carts, and restaurants rely on time and money. Taco trucks complement restaurants because they offer a convenient option for people on the go.

8. She has several newspaper clippings from the *San Francisco Chronicle* featuring her work. In 2008 the Obama administration even awarded her the Jefferson Medal for her public service.

9. I use the term houseless instead of homeless. Many of the people I talked with who live on the street are not homeless. They have a place they call home and often have a social network that they interact with. They have a familiarized place and feel they belong somewhere. Homeless evokes the notion that these people do not have a social network or a place they can call home.

10. Personal interview, Nancy Marcus, March 14, 2013, and multiple e-mail interviews between December 2013 and May 2014.

11. In January 2015 the State of California permitted nondocumented immigrants to apply for a driver's license.

12. Most counties have just one Health Department officer who works with mobile food vending.

13. Atkinson-Adams is also referring to an increase in gourmet food trucks, which chapter 2 addresses.

14. The *East Bay Express* reported in 2011, "Is Fruitvale the New Hipster Hangout? Forget the Mission. UC Berkeley students now flock to east Oakland for tacos and shopping" (Pennick 2011).

Chapter 2. Formalizing San Francisco's Informal Street Food Vendors

1. Caleb Zigas interview, March 3, 2014.
2. A former military base.

Chapter 3. Making Sacramento into an Edible City

1. The city of Sacramento and its residents no longer have to deal with the threat of seasonal flooding. However, the levees have created vast tracts of land—many of them housing developments that are below water level and therefore prone to inundation.

2. I use "city of Sacramento" to encompass all individuals who contribute directly to shaping the city's image, including the city council, city staff, economic developers, city planners, and city boosters.

3. As of 2018, this restaurant is now being changed and renovated yet again into another dining concept.

4. The restaurants' origin can be traced back to Paris, France. Before restaurants became spaces of status and power, they were places for invalids to get nourishment (Spang 2001).

Chapter 4. Landscape, Labor, and the Lonchera

1. In Sacramento, the Department of Finance writes and enforces food truck vending ordinances. In Oakland, it is Special Events Permitting; in San Francisco, it used to be the Police Department, but now it is the Planning Department. In the entire state of Ohio and in Austin, Texas, it is the Health Department.

2. The taco truck's history in Sacramento can only be traced back to 1975. However, other forms of Mexican street-food vending may have been present several decades prior to 1975.

3. George Azar interview, May 30, 2013.

4. For another version where I define the differences between taco trucks and gourmet food trucks, see Julian Agyeman, ed., *From Loncheras to Lobsta Love: Food Trucks, Cultural Identity, and Social Justice* (MIT Press). In the chapter titled "The Spatial Practices of Food Trucks" I make an argument that culinary culture should also be evaluated as a spatial practice.

5. Taken from multiple interviews with taco truck owners in Sacramento.

6. Interview with Jaime Quintero was conducted in Spanish and translated into English by the author.

7. Unlike San Francisco and Oakland, who try to regulate mobile food vending under the guise of public safety, Sacramento does not. The City of Sacramento writes their mobile food-vending ordinances as they see fit.

8. In Sacramento, you must look diligently to find taco trucks. Occasionally, you will drive by one, but most of the time you have to seek them out. They are located all over the city and seldom close together. Other than using Yelp for my search, I once followed a taco truck back to a large commissary garage. In the massive garage were about sixty food trucks—of all types—in operation. Some of those trucks were traditional taco trucks that would leave early each morning and park in one spot throughout the day.

9. Interview with Areolo Torres Hurelio was conducted in Spanish and translated into English by the author.

10. Interview with Luis Bueno was conducted in Spanish and translated into English by the author.

11. Some of the new regulations read as if they are designed to protect restaurants from competition from food trucks. Others seem to be continuing to keep food trucks from permanently parking on lots in the downtown area.

12. Cosgrove and Daniels (1988) posit that property owners control the iconography of landscape. This is certainly true of Sacramento. Sacramento's restaurateurs have considerable power and influence over the city council and over the manner in which they homogenize the urban landscape. As Mitchell (1996, 27) maintains, "Landscapes transform the facts of place into a controlled representation, an imposition of order in which one (or perhaps a few) dominant ways of seeing are substituted for all ways of seeing and experiencing." Within the context of California's agrarian landscape, Mitchell (1996) also asserts, "there can be no beauty without a simultaneous damning." This quote holds true for California's agricultural aesthetics and urban landscapes alike.

Chapter 5. Community Conflict and Cuisine in Columbus

1. This was according to many citizens I spoke with as well as planners. City planners Vince Papsidero (principal city planner) and Chris Presutti (zoning administrator) noted that Columbus's citizens struggled with defining the city's sense of place.

2. These numbers are estimated from interviews taken with 15 taco truck owners and with Ohio Hispanic Coalition president Josué Vicente.

3. Based on my interviews with taco truck owners. Trucks ranged in price from $7,000 to $40,000. Most, however, cost between $15,000 and $20,000.

4. *Huarache* is Spanish for sandal. It is also a type of street food in Mexico City. It's a thick corn tortilla topped with vegetables and meat. It's called *huarache* because of its shape: it looks like a sandal.

5. The phrase "A taco truck on every corner" was made popular on an MSNBC interview in 2016 with Marco Gutiérrez, who founded Latinos for Trump. In sum, he claimed that immigration from Mexico needed to be regulated; otherwise, Mexican immigrants would impose their undesirable culture onto the American landscape. Perhaps his opinion would have resonated with the Greater Hilltop community a decade prior. "Trump Supporter Warns of 'Taco Trucks on Every Corner.'" (2016) MSNBC.com. https://www.msnbc.com/all-in/watch/taco-trucks-on-every-corner-756382787934.

6. Interview with Lidia Flores was conducted in Spanish and translated into English by author.

Chapter 6. Cooking Up Multiculturalism

1. When I use the term "white" throughout this chapter, I specifically mean Anglo, middle-class non-Latinos. It should be noted that the U.S. Census and professional demographers technically categorize Latinos as "Caucasian." However, because Mexicans are mostly brown in skin color, aspects of race in common discourse among Anglos and Latinos is prevalent. Both groups speak of racial differences and discrimination. The idea of race, or at least the differences of ethnicity between mostly brown Latinos and pale Anglos, should be fleshed out to reflect how society most often frames it.

2. In 2012, shortly after my interviews, some minor controversies began over where on city streets gourmet food trucks could park. The controversy emerged due to altercations between food-truck owners and brick-and-mortar establishments that sold similar foods in the same place. The city created a pilot program that specified that food trucks could not park within a block of a restaurant that serves similar cuisine. In addition, food trucks were only permitted to park in designated parking spots on downtown streets. By 2014, controversies over food vending had come to a close. Food trucks are permitted to park on any public street, and any restaurateur who objects can use an appeals process to ask for the food truck parking spot to be made unavailable.

3. Again, I use white in this context to read *non-Latino*.

Chapter 7. Food, Fear, and Dreams

1. Deporting undocumented immigrants regardless of whether they have a criminal background is part of a larger overall deportation initiative. It is the result of the Immigration Reform and Immigrant Responsibility act of 1996, which made it easier to deport immigrants who are in the country without papers.

2. The fruits and vegetables were grown in Mexico and shipped through Chicago's produce market.

3. Interview with Alejandra Hernandez was conducted in Spanish and translated into English by the author.

4. This policy has not changed under the Trump administration. During the time of this research, the Obama administration had deported more immigrants than both Bill Clinton and George W. Bush. In fact, during Obama's first term he deported more than 1.5 million people (ICE removal statistics).

5. Interview with Ricardo Diaz was conducted in Spanish and translated into English by the author.

6. See the discussions of immobile mobility in chapter 4 and chapter 5 for more details about the ways in which taco trucks move.

7. *Al Pastor* is pork marinated in achiote paste and cooked on a vertical spit. It is then served in the form of a taco.

8. A *comal* is flat cookware with the edges slightly bent upward. This allows the cook to use the center for cooking food in oil, while allowing foods to stay warm at the edges but not continue to cook. It is also very portable.

9. The example of Lisa's and Luis taco truck is deconstructed in a different context and through a different spatial framework in a chapter I (Lemon 2017) wrote for Julian Agyeman, ed., *From Loncheras to Lobsta Love: Food Trucks, Cultural Identity, and Social Justice* (MIT Press). The chapter is titled, "The Spatial Practices of Food Trucks."

10. Lisa's interview was in English and I interviewed Luis separately that afternoon in Spanish.

11. Tamales potosinos are made with banana leaves, similar to Oaxaca-style tamales.

12. "Eyes on the street" is a phrase used by Jane Jacobs in "Death and Life of the American City" to refer to social knowledge of one's neighborhood, specifically the ability to recognize who is part of the community and who is not.

13. ICE is not the sole reason many Mexican immigrants wished to move across the city. There are other work opportunities on the east side of Columbus in which Mexican labors wished to take part in.

Conclusion

1. In Austin, large trailers seem to be just as popular as trucks. All trailers have to prove their mobility to the Health Department on an annual basis.

2. It should be noted that flour tortillas *are* found in Mexico, especially within wheat growing regions throughout Northern Mexico.

3. A bus ticket from Austin to Monterrey, Mexico, costs US $120 (cash only).

REFERENCES

Adams, Paul C. 2005. *The Boundless Self: Communication in Physical and Virtual Spaces*. Illus. ed. Syracuse, N.Y.: Syracuse University Press.

Adema, Pauline. 2009. *Garlic Capital of the World: Gilroy, Garlic, and the Making of a Festive Foodscape*. Jackson: University Press of Mississippi.

Alameda County Environmental Health. 2014. "Food Safety." http://www.acgov.org/aceh/food/mobile_food_units.htm.

Amin, Ash, and Nigel Thrift. 2009. *Cities: Reimagining the Urban*. Malden, Mass.: Blackwell.

Anderson, Cathie. 2013. "Cathie Anderson: New Restaurant Seeks to Bridge Downtown, Midtown." *Sacramento Bee*, April 6.

Anderson, Mark. 2013. "Cattle Drive across Tower Bridge to Kick off Farm-to-Fork Week." *Sacramento Business Journal*, July 9. http://www.bizjournals.com/sacramento/news/2013/07/09/cattle-drive-across-tower-bridge-to.html.

Arellano, Gustavo. 2013. *Taco USA: How Mexican Food Conquered America*. New York: Scribner.

Arreola, Daniel. 2002. *Tejano South Texas: A Mexican American Cultural Province*. 1st ed. Austin: University of Texas Press.

Bagwell, Beth. 1996. *Oakland: The Story of a City*. Repr. ed. Oakland, Calif.: Oakland Heritage Alliance.

Barajas v. City of Anaheim. 1993. 15 Cal. App. 4th 1808 [19 Cal. Rptr. 2d 764]. Justia Law. http://law.justia.com/cases/california/caapp4th/15/1808.html.

Barbas, Samantha. 2003. "'I'll Take Chop Suey': Restaurants as Agents of Culinary and Cultural Change." *Journal of Popular Culture* 36, no. 4 (Spring): 669–86.

Barth, Gunther Paul. 1988. *Instant Cities: Urbanization and the Rise of San Francisco and Denver*. Albuquerque: University of New Mexico Press.

Bauch, Nicholas. 2005. "Food and Place: Consuming Parma, Italy." Master's thesis, Department of Geography, University of Wisconsin Madison.

Bayless, Rick. 2007. *Authentic Mexican: Regional Cooking from the Heart of Mexico*. 20th anniversary ed. New York: William Morrow Cookbooks.

Belcher, Colleen. 2009. "City Council Meeting to Determine Fate of K Street Redevelopment Project." *Sacramento Press*, March 10. http://sacramentopress.com/2009/03/10/city-council-meeting-to-determine-fate-of-k-street-redevelopment-project/.

Bell, David, and Gill Valentine. 1997. *Consuming Geographies: We Are Where We Eat*. New York: Routledge.

Beriss, David. 2007. "Authentic Creole: Tourism, Style and Calamity in New Orleans Restaurants." In Beriss and Sutton, *Restaurants Book*, 151–66.

Beriss, David, and David Sutton, eds. 2007. *The Restaurants Book: Ethnographies of Where We Eat*. Oxford: Bloomsbury Academic.

Berman, Marshall. 1988. *All That Is Solid Melts into Air: The Experience of Modernity*. New York: Penguin.

Binnie, Jon, Julian Holloway, Steve Millington, and Craig Young. 2006. *Cosmopolitan Urbanism*. New York: Routledge.

Bost, Suzanne. 2003. "Women and Chile at the Alamo: Feeding U.S. Colonial Mythology." *Nepantla: Views from South* 4, no. 3: 493–522.

Bourdieu, Pierre. 1984. *Distinction: A Social Critique of the Judgement of Taste*. Cambridge, Mass.: Harvard University Press.

Boyer, M. Christine. 1986. *Dreaming the Rational City: The Myth of American City Planning*. Cambridge, Mass.: MIT Press.

"Brand Columbus 2012." 2012. Columbus Brand Marketing Committee. http://www.brandcolumbus.com.

Brechin, Gray. 2006. *Imperial San Francisco: Urban Power, Earthly Ruin*. Berkeley: University of California Press.

Caldwell, Alison. 2011. "Will Tweet for Food: Microblogging Mobile Food Trucks—Online, Offline, and In Line." In *Taking Food Public: Redefining Foodways in a Changing World*, edited by Psyche Williams-Forson and Carole Counihan, 306–21. New York: Routledge.

California Department of Food and Agriculture. 2013. "California Agricultural Statistics Overview 2012–2013." http://www.cdfa.ca.gov/statistics/pdfs/2013/FinalDraft2012-2013.pdf.

California Department of Motor Vehicles. 2009. "VC Section 22455 Vending from Vehicles." January 1.

Certeau, Michel de. 1984. *The Practice of Everyday Life*. Berkeley: University of California Press.

City of Columbus Planning Division. "INFO Base: Area and Demographics."

Columbus Commons. 2012. http:// http://columbuscommons.org.

"Columbus Food Tours and Culinary Walking Tours | Guided Columbus Tours - Columbus Events and Attractions (Columbus Ohio)." 2014. http://columbusfood adventures.com/.

"Columbus, Santa Maria." The Santa Maria Webpage, Columbus, Ohio.http://www .santamaria.org.

Cook, Ian, and Philip Crang. 1996. "The World on a Plate Culinary Culture, Displacement and Geographical Knowledges." *Journal of Material Culture* 1, no. 2: 131–53.

Cosgrove, Denis E. 1998. *Social Formation and Symbolic Landscape*. Madison: University of Wisconsin Press.

Cosgrove, Denis, and Stephen Daniels, eds. 1989. *The Iconography of Landscape: Essays on the Symbolic Representation, Design and Use of Past Environments*. Repr. ed. Cambridge: Cambridge University Press.

Cresswell, Timothy. 1996. *In Place / Out of Place: Geography, Ideology, and Transgression*. Minneapolis: University of Minnesota Press.

——. 2006. *On the Move: Mobility in the Modern Western World*. New York: Routledge.

——. 2010. "Towards a Politics of Mobility." *Environment and Planning D: Society and Space* 28, no. 1: 17–31.

Cronon, William. 1992. *Nature's Metropolis: Chicago and the Great West*. Repr. ed. New York: Norton.

Darnell, Brandon. 2012. "K Street's Resurgence." *Sacramento Press*, May 9. http:// sacramentopress.com/2012/05/09/k-streets-resurgence/.

Department of Homeland Security. Office of Immigration Statistics. 2014. https:// www.dhs.gov/immigration-statistics/population-estimates/unauthorized -resident.

Dermer Behrendt Legal Advisors. 2011. http://www.dermerbehrendt.com/index.html.

Didion, Joan. *Where I Was From*. 2004. Repr. ed. New York: Vintage.

Dinin' Hall. 2012. https://www.hugedomains.com/domain_profile.cfm?d=dininhall &e=com.

Downtown Grid Sacramento. 2014. "Sacramento Restaurants, Sacramento Events, Downtown Dining, Sacramento Shopping." http://sacramento.downtowngrid.com/.

Duncan, James, and Nancy Duncan. 2003. *Landscapes of Privilege: The Politics of the Aesthetic in an American Suburb*. New York: Routledge.

Duncan, James S. 2005. *The City as Text: The Politics of Landscape Interpretation in the Kandyan Kingdom*. Cambridge: Cambridge University Press.

Duncan, James S., and David Ley, eds. 1997. *Place/Culture/Representation*. London : Routledge.

Duneier, Mitchell. *Sidewalk*. 2001. 1st ed. New York: Farrar, Straus and Giroux.

Dunteman, Dayna. 2008. "The Power and Influence 100." *Sacramento Magazine*, August 15. http://www.sacmag.com/Sacramento-Magazine/September-2008/The-Power -Influence-100/.

Durand, Jorge, and Douglas Massey. 1992. "Mexican Migration to the United States: A Critical Review." *Latin American Research* 27, no. 2: 3–42.

Durand, Jorge, Douglas S. Massey, and Chiara Capoferro. 2005. "The New Geography of Mexican Immigration." In *New Destinations: Mexican Immigration in the United States*, edited by Victor Zúñiga and Rubén Hernández-León, 1–20. New York: Sage.

Dyer, Amanda. 2006. "Move It or Lose It: City Cracks Down on Food Trucks, Vendors Cry 'Ethnic Cleansing.'" *Sacramento News and Review*, April 27.

Engber, Daniel. 2014. "Who Made That Food Truck?" *New York Times*, May 2. http://www.nytimes.com/2014/05/04/magazine/who-made-that-food-truck.html.

Esquivel, Laura. *Like Water for Chocolate*. 1992. New York: Doubleday.

"Farm To Fork Capital of America." 2014. http://farmtofork.com.

Ferenchik, Mark. 2007. "Food Wagons an Acquired Taste: Mobile Stands Bother Some Neighborhoods; City Considers Regulations." *Columbus Dispatch*. December 6.

Ferrero, Sylvia. 2001. "*Comida sin par*. Consumption of Mexican Food in Los Angeles: 'Foodscapes' in a Transnational Consumer Society." In *Food Nations: Selling Taste in Consumer Societies*, edited by Warren Belasco and Philip Scranton, 194–219. New York: Routledge.

Finkelstein, Joanne. 1991. *Dining Out: An Observation of Modern Manners*. New York: New York University Press.

Florida, Richard L. 2012. *Cities and the Creative Class*. Ann Arbor, Mich.: Psychology Press, 2005.

"Food Trucks vs. The Establishment: Attorney Jeffrey Dermer on the Legalities of Mobile Vending." 2012. http://www.youtube.com/watch?v=QeUh1krc0Ms&feature=youtube_gdata_player.

Foxworthy, Jeff. 1993. *Jeff Foxworthy: Check Your Neck*. Dir. Keith Truesdell. New York: Showtime Presents.

Fyfe, Nicholas, ed. 1998. *Images of the Street: Planning, Identity and Control in Public Space*. New York: Routledge.

Gibson, Michael. 2010. *The Sommelier Prep Course: An Introduction to the Wines, Beers, and Spirits of the World*. 1st ed. Hoboken, N.J.: Wiley.

Goffman, Erving. 1959. *The Presentation of Self in Everyday Life*. New York: Anchor.

Gregory, Derek. 1994. *Geographical Imaginations*. Malden, Mass.: Wiley-Blackwell.

Groth, Paul. 1994. *Living Downtown: The History of Residential Hotels in the United States*. Berkeley: University of California Press.

———. 2008. "Lecture 12: Urbane Alternatives to the Single Family House: Hotels, Apartments, Flats." Lecture from "American Cultural Landscapes, 1900 to the Present." Spring semester. Department of Geography, University of California, Berkeley.

Groth, Paul, and Todd W. Bressi. 1997. *Understanding Ordinary Landscapes*. Annotated ed. New Haven, Conn.: Yale University Press.

Guthman, Julie. 2004. *Agrarian Dreams: The Paradox of Organic Farming in California*. Berkeley: University of California Press.

———. 2008. "'If They Only Knew': Color Blindness and Universalism in California Alternative Food Institutions." *Professional Geographer* 60, no. 3 (June 4): 387–97.

Gutman, Richard J. S. 2000. *American Diner Then and Now*. Baltimore, Md.: Johns Hopkins University Press.

Haley, Andrew P. 2011. *Turning the Tables: Restaurants and the Rise of the American Middle Class, 1880–1920*. Chapel Hill, N.C.: University of North Carolina Press.

Harvey, David. 1989a. "From Managerialism to Entrepreneurialism: The Transformation in Urban Governance in Late Capitalism." *Geografiska Annaler: Series B, Human Geography* 71, no. 1: 3–17.

———. 1989b. *The Urban Experience*. Baltimore, Md.: Johns Hopkins University Press.

———. 1990. "Between Space and Time: Reflections on the Geographical Imagination." *Annals, Association of American Geographers* 80, no. 3: 418–34.

———. 1991. *The Condition of Postmodernity: An Enquiry into the Origins of Cultural Change*. Malden, Mass.: Wiley-Blackwell.

———. 2003. "The Right to the City." *International Journal of Urban and Regional Research* 27, no. 4: 939–41.

Heitner, Darin. 2014. "Sacramento Kings Arena Construction Receives Approval with Anticipated 2016 Completion." *Forbes*, May 27. http://www.forbes.com/sites/darren heitner/2014/05/27/sacramento-kings-arena-construction-receives-approval-with -anticipated-2016-completion/.

Heldke, Lisa M. 2003. *Exotic Appetites: Ruminations of a Food Adventurer*. New York: Routledge.

Hernandez-Lopez, Ernesto. 2010. "LA's Taco Truck War: How Law Cooks Food Culture Contests." SSRN Scholarly Paper. Rochester, N.Y.: Social Science Research Network, October 19.

Hines, Lauren. 2013. "Moving Out of the Shadows: Resistance and Representation in the Struggle for Migrant Rights." Master's thesis, Department of Geography, Ohio State University.

hooks, bell. 1992. *Black Looks: Race and Representation*. 3rd ed. Boston: South End.

ICE Removal Statistics. https://www.ice.gov/removal-statistics/2016.

Jackson, John Brinckerhoff. 1986. *Discovering the Vernacular Landscape*. 8th ed. New Haven, Conn.: Yale University Press.

———. *Landscape in Sight: Looking at America*. 2000. Edited by Helen Lefkowitz Horowitz. New Haven, Conn.: Yale University Press.

Jacobs, Jane. 1992. *The Death and Life of Great American Cities*. New York: Vintage.

Johnston, Josée, and Shyon Baumann. 2009. *Democracy and Distinction in the Gourmet Foodscape*. London: Routledge.

Keegan, Rebecca Winters. 2008. "The Great Taco Truck War." *Time*, April 25. http://content.time.com/time/nation/article/0,8599,1735104,00.html.

Kelling, George L., and James Q. Wilson. 1982. "Broken Windows." *Atlantic Monthly*, March. http://www.theatlantic.com/magazine/archive/1982/03/broken-windows/304465/.

Kennedy, Diana. 2009. *The Essential Cuisines of Mexico*. Rev. ed. New York: Clarkson Potter.

———. 2013. *My Mexico: A Culinary Odyssey with Recipes*. Updated ed. Austin: University of Texas Press.

Kraft, Kraig. 2009. *"Sacramento's Vanishing Taco Trucks."* *Edible Sacramento*, April. http://ediblenetwork.com/sacramento/online-magazine/spring-2009/sacramentos-vanishing-taco-trucks/.

Latham, Alan. 2006. "Sociality and the Cosmopolitan Imagination: National, Cosmopolitan and Local Imaginaries in Auckland, New Zealand." In *Cosmopolitan Urbanism*, edited by Jon Binnie, Julian Holloway, Steve Millington, and Craig Young, 89–111. London: Routledge.

Lefebvre, Henri. 1991. The *Production of Space*. Oxford: Wiley-Blackwell.

———. 1996. *Writings on Cities*. Translated and edited by Eleonore Kofman and Elizabeth Lebas. Oxford: Wiley-Blackwell.

Lemon, Robert D. 2016. "The Budding Aromas from Taco Trucks: Taste and Space in Austin, Texas." *Transnational Marketing Journal* 4, no. 2: 100–109.

———. 2017. "The Spatial Practices of Food Trucks." In *From Food Trucks, Cultural Identity, and Social Justice*, edited by Julian Agyeman, Caitlin Matthews, and Hannah Sobel, 169–88. Cambridge, Mass.: MIT Press.

Lewis, Peirce. 1979. "Axioms for Reading the Landscape." In *The Interpretation of Ordinary Landscapes: Geographical Essays*, edited by Donald W. Meinig, 11–32. New York: Oxford University Press.

Ley, David. 2004. "Transnational Space and Everyday Lives." *Transactions of the Institute of British Geographers* 29:151–64.

Lillis, Ryan. 2012. "City Beat: Sacramento Touted as America's 'Farm-to-Fork Capital.'" *Sacramento Bee*, October 31.

Linnekin, Baylen J., Jeffrey Dermer, and Matthew Geller. 2011. "The New Food Truck Advocacy: Social Media, Mobile Food Vending Associations, Truck Lots, and Litigation in California and Beyond." *Nexus: Chapman's Journal of Law and Policy* 17:35.

Logan, John R., and Harvey L. Molotch. 2007. *Urban Fortunes: The Political Economy of Place*. 20th anniversary ed. Berkeley: University of California Press.

Macias, Chris. 2010. "Mobile Food Vendors Feel Threatened: Restaurant Owners, City Officials Seek to Keep Catering Operations Moving.'" *Sacramento Bee*, August 23.

Magee, Richard M. 2007. "Food Puritanism and Food Pornography: The Gourmet Semiotics of Martha and Nigella." *Americana: The Journal of American Popular Culture* 6 (Fall): 2.

Maly, Michael. 2008. *Beyond Segregation: Multiracial and Multiethnic Neighborhoods*. Philadelphia: Temple University Press.

McBride, Anne E. 2010. "Food Porn." *Gastronomica: The Journal of Critical Food Studies* 10, no. 1 (February 1): 38–46. doi:10.1525/gfc.2010.10.1.38.

McWilliams, Carey, and Douglas Cazaux Sackman. 2000. *Factories in the Field: The Story of Migratory Farm Labor in California*. Berkeley: University of California Press.

Mead, George Herbert, and Charles William Morris. 1962. *Mind, Self and Society from the Standpoint of a Social Behaviorist*. Chicago: University of Chicago Press.

Meinig, Donald W. 1979. "The Beholding Eye." In *The Interpretation of Ordinary Land-scapes: Geographical Essays*, edited by Donald W. Leinig, 33–50. New York: Oxford University Press.

Mendick, Jonathan. 2009. "City Council Meeting Draws Hundreds." *Sacramento Press*, March 11. http://sacramentopress.com/2009/03/11/city-council-meeting-draws -hundreds/.

Miller, Nick. 2011. "What the Truck?!!" *Sacramento News and Review*, April 28. http:// www.newsreview.com/sacramento/what-the-truck/content?oid=1967333.

Mitchell, Don. 1995. "There's No Such Thing as Culture: Towards a Reconceptualiza-tion of the Idea of Culture in Geography." *Transactions of the Institute of British Geog-raphers* 20, no. 1: 102–16.

———. 1996. *The Lie of The Land: Migrant Workers and the California Landscape*. Minneapolis: University of Minnesota Press.

———. 2003. *The Right to the City: Social Justice and the Fight for Public Space*. New York: Guilford.

———. 2005. "The S.U.V. Model of Citizenship: Floating Bubbles, Buffer Zones, and the Rise of the 'Purely Atomic' Individual." *Political Geography* 24, no. 1 (January): 77–100.

———. 2008. "New Axioms for Reading the Landscape: Paying Attention to Political Economy and Social Justice." In *Political Economies of Landscape Change: Places of Integra-tive Power*, edited by James L. Wescoat and Douglas M. Johnston, 29–50. GeoJournal Library. Dordrecht, Neth.: Springer. https://doi.org/10.1007/978-1-4020-5849-3_2.

Montaño, Ralph. 2006. "Mobile Food Vendors Feel Threatened: Restaurant Owners, City Officials Seek to Keep Catering Operations Moving.'" *Sacramento Bee*, April 20.

Mumford, Lewis. 1989. *The City in History: Its Origins, Its Transformations, and Its Prospects*. New York: Mariner.

Oakland, California, Code of Ordinance. Business Taxes, Permits and Regulations. Chapter 5.49: Pushcart Food Vending Pilot Program. https://library.municode.com.

Oakland, California, Code of Ordinance. Business Taxes, Permits and Regulations. Chapter 8.09: Vehicular Food Vending. https://library.municode.com.

Paragary Restaurant Group. "Esquire Grill." 2014a. http://www.esquiregrill.com/.

Paragary Restaurant Group. "Hock Farm." 2014b. http://www.paragarys.com/sacramento -restaurants/hock-farm/.

Paragary Restaurant Group. "KBAR." 2014c. http://www.paragarys.com/sacramento-restaurants/k-bar/.

Paragary Restaurant Group. "Paragary Restaurant Group." 2014d. http://www.paragarys .com/team.

Pardue, Derek. 2007. "Familiarity, Ambiance and Intentionality: An Investigation into Casual Dining Restaurants in Central Illinois." In Beriss and Sutton, *Restaurants Book*, 65–78. Oxford: Bloomsbury Academic.

Parsons, James J. 1986. "A Geographer Looks at the San Joaquin Valley." *Geographical Review* 76, no. 4: 371–89.

Pennick, Bailey. n.d. "Fruitvale the New Hipster Hangout?" *East Bay Express*. Accessed October 26, 2018. https://www.eastbayexpress.com/oakland/fruitvale-the-new -hipster-hangout/Content?oid=2491920.

Peralta Hacienda Historical Park. 2012. "Peralta Family History." http://www.peralta hacienda.org/pages/main.php?pageid=69&pagecategory=3.

Peters, Erica J. 2013. *San Francisco: A Food Biography*. Lanham, Md.: Rowman and Little-field.

Pilcher, Jeffrey M. 1998. *Que Vivan Los Tamales! Food and the Making of Mexican Identity*. Albuquerque: University of New Mexico Press.

———. 2008. "Was the Taco Invented in Southern California?" *Gastronomica: The Journal of Food and Culture* 8, no. 1 (February 1): 26–38.

———. 2012. *Planet Taco: A Global History of Mexican Food*. Oxford: Oxford University Press.

Pile, Steve. 2005. *Real Cities: Modernity, Space and the Phantasmagorias of City Life*. London: Sage.

Pile, Steve, and Nigel Thrift, eds. 1995. *Mapping the Subject: Geographies of Cultural Transformation*. London: Routledge.

Pillsbury, Richard. 1990. *From Boarding House to Bistro: The American Restaurant Then and Now*. Boston: Routledge.

———. 1998. *No Foreign Food: The American Diet in Time and Place*. Boulder, Colo.: Westview.

Pulido, Laura. 2000. "Rethinking Environmental Racism: White Privilege and Urban Development in Southern California." *Annals of the Association of American Geographers* 90, no. 1 (March 1): 12–40.

Ray, Krishnendu. 2007. "Domesticating Cuisine: Food and Aesthetics on American Television." *Gastronomica* 7, no. 1: 50–63. doi:10.1525/gfc.2007.7.1.50.

Relph, Edward. 1984. "Seeing, Thinking, Describing Landscapes," In *Environmental Perception and Behavior: An Inventory and Prospect*, edited by Thomas F. Saarinen, David Seamon, James L. Sell, 209–24. Chicago: University of Chicago Department of Geography Research Paper No. 209.

———. 2008. *Place and Placelessness*. London: Pion.

Rofe, M. W. 2003. "'I Want to Be Global': Theorizing the Gentrifying Class as an Emergent Elite Global Community." *Urban Studies* 40:2511–26.

Rogers, Elizabeth Barlow. 2001. *Landscape Design: A Cultural and Architectural History*. New York: Harry N. Abrams.

Rogers, John. 2008. "LA County Judge Tosses Out Taco Truck Restrictions." *USA Today*, August 28. http://usatoday30.usatoday.com/news/nation/2008-08-28 -2917838081_x.htm.

Rojas, James. 2003. "The Enacted Environment: Examining the Streets and Yards in East Los Angeles." In *Everyday America: Cultural Landscape Studies after J. B. Jackson*, edited by Chris Wilson and Paul Groth, 275–92. Berkeley: University of California Press.

Sacramento City Code. Chapter 5.68: Food Vending Vehicles. http://www.qcode.us/ codes/sacramento/view.php?topic=5–5_68&showAll=1.

Sacramento City Code. Ordinance No. 2015–0016. Amendments to Chapter 5.68: Food Vending Vehicles. https://qcode.us/codes/sacramento/revisions/2015-0016 .pdf.

Sacramento Economic Development Strategy 2007. City of Sacramento, Economic Development. http://portal.cityofsacramento.org/Economic-Development/Publications.

Sacramento Economic Development Strategy 2013. City of Sacramento, Economic Development. http://portal.cityofsacramento.org/Economic-Development/Publications.

San Francisco Street Food Festival's Webpage. 2014. http://www.sfstreetfoodfest.com/sponsors.php.

Sauer, Carl Ortwin. 1967. "The Morphology of Landscape." (1925). In *Land and Life: A Selection from the Writings of Carl Ortwin Sauer*, by Carl Ortwin Sauer, 104–17. Berkeley: University of California Press.

"Saveourtacotrucks.org | Sign The Petition - Page 4 | Carne Asada Is Not a Crime." 2008. http://saveourtacotrucks.org/2008/05/05/sign-the-petition-page-4/.

SB 946 Sidewalk Vendors. https://leginfo.legislature.ca.gov/faces/billVersionsCompareClient.xhtml?bill_id=201720180SB946

Schein, Richard H. 2006. *Landscape and Race in the United States*. New York: Routledge.

Schoenfeld, Bruce. 2011. "How the Farm-to-Table Movement Is Helping Grow the Economy." *Entrepreneur*, September 21. https://www.entrepreneur.com/article/220357.

Self, Robert O. 2003. *American Babylon: Race and the Struggle for Postwar Oakland*. Princeton, N.J.: Princeton University Press.

Selland's. 2014. http://www.sellands.com.

Shaw, Hillary J. 2006. "Food Deserts: Towards the Development of a Classification." *Geografiska Annaler: Series B, Human Geography* 88, no. 2: 231–47.

Shaw, S., Bagwell, S. and Karmowska, J. 2004. "Ethnoscapes as Spectacle: Reimagining Multicultural Districts as New Destinations for Leisure and Consumption." *Urban Studies* 41, no. 10: 1983–2000.

Sibley, David. 1995. *Geographies of Exclusion: Society and Difference in the West*. London: Routledge.

Sims, Rebecca. 2011. "Food, Place and Authenticity: Local Food and the Sustainable Tourism Experience." In *Taking Food Public: Redefining Foodways in a Changing World*, edited by Psyche Williams Forson and Carole Counihan, 492–508. New York: Routledge.

Slocum Rachel. 2006. "Anti-Racist Practice and the Work of Community Food Organizations." *Antipode* 38, no. 2: 327–49.

———. 2007. "Whiteness, Space and Alternative Food Practice." *Geoforum: Special Issue, Post-Communist Transformation* 38, no. 3 (May): 520–33.

———. 2011. Race in the Study of Food. *Progress in Human Geography* 35, no. 3: 303–27.

"Slow Food International." *Slow Food International*. http://www.slowfood.com/.

Smith, Michael Ernest. 2003. *The Aztecs*. Malden, Mass.: Blackwell.

Sochat, Anne, and Tony Cano. 1997. *Chuck Wagon Heyday*. Canutillo, Tex.: Reata.

Soja, Edward W. 1989. *Postmodern Geographies: The Reassertion of Space in Critical Social Theory*. 2nd ed. London: Verso.

———. 2000. *Postmetropolis: Critical Studies of Cities and Regions*. Malden, Mass.: Blackwell.

Spang, Rebecca L. 2001. *The Invention of the Restaurant: Paris and Modern Gastronomic Culture*. Cambridge, Mass.: Harvard University Press.

Steinhauer, Jennifer. 2008. "In Taco Truck Battle, Mild Angelenos Turn Hot." *New York Times*, May 3.

Swanbrow, Diane. 2014. "Study Identifies Factors that Contribute to Food Trucks' Fast Spread." *Michigan News*, August 16. http://ns.umich.edu/new/releases/22337-study-identifies-factors-that-contribute-to-food-trucks-fast-spread.

Trubek, Amy B. 2009. *The Taste of Place: A Cultural Journey into Terroir*. Berkeley: University of California Press.

"Trump Supporter Warns of 'Taco Trucks on Every Corner.'" 2016. *MSNBC.com*. https://www.msnbc.com/all-in/watch/taco-trucks-on-every-corner-756382787934.

Tuan, Yi-Fu. 1990. *Topophilia: A Study of Environmental Perception, Attitudes, and Values*. New York: Columbia University Press.

———. 2001. *Space and Place: The Perspective of Experience*. Minneapolis: University of Minnesota Press.

———. 2013. *Landscapes of Fear*. Repr. ed. Minneapolis: University of Minnesota Press.

U.S. Census Bureau. 2010 Census. https://www.census.gov/programs-surveys/decennial-census/decade.2010.html.

U.S. Census Bureau Public Information. 2012. "U.S. Census Bureau Projections Show a Slower Growing, Older, More Diverse Nation a Half Century from Now." http://www.census.gov/newsroom/releases/archives/population/cb12-243.html.

U.S. Immigration and Customs Enforcement. 2012. "Secure Communities: Monthly Statistics through August 31, 2012; IDENT/IAFIS Interoperability Statistics." http://www.ice.gov/doclib/foia/sc-stats/nationwide_interop_stats-fy2012-to-date.pdf.

van den Berghe, Pierre L. 1994. *The Quest for the Other: Ethnic Tourism in San Cristobal, Mexico*. Seattle: University of Washington Press.

Walker, Richard. 2004. *The Conquest of Bread: 150 Years of Agribusiness in California*. New York: New Press.

Willow, Molly. 2011. "Touring the Taco Trucks." *Columbus Monthly*, June. http://www.columbusmonthly.com/content/stories/2011/06/touring-the-taco-trucks.html.

Wilson, James E. 2012. *Terroir: The Role of Geology, Climate, and Culture in the Making of French Wines*. Berkeley, Calif.: Wine Appreciation Guild.

Yelp Review. 2013. La Bamba Taco Truck, Sonoma, California, April 26. https://www.yelp.com/biz/la-bamba-taco-truck-sonoma.

Zelinsky, Wilbur. 1994. *Exploring the Beloved Country: Geographic Forays into American Society and Culture*. Iowa City: University of Iowa Press.

Zimmerman, Steve. 2009. *Food in the Movies*. 2nd ed. Jefferson, N.C.: McFarland.

Zukin, Sharon. 1993. *Landscapes of Power: From Detroit to Disney World*. Berkeley: University of California Press.

———. 1996. *The Cultures of Cities*. Malden, Mass.: Blackwell.

INDEX

ROBERT LEMON is an urban and social researcher and documentary filmmaker. His films include *Transfusión*.

The University of Illinois Press
is a founding member of the
Association of University Presses.

_____

Composed in 10.23/13 Marat Pro
with BarberinoCleanTT display
by Lisa Connery
at the University of Illinois Press
Cover designed by Jennifer S. Fisher
Cover images: Taco truck in Tulsa Oklahoma
(photo by Robert Lemon); skyline background image
(© iStock.com/Terriana).
Manufactured by Sheridan Books, Inc.

University of Illinois Press
1325 South Oak Street
Champaign, IL 61820-6903
www.press.uillinois.edu